Benefits for Children: A Four Country Study

Ken Battle
Michael Mendelson
Daniel Meyer
Jane Millar
Peter Whiteford

Edited by Ken Battle and Michael Mendelson

ISBN# 1-894598-31-8

Published by:

The Caledon Institute of Social Policy
1600 Scott Street, Suite 620
Ottawa, Ontario, Canada
K1Y 4N7
Phone: (613) 729-3340
Fax: (613) 729-3896
www.caledoninst.org

Supported by:

Joseph Rowntree Foundation
The Homestead
40 Water End
York
YO30 6WP
United Kingdom
www. jrf.org.uk

The Joseph Rowntree Foundation has supported this project as part of its programme of research and innovative development projects, which it hopes will be of value to policy makers, practitioners and service users. The facts presented and views expressed in this report, however, are those of the authors and not necessarily those of the Foundation.

Caledon publications are available from:
Renouf Publishing Company Limited
5369 Canotek Road
Ottawa, Ontario
K1J 9J3
Phone: (613) 745-2665
Fax: (613) 745-7660

and from Renouf stores at:
71 1/2 Sparks Street, Ottawa (613) 238-8985
12 Adelaide St. West, Toronto (416) 363-3171

BENEFITS FOR CHILDREN: A FOUR COUNTRY STUDY

Table of Contents

ACKNOWLEDGEMENTS

The authors thank the following for their assistance in helping us with this project:

Gary Bagley, Human Resources Development Canada
Barbara Ballard, Joseph Rowntree Foundation
Matt Barnes, University of Bath
Gillian Campbell, Human Resources Development Canada
Alain Denhez, Human Resources Development Canada
Department of Family and Community Services, Australia
Chris Foster, Australian Permanent Delegation to the OECD
Donald Hirsch, Joseph Rowntree Foundation
Andrée Houde, Finance Canada
Sharon Irwin, Human Resources Development Canada
Rob Kanasay, Canada Customs and Revenue Agency
Marta Morgan, Human Resources Development Canada
Robert Mundie, Human Resources Development Canada
Doug Murphy, Human Resources Development Canada
Lise Potvin, Finance Canada
Louise Roussel, Caledon Institute of Social Policy
Wendell Primus, Centre on Budget and Policy Priorities, Washington, D.C.
John Karl Scholz, Institute for Research on Poverty of the University of Wisconsin
David Stanton, Australian Institute of Family Studies
Kathy Turner, Canada Customs and Revenue Agency

The Caledon Institute of Social Policy gratefully acknowledges the financial support of the Joseph Rowntree Foundation in the UK and the Departments of Finance and Human Resources Development in Canada.

INTRODUCTION

Few aspects of social policy are more important than the programs we provide to support our children. The opportunity for every child to enjoy a happy and enriching childhood is surely one of the most cherished goals of a just society. Not only should we be interested in the well-being of children because they will become the citizens of tomorrow, but children deserve a good childhood just because they are children.

For the most part, though, even the richest nations on earth are far from this goal for every child. However, there is today renewed attention in many countries to issues such as poverty in childhood and fair treatment for families with children. Consequently, reform of programs that pay benefits on behalf of children has become a higher priority in many countries, as we struggle with such contentious issues as the boundary between societal and familial responsibilities, and the need for compensatory government income support to remedy the long-standing inability of the labour market to provide adequate earnings for many families with children.

Reflecting this renewed emphasis, income security programs for children are undergoing a time of rapid change in most English-speaking countries. Prior to the 1970s, income benefits paid on behalf of children typically were embedded within the payment schedule of other programs, such as social assistance or unemployment insurance, or hidden within the income tax system as an exemption providing tax savings for taxpayers with children. The only stand-alone programs providing benefits solely for children were universal, paying a cash payment (taxed or tax-free) to all families at all income levels.

The 1970s saw the creation of new income-tested programs such as the Earned Income Tax Credit in the United States, the Family Income Supplement in the United Kingdom and the refundable child tax credit in Canada that calculated eligibility for and the amount of benefit on the basis of family earnings or income, excluding families above a certain level. These and other benefits for children evolved over the subsequent decades, and now Australia, Canada and the United Kingdom are all in the midst of major reforms to their systems, with income-related programs as the centrepiece. While the United States is not currently contemplating a significant change in its child income programs – indeed, tends not to see its tax-delivered benefits for children as child benefits *per se* – the 'Anglo-American' countries have been influenced to some extent by the experience and evaluations of the US Earned Income Tax Credit.

Child poverty is persistent and extensive in all four countries. While the issue has been a prime impetus for the comprehensive reform of child benefits in Australia, Canada and the UK, the same cannot be said for the US, where child benefit programs remain unintegrated and child poverty is a less compelling public issue. Nonetheless, the American emphasis on market solutions to poverty, as exemplified by the use of earnings supplementation through the Earned Income Tax Credit, has played a part in the debate and to some extent the shape of child benefit reform in the other countries. This mix of similar but also different income support policies for children among countries that share both a linguistic and historical inheritance has created a potentially productive opportunity for each country to learn from the others. The Caledon Institute of Social Policy, in collaboration with the Joseph Rowntree Foundation in the United Kingdom, initiated the project

Benefits for Children: A Four Country Study to take advantage of this opportunity.

This volume represents the work of experts in child benefits from each country. The authors not only have written about their own system of benefits for children, but also have provided extensive comments on and input into the other national papers, as well as the introductory comparative analysis that follows. In working closely together, we developed a common template for the national papers and attempted to write in a manner that is readable and understandable in all four countries.

In addition to this report, *A credit to children – The UK's radical reform of children's benefits in an international perspective,* an analysis of the international experience specifically in relation to current UK policy concerns, is being published by the Joseph Rowntree Foundation [Donald Hirsch, Joseph Rowntree Foundation/York Publishing Services, York 2000].

Comparing social programs

It is notoriously difficult to undertake comparative international research on social programs. Researchers must fight their way through a dense undergrowth of incompatible definitions, untranslatable terminology, different institutional and jurisdictional arrangements, and many other factors unique to each country. Perhaps as a result, most international social policy analysis consists largely of an evaluation of overall inputs and outputs across a number of countries – e.g., what percentage of GDP does each country spend on social programs and what does this mean for measures of inequality? These are 'high level' comparisons of aggregate inputs and outputs that, while often useful, tell us relatively little about the *programs* themselves (e.g., their objectives, design and delivery). Only rarely do international studies attempt to compare the structure and functioning of programs *per se*; instead, most treat social programs themselves as a 'black box' without delving into what happens inside the black box. In this project, by contrast, we are attempting to open up the black box and reveal what is inside. Furthermore, we are aiming to do so in sufficient depth and detail to be useful to the government officials who design and deliver child benefits.

Looking into the 'black box' in other countries is not easy. For the United States and Canada, where both the national and sub-national levels of government deliver income security programs, this is a familiar problem to researchers attempting to compare social programs among states or provinces. Yet it is infinitely more challenging to compare programs in different countries than in different states or provinces within the same country. To do so requires a deep understanding of each country's history and policy context including, for example, its tax system, the respective roles of different levels of government, and the countless institutional details that make up the fabric of public policy.

It was partly because of these challenges that this project selected Australia, Canada, the United Kingdom and the United States. These countries share a common heritage; they are English speaking (or, in Canada's case, English and French speaking) and, as noted above, they are all undertaking major child benefit reform, with the exception of the US. All of these countries rely primarily on 'state-delivered' income security, rather than the more 'corporatist' models of other European countries or the non-state models of Asia, and in many important ways their income security philosophies and systems are similar. In studying four countries that are so much alike in so many ways, we hope to be able to derive practical ideas and insights from one another's experience that can be adapted to our respective countries.

Nevertheless, even among these four related countries, there are numerous challenges in undertaking meaningful comparative analysis. For example, to note just one minor difference that can cause confusion, the term 'welfare' generally means the whole income security system in the UK and in Australia, while it has quite another, narrower meaning (i.e., the income security program of last resort) in Canada and the US. Another example: The British income tax system is primarily 'Pay-As-You-Earn' (i.e., the exact income tax owed is deducted from paycheques and most ordinary taxpayers never fill out a tax form) while in the other three countries most adults complete a tax form annually. We believe that we have surmounted these kinds of problems by working together with a common template and through mutual review of each other's work.

While this report attempts to delve deeply into the structure of benefits for children in each of the four countries, it is emphatically *not* an attempt to rank systems and judge which is 'best.' We have not attempted to develop and apply any over-arching evaluative framework or set of cross-national objectives against which to weigh each country's system. Rather, we seek to understand and learn from what each country is doing about child benefit reform by focusing on the programs themselves. And 'reform' is the operative word: Our main objective is to compare and contrast the countries' different approaches to the reform of benefits for children.

Which programs is this report about?

This volume examines income benefits for children, focusing on new income-tested programs that exist or are being introduced in all four countries. In Australia, the main program is the Family Tax Benefit Parts A and B. In Canada, it is the federal Canada Child Tax Benefit, though we also discuss the emerging child benefits and earnings supplements offered by most provincial governments. In the UK, it is the still to be implemented Integrated Child Credit and the existing universal Child Benefit. The American child benefit system is best known for its Earned Income Tax Credit, though it recently added a nonrefundable child tax credit and also continues to offer child-related preferences in its income tax system. But these programs cannot be discussed in isolation from the rest of each nation's income security system, which may contain substantial additional benefits for children that fit – or fail to fit – together to form a coherent picture. Therefore, the country reports that follow include a detailed review of all income child benefits delivered either in the form of cash (cheques or direct bank deposit) or income tax reductions.

The four countries in the study also provide various in-kind benefits – i.e., services or subsidies – on behalf of children, though their importance varies from one nation to another. However, in order to draw the line somewhere, we decided that detailed review would be confined to income benefits paid on behalf of children, whether delivered through the tax system or by individual programs. Consequently, each paper only briefly describes in-kind benefits for children, to provide contextual information that rounds out the picture of supports for children in each country. Similarly, some general information on broader income security and other social programs is given as necessary background to help make sense of how each country's child benefit system operates.

How do we define 'child benefits'?

To undertake this study, we first had to develop a workable and consistent definition of 'child benefits.' Despite the similarities of the four countries, this task has proved surprisingly difficult. We ended up using two definitions.

One approach defines child benefits as income benefits *formally designated* to help pay for children's expenses. For example, a single childless individual in a Canadian province might get, say (these are purely hypothetical amounts), $500 a month from social assistance, while a lone parent might get an adult benefit of $700 and a benefit intended for the child of $100 a month. Using the 'designated benefits' methodology, the children's benefit would be $100 a month in this hypothetical example.

The other approach to defining child benefits is to look strictly at the *difference* between what a household gets when a child is added on. Using the 'difference method' in the above example, the children's benefit would be the difference between what an adult gets with a child and what the same adult would get without a child and everything else being equal. Using this definition, the child benefit would be $300 a month (i.e., $700 for the parent plus $100 for the child equals $800 for the lone-parent family, minus $500 for the single adult).

Both definitions have pros and cons. The designated benefit definition may represent more accurately the intentions of the designers of income security programs. It might be argued that the reason for the $300 difference between the childless adult and the lone-parent family has nothing to do with the child *per se*: Rather, it is a reflection of society's relative disapproval of single, unattached adults relying on social assistance. On the other hand, the difference method is objective in that it can be applied purely following a formula and will always get the same answer. The difference method does not rely upon a subjective interpretation of intentions. And the difference method can capture more accurately the reality of social policy, which typically entails complex interrelations among various programs with varying objectives, designs and delivery mechanisms.

We resolved this problem by using both definitions when appropriate and, when national circumstances dictate, one or the other approach. Throughout, we clarify which method we are using at any given time.

How do we compare currencies across countries?

For the most part, we are more interested in comparing the way benefits for children have evolved and how they are designed, than the specific amounts they pay. After all, once a program is up and running, changing the amount of the benefit is relatively simple – just a stroke of a pen and an attendant increase (or reduction) in budget. More difficult is setting up programs in the first place and deciding how they fit into a country's income security system. Nevertheless, it is necessary to show the value of payments, to help understand the structure and impact of a program. To do this across countries requires converting the denominations of money into a common currency. Although three of the four countries call their currency 'dollars,' we should not be misled by the name. All are different currencies with different values within each country. 1,000 Australian dollars are not the same as $1,000 Canadian or $1,000 US, and certainly not £1,000 UK. So how do we measure these currencies across nations?

The method for conversion to a common currency that we use in this study is 'Purchasing Power Parity' or PPP for short. Purchasing Power Parity is the amount of money in each national currency needed to buy a common basket of goods and services. It is not the same as the exchange rate. The exchange rate is not a good measure of comparative purchasing power as it is highly responsive to other influences having nothing to do with the purchasing power of the currency, such as short-term flows of investment capital.

The Purchasing Power Parity equivalencies used here are from the Organization for Economic Development and Co-operation, which defines them as follows:

> …the rates of currency conversion that equalise the purchasing power of different currencies by eliminating the differences in price levels between countries. In their simplest form PPPs are nothing more than price relatives. For example, if the price of a cauliflower in France is 8.00 francs and in the United States it is 1.50 dollars, then the PPP for cauliflower between France and the United States is 8.00 francs to 1.50 dollars or 5.33 francs to the dollar. This means that for every dollar spent on cauliflower in the United States, 5.33 francs would have to be spent in France to obtain the same quantity and quality – or, in other words, the same volume – of cauliflower [http://www.oecd.org//std/ppp/pppbackground.htm].

Purchasing Power Parity figures are published quarterly by the Organization for Economic Development and Co-operation.

The most recent published PPP equivalences used in this report, for 1999, are:

Table 1
Purchasing Power Parity Equivalences

	1 $Australia	1 $Canada	1 £UK	1 $US
1$US	$1.30	$1.17	£0.67	$1.00
1£UK	$1.93	$1.74	£1.00	$1.49
1$C	$1.11	$1.00	£0.58	$0.85
1$A	1.00	$0.90	£0.52	$0.77

Source: Organization for Economic Co-operation and Development, July 2000. *Purchasing Power Parities – Comparative Price Levels – Main Economic Indicators.* See http://www.oecd.org//std/ppp1.pdf.

For example, the purchasing power of one Canadian dollar is equal to the purchasing power of 1.11 Australian dollars, 0.58 British pounds and 0.85 United States dollars.

While there are other choices of conversion available, Purchasing Power Parity is the most appropriate measure for this study because it is as close as we can get to showing how much a particular level of child benefits can buy in each country compared to the others. As with all measures, there are weaknesses in the use of Purchasing Power Parity. It includes a full basket of goods and services, not just consumer goods, so that the equivalencies reflect, for example, construction costs and equipment that are not normally part of a family's purchases. Moreover, the purchasing patterns of low-income families tend to be different than those of higher-income families, with more weight on food and shelter and less on items such as clothing, entertainment and travel. Nevertheless, if we want to obtain a sense of the comparative extent to which each country's benefits allows a household to buy goods and services, Purchasing Power Parity is the best available measure.

Organization of the volume

This volume begins with a comparative analysis of the structure of major benefits for children in the four countries. Four papers then follow on child benefits in each of the countries. Each of the national papers is written to a similar outline, beginning with a brief account of the historical evolution of the philosophy, goals and design of child benefit programs. The papers go on to describe the main income programs on behalf of children, followed by a brief description of in-kind benefits where these are relevant and important in understanding the overall system of supports for families with children. A discussion of inputs and outcomes comes next, then a concluding review of key policy issues.

THE STRUCTURE OF INCOME BENEFITS FOR CHILDREN IN AUSTRALIA, CANADA, THE UK AND THE US

Michael Mendelson and Ken Battle

As discussed in the introduction, this volume focuses mainly on income-tested programs that, in three of the four countries (Australia, Canada and the UK), are at the heart of comprehensive reform of their child benefit systems. Drawing upon the results of the four country studies, this paper compares the structure of the following major child benefit programs:

Australia
Family Tax Benefit Parts A and B

Canada
The federal government's Canada Child Tax Benefit (comprised of the basic Child Tax Benefit and the National Child Benefit Supplement) and, for lone-parent families, the spousal equivalent nonrefundable tax credit payable on behalf of the first child

United Kingdom
The existing universal Child Benefit and the Integrated Child Credit (to be introduced in 2003, assuming that the government after the next election continues with these plans)

United States
The national government's Earned Income Tax Credit, non-refundable child tax credit and preferences for families with children that are embedded in the income tax system

For Canada and the US, in a separate section we also examine the combined federal-provincial/state structure of child benefits for two examples – the province of British Columbia and the state of Wisconsin.

The purpose of this section is primarily to understand how the major child benefits work in each country, along with any remaining tax preferences and exemptions. But a picture of these programs does not provide a basis for comparison of the whole system of supports for families with children of the four countries in this study. For example, the US's Earned Income Tax Credit could be less generous than other countries' child benefit programs, but its food stamp scheme, not discussed in this paper, is unique and provides significant additional benefits to the low-income population. As another example, Australia and the UK both have very extensive rental assistance that benefits most of their low-income population, and this is not included in the comparisons in this paper. Therefore, one could not draw any conclusion about the countries' treatment of their low-income families just from the comparisons made in this section.

In the following discussion, all figures have been converted to US dollars using Purchasing Power Parity as set out in Table 1. All figures are for two types of households, unless otherwise stated: lone-parent families with one child under five years of age, and two-parent, single-earner families with one child under five years old and another child between seven and thirteen years.

The vertical y-axis in all figures – setting out the value of child benefits in US dollars – is fully comparable, at least to the extent that Purchasing Power Parity can be treated as a reliable means of conversion. Unfortunately, the horizontal x-axis cannot be made quite so precisely comparable among the four countries. While the x-axis provides a common comparison of the income levels used to determine a given level of benefits across all four countries, each country uses somewhat different definitions for that income. For example, as explained in the Canada paper, Canada pays its federal Canada Child Tax Benefit and various provincial income-tested child benefits not according to total or gross income, but rather a definition of 'net income' that allows for certain commonplace and often substantial deductions (e.g., private pension contributions and child care expenses). The other countries all have slightly different deductions netted out from gross income; for example, the UK at present subtracts income tax, which the other countries do not. As well, the Canadian and American income definitions are retrospective, using last year's income as assessed on the income tax form. Australia's income definition, in contrast, is prospective using an estimate of income in the coming year. There are other inconsistencies in detail in the definition of income according to which each country sets its benefit amounts. All this means that the level of child benefits at any given income level should be treated more as a 'band' than an exact number.

The following analysis is built upon a common quantitative model we have constructed to calculate child benefits in all four countries. To our knowledge this is the first time such a model has been used to permit a deeper level of detailed comparative review across countries than otherwise would be possible.

One-parent families

Figure 1 shows child benefits for one-parent families with one child under age five. All figures are in US dollars unless otherwise indicated. All four countries' benefits continue beyond the $80,000 level due to the effect of the universal Child Benefit in the UK, the Family Tax Benefit Part B for single earners in Australia, the spousal equivalent nonrefundable tax credit for lone parents in Canada, and the preferences built into the US income tax system for families with children (there are no longer analogous tax preferences in the other three countries).

As the final configuration for the Integrated Child Credit in the UK has not yet been decided, we show here the shape of the impending (2003) Integrated Child Credit and existing Child Benefit based on current benefit rates, as described in the UK paper. This results in a three-tiered structure with three plateaus connected by two steep slopes (the first more precipitous than the second) where high reduction rates cause rapid declines in benefits to the next plateau. Median income for one-parent families in the UK is equivalent to about US$15,000, so most will find themselves on the first plateau.

The Australian structure of benefits for lone-parent families is very similar to that in the UK. Australia also has three plateaus connected by slopes so steep as to resemble cliffs. The main difference between the Australian and UK configurations of child benefits for this family type is that the British payments to the poorest families are higher, and are somewhat higher for the other two plateaus as well.

Both Canada and the United States have tax preferences built into their systems. In Canada's case, a spousal equivalent nonrefundable tax credit is provided for lone parents so that they can treat their first child the same as a dependent spouse for the purposes of claiming a reduction in federal and provincial income taxes. In the US, there is a $500 per child nonrefundable tax credit as well as preferences for families with children embedded within the exemption and rate structure of the tax system. As a result of these elements, both the Canadian and US systems provide tax-delivered child benefits that extend income tax savings to upper-income families, though only in the case of one-parent families in Canada. Because of these tax measures, child benefits for lone-parent families in both countries ramp up after the tax system cuts in at roughly $7,000 to $8,000, with a peak followed by a slope (due to reductions in other income-tested child benefit programs).

Unlike the US system, Canadian child benefits for lone-parent families form a plateau at low income levels (because of the Canada Child Tax Benefit which pays equal amounts to all low-income families, whether on social assistance or in the work-force), followed by a peak due to the spousal equivalent nonrefundable tax credit adding to the Canada Child Tax Benefit, and then a slope downwards as the income-tested Canada Child Tax Benefit diminishes, until all that remains is the spousal equivalent tax credit that continues to benefit all lone-parent families at the upper end of the income range (admittedly a small group, given the modest incomes of most lone-parent families). Although Canadian child benefits are generally much smaller than those in Australia and the UK, Canada's benefits for lone-parent families are actually highest of all four countries for the income range of about $25,000 to $35,000.

The US benefit structure is unique in providing no payments to families without any income and maintaining a rising benefit structure up to a pronounced peak, followed by a decline and a valley, only to have benefits rise again starting at about $32,000. With the median income for female lone-parent families about

$20,700 (figures are unavailable for male lone-parent families), most lone-parent families are likely on the downward slope of the benefits structure before the valley.

Australian, Canadian and British per capita Gross Domestic Product (in US dollars converted using Purchasing Power Parity) is in a cluster of $24,192, $25,179 and $21,673, respectively. US per capita GDP is much higher at $32,184. There is no obvious pattern of benefits related to per capita GDP. However, each country's first plateau of child benefits falls below its per capita GDP figure.

Two-parent families

Figure 2 shows the structure of child benefits for two-parent single-earner families with two children (one under five and the other between seven and thirteen). Canada is alone in not paying child benefits to high-income couples: The Canada Child Tax Benefit ends at net family income of about US$69,000 for one or two children. (While a Canadian two-parent single-earner family will get the same nonrefundable tax credit as the spousal equivalent credit, in respect of the non-earning spouse, this tax break is available regardless of whether children are present, so this credit cannot be counted as a child-related benefit.) The UK's benefits extend into the upper income ranges because of the universal Child Benefit payment. Australia's Family Tax Benefit Part B provides flat rate universal assistance to all single-earner families with dependent children, so Australia also pays benefits through this program to those in higher income ranges – though *not* in the case of two-earner families. In the US, the $500 per child nonrefundable tax credit is phased out at $100,000 income for a family with two

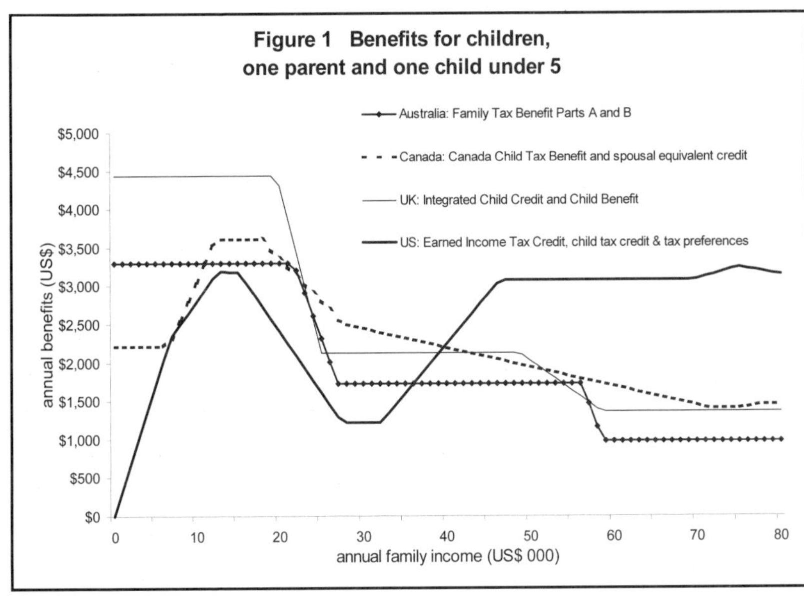
Figure 1 Benefits for children, one parent and one child under 5
Australia: Family Tax Benefit Parts A and B
Canada: Canada Child Tax Benefit and spousal equivalent credit
UK: Integrated Child Credit and Child Benefit
US: Earned Income Tax Credit, child tax credit & tax preferences
annual benefits (US$)
$5,000
$4,500
$4,000
$3,500
$3,000
$2,500
$2,000
$1,500
$1,000
$500
$0
0
10
20
30
40
50
60
70
80
annual family income (US$ 000)

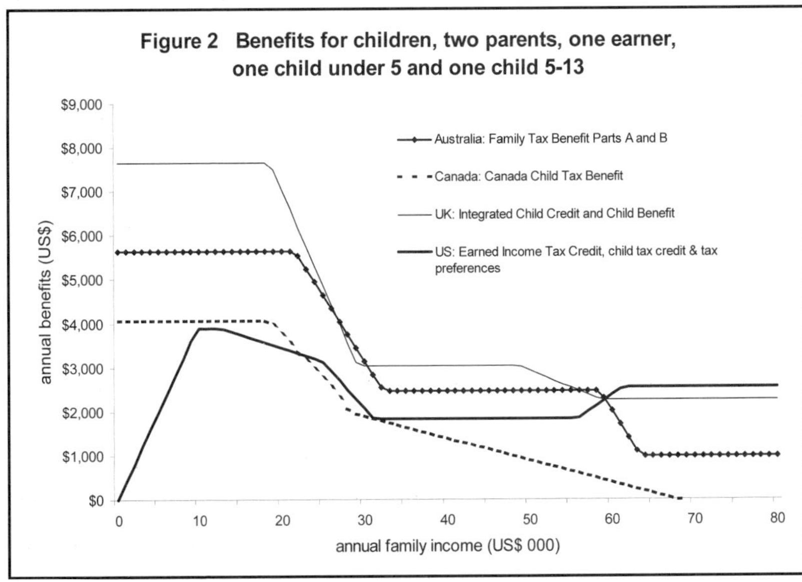
Figure 2 Benefits for children, two parents, one earner, one child under 5 and one child 5-13
Australia: Family Tax Benefit Parts A and B
Canada: Canada Child Tax Benefit
UK: Integrated Child Credit and Child Benefit
US: Earned Income Tax Credit, child tax credit & tax preferences
annual benefits (US$)
$9,000
$8,000
$7,000
$6,000
$5,000
$4,000
$3,000
$2,000
$1,000
$0
0
10
20
30
40
50
60
70
80
annual family income (US$ 000)

children and disappears entirely at $120,000, but this loss is offset by the tax preferences for families with children, which are more advantageous to those with higher incomes since their value rises with increasing marginal tax rates. However, some of the US tax preferences also phase out at very high incomes.

In Australia and the UK child benefits for two-parent families show the same 'three plateaus, two slopes' structure as for lone-parent families. It is probably not just coincidental that Australia and the UK both pay relatively generous benefits to low-income families. A 'stepped' shape (e.g., three plateaus and two sharp slopes) is necessary to limit costs in systems that pay relatively large benefits to lower-income families. If they were to use the Canadian model, which reduces benefits more gently for non-poor families and thus results in a smooth downward slope, the result would be a substantial increase in benefits for all families between $20,000 and $60,000. This design doubtless would be very expensive due to the large percentage of families in that income range.

Were the generosity of Canadian benefits to be increased to the levels in the UK or Australia, with no change in design, the result would be a more costly system in Canada than in Australia or the UK. But there are advantages to Canada's smooth structure as opposed to a stepped structure. A smooth structure does not impose such high effective marginal tax rates on families that fall on the slopes. A smooth structure relates the amount of benefits progressively to the amount of income for non-poor families, whereas stepped structures result in vertical inequities (families at the end of one plateau and the beginning of the next plateau get very different amounts of child benefit even though their incomes are not as different, while families at either end of each plateau receive similar amounts even though their incomes are very different). In short, as in almost all areas of public policy, there is a trade-off between what might be a preferable design were budgets unconstrained, and what might be an achievable design given the reality that budgets *are* constrained.

The American system is unique. Child benefits for two-parent families show a rising slope, followed by a peak, albeit gentler than in the case of lone-parent families, then a valley and slight increase for upper income ranges. The US system provides nothing for the poorest, relatively high benefits for a narrow range of the working poor, less for middle-income groups and more for high-income families. At the upper income ranges, the US provides the most generous child benefits of the four countries.

The Australian system treats single-earner families more generously than two-earner families, at least with respect to the range of programs discussed in this paper. This differential treatment results from the historical evolution of tax exemptions into the existing system, which provides a refundable tax credit of the same amount to all single-earner families as a way to distribute tax breaks without favouring the wealthiest. However, while accurate, Figure 2's illustration of preferential treatment for single-earner families does not give a representative view of the Australian system overall, since in reality only a minority of two-parent families in the middle and upper income ranges have just one earner, at least for any length of time.

Figure 3 provides a view of child benefits for two-parent, two-earner families in Australia, assuming that the second parent begins earning an income at about US$15,500 (i.e., when the first earner is making roughly A$20,000, the second earner begins to add to the family income, so that at about A$40,000 both are making about A$20,000), after which all additional income is attributed to the second parent. For this family type, the Australian system is even more clearly progressive in its distribution of benefits, with one of the three plateaus lopped off. However, there is no difference in child benefits for one-earner and two-earner couples with the same incomes in the other three countries.

State and provincial programs

Income security programs in the UK and Australia are operated exclusively by the central government. In both Canada and the US, sub-national governments play important roles in the income security system as a whole. While the Canadian and American child benefit programs that are the primary focus of this paper are predominately federal, there are significant provincial and some state supplements.

In Canada, every province and territory except for one jurisdiction (Prince Edward Island) now provides income-tested child benefit programs and/or employment earnings supplements for families with children. These new programs are intended ultimately to replace most or all of social assistance child-related benefits that used to go only to families on assistance. Fully integrated child benefit programs – replacing most social assistance payments on behalf of children and extending provincial child benefits to the working poor and, in some instances, modest-income families – are now operating in British Columbia, Saskatchewan, Quebec and Newfoundland. As noted in Daniel Meyer's paper on the US, in 1999 11 states provided supplements to the federal Earned Income Tax Credit.

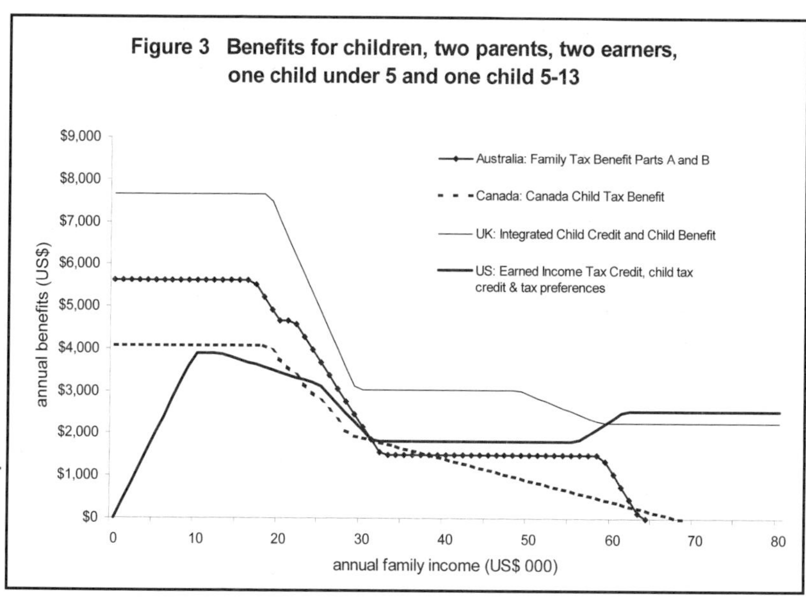
Figure 3 Benefits for children, two parents, two earners, one child under 5 and one child 5-13
$9,000
$8,000
$7,000
$6,000
$5,000
$4,000
$3,000
$2,000
$1,000
$0
annual benefits (US$)
0
10
20
30
40
50
60
70
80
annual family income (US$ 000)
Australia: Family Tax Benefit Parts A and B
Canada: Canada Child Tax Benefit
UK: Integrated Child Credit and Child Benefit
US: Earned Income Tax Credit, child tax credit & tax preferences

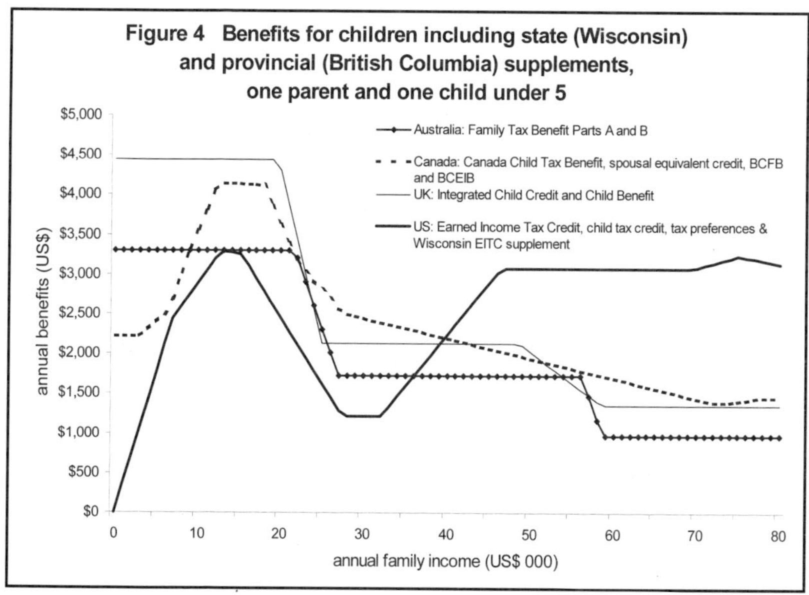
Figure 4 Benefits for children including state (Wisconsin) and provincial (British Columbia) supplements, one parent and one child under 5
$5,000
$4,500
$4,000
$3,500
$3,000
$2,500
$2,000
$1,500
$1,000
$500
$0
annual benefits (US$)
0
10
20
30
40
50
60
70
80
annual family income (US$ 000)
Australia: Family Tax Benefit Parts A and B
Canada: Canada Child Tax Benefit, spousal equivalent credit, BCFB and BCEIB
UK: Integrated Child Credit and Child Benefit
US: Earned Income Tax Credit, child tax credit, tax preferences & Wisconsin EITC supplement

Figure 4 illustrates, for lone-parent families with one child less than five years old, combined federal-state child benefits for the state of Wisconsin and federal-provincial child benefits for the province of British Columbia. Wisconsin's earnings-tested supplement to the Earned Income Tax Credit adds 4 percent to the Credit for one-parent families and 14 percent for two-parent families. British Columbia's provincial programs are more complex, consisting of an income-tested child benefit (the BC Family Bonus) and an earnings-tested supplement (the BC Earned Income Benefit).

With these additional state/provincial programs, the upward slope, peak and downward slope configurations of child benefits in Canada and the US become even more pronounced. For the province of British Columbia, Canada now shows the highest benefits among the four countries for one-parent families with incomes ranging from about $24,000 to $40,000. American child benefits also appear more generous for the working poor once Wisconsin's supplement to the federal Earned Income Tax Credit is included. In British Columbia's case, maximum federal and provincial child benefits (including the spousal equivalent nonrefundable tax credit for lone-parent families) for lone-parent families are within sight of the level of benefits envisaged for the UK once the Integrated Child Credit is implemented and higher than those in effect in Australia.

Figure 5 shows combined federal-state/provincial child benefits for families with two parents and two children. Because the spousal equivalent nonrefundable credit is not available to couples with children, the Canadian peak is much less pronounced, reflecting only the effect of the BC Earned Income Benefit (which is structurally similar to the Earned Income Tax Credit in the US, with a phase-in, plateau and phase-out), and there are no benefits at the upper income level. The American system looks much the same as in the previous figures that did not include state benefits, except of course it is more generous when Wisconsin's Earned Income Tax Credit supplement is included.

Just the income-tested stand-alone child benefit programs

Much of the reform effort in these countries has concentrated on developing new programs to provide income-related payments on behalf of children outside of the traditional income security system, in most cases using the tax system to assess income and deliver benefits. The key instances of this type of reform are the Australian Family Tax Benefit Part A, the Canada Child Tax Benefit, the UK Integrated Child Credit and the US Earned Income Tax Credit.

Figure 6 shows the structure of benefits for these four programs, isolated from the rest of the child benefit system, for one-parent families with one child. Again, we caution against drawing conclusions about the relative generosity of benefits among countries because the programs illustrated represent only part of a system of child benefits and the programs fit into the whole differently in each country (varying from the large part in Australia and Canada to a significant part in the UK and a smaller part in the US). Nevertheless, Figure 6 is useful in understanding the design features and distributional impact of each of these income-tested child benefits.

The Australian Family Tax Benefit Part A and the UK's planned Integrated Child Credit structurally are almost identical,

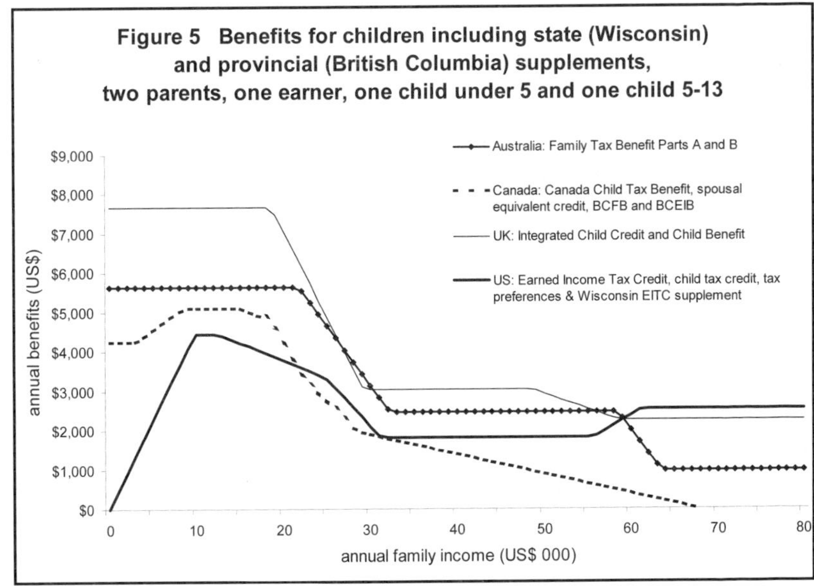
Figure 5 Benefits for children including state (Wisconsin) and provincial (British Columbia) supplements, two parents, one earner, one child under 5 and one child 5-13
Australia: Family Tax Benefit Parts A and B
Canada: Canada Child Tax Benefit, spousal equivalent credit, BCFB and BCEIB
UK: Integrated Child Credit and Child Benefit
US: Earned Income Tax Credit, child tax credit, tax preferences & Wisconsin EITC supplement
$9,000
$8,000
$7,000
$6,000
$5,000
$4,000
$3,000
$2,000
$1,000
$0
annual benefits (US$)
0
10
20
30
40
50
60
70
80
annual family income (US$ 000)

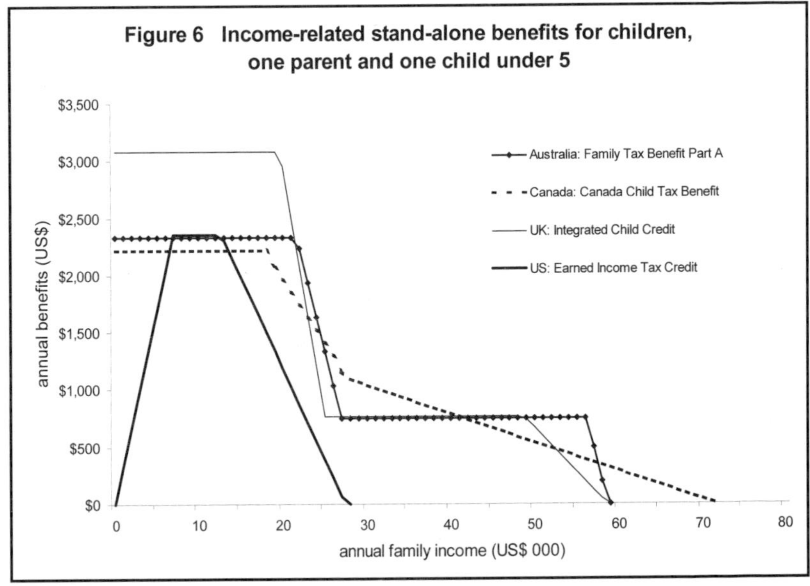
Figure 6 Income-related stand-alone benefits for children, one parent and one child under 5
Australia: Family Tax Benefit Part A
Canada: Canada Child Tax Benefit
UK: Integrated Child Credit
US: Earned Income Tax Credit
$3,500
$3,000
$2,500
$2,000
$1,500
$1,000
$500
$0
annual benefits (US$)
0
10
20
30
40
50
60
70
80
annual family income (US$ 000)

differing primarily in a steeper reduction rate at the upper income phase-out level in Australia. The Canada Child Tax Benefit differs from Australia and the UK in having a gentler slope after the first low-income plateau, but this is because Canada has no second plateau for middle-income families; instead, it employs a fairly steep taper for the portion of benefits targeted to low-income families and a very gradual taper for benefits to non-poor families. The US structure is unique in providing no child benefits to families with no income.

Figure 7 shows the same programs for Australia and the UK but includes sub-national programs for Canada (British Columbia) and the US (Wisconsin). When British Columbia's provincial benefits are added to the federal Canada Child Tax Benefit, Canada's system resembles much more closely Australia's and the UK's. Indeed, the UK also will have an 'earned income' component in its new system, which will operate something like BC's Earned Income Benefit, except that the British program also will serve households without children. This earned income component in the UK will make its system even more similar to that of Canada/British Columbia, the main difference being the presence of a second plateau in the UK.

Benefit reduction rates in the child benefit programs

To better see the design of the key child benefit programs, Figure 8 shows the child benefit reduction rates for one-parent, one-child families for the national programs listed above (i.e., not including sub-national programs). 'Reduction rates' are the rates at which benefits fall as incomes increase; for example, if benefits are decreased by $100 when income increases by $1,000, this results in a 10 percent reduction rate.

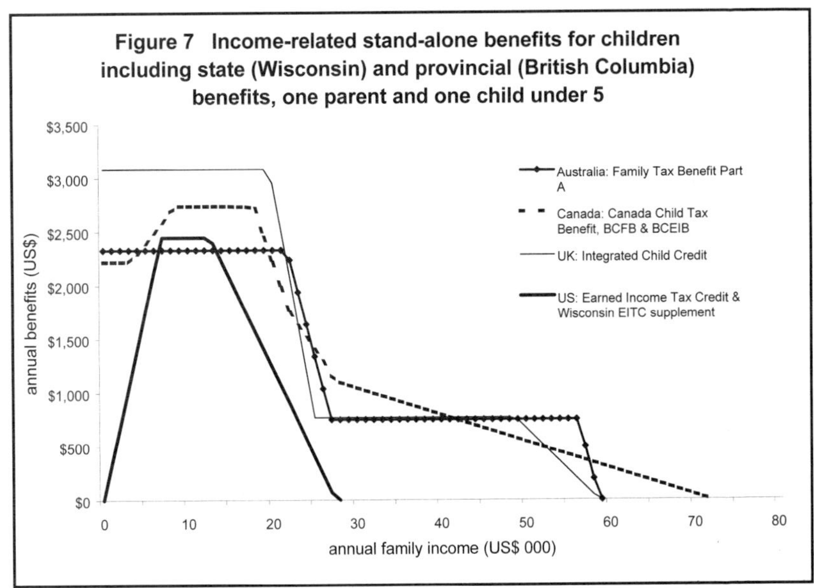
Figure 7 Income-related stand-alone benefits for children including state (Wisconsin) and provincial (British Columbia) benefits, one parent and one child under 5
$3,500
$3,000
$2,500
$2,000
$1,500
$1,000
$500
$0
annual benefits (US$)
0
10
20
30
40
50
60
70
80
annual family income (US$ 000)
Australia: Family Tax Benefit Part A
Canada: Canada Child Tax Benefit, BCFB & BCEIB
UK: Integrated Child Credit
US: Earned Income Tax Credit & Wisconsin EITC supplement

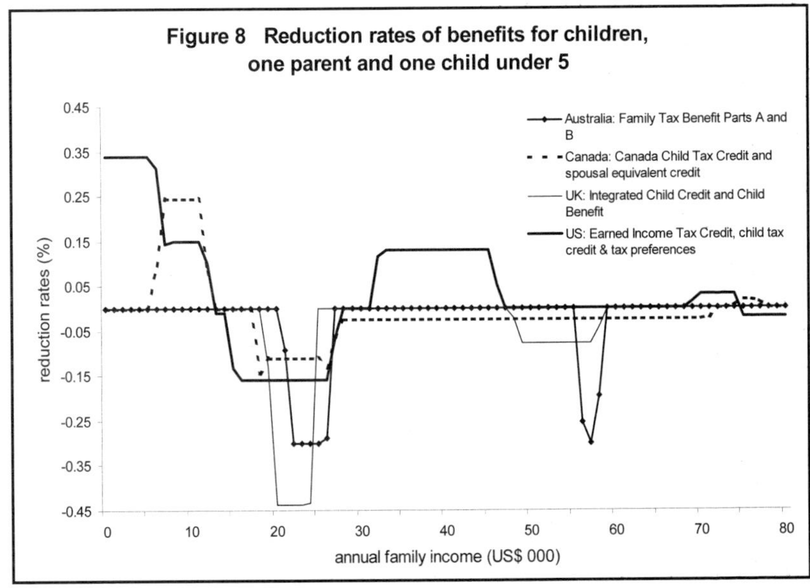
Figure 8 Reduction rates of benefits for children, one parent and one child under 5
0.45
0.35
0.25
0.15
0.05
-0.05
-0.15
-0.25
-0.35
-0.45
reduction rates (%)
0
10
20
30
40
50
60
70
80
annual family income (US$ 000)
Australia: Family Tax Benefit Parts A and B
Canada: Canada Child Tax Credit and spousal equivalent credit
UK: Integrated Child Credit and Child Benefit
US: Earned Income Tax Credit, child tax credit & tax preferences

Neither Australia nor the UK have any areas of 'positive' reduction rates (a 'positive' rate being an *increase* in benefit as income increases) because neither has any programs where the amount of child benefit increases with income. However, both Canada and the US have some income ranges in which there are positive reduction rates. In Canada's case, this is a relatively small range of low income and is due entirely to the phasing in of the spousal equivalent nonrefundable tax credit for lone-parent families. In the case of the US, reduction rates are more varied than for the other countries, with substantial income ranges of positive rates due to the Earned Income Tax Credit, the child tax credit and, in upper income ranges, the tax system's exemptions and higher tax thresholds for families with children.

Australia and the UK both concentrate their negative reduction rates in two very narrow bands of income, from about $20,000 to $25,000, and again between roughly $50,000 and $60,000. This is a reflection of the 'three plateaus' structure in Australia and the UK. In contrast, Canada is the only country with a small negative reduction rate for a wide range of income (i.e., for all non-poor families that receive the basic Child Tax Benefit), as the latter program's design employs a longer, very gradual phase-out with no second plateau.

The pattern is even clearer for two-parent families, as can be seen in Figure 9. Other than in the US, there are no positive reduction rates. Most negative rates are concentrated in a relatively narrow band of income; indeed, there is much convergence among countries. Only Canada has a long band of low but negative reduction rates under its income-tested Canada Child Tax Benefit.

The relationship of child benefit reduction rates to the broader income security and tax systems, particularly social assistance, is

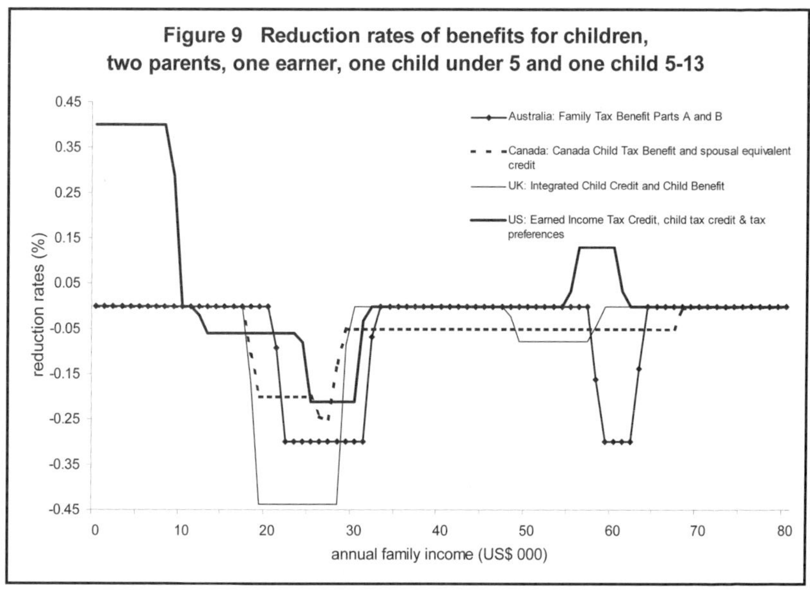

not shown here. The highest effective marginal tax rates (i.e., the percentage of additional income that is lost as a result of income-tested social programs and income and payroll taxes) traditionally have been found in the transition from social assistance to work, where benefits are wholly or largely eliminated as employment earnings increase. With child benefits in Australia being available at the same rate for families whether they are on social assistance or working, and with the implementation of the fully portable Integrated Child Credit in the UK that also will allow child benefits to be maintained whether working or on assistance, effective marginal tax rates for Australian and British families moving from assistance to work are (or, in the UK, will be) much lower than they would be were child benefits unavailable to those who are working.

In most of Canada's provinces, child benefits in social assistance to date have been only partly replaced by the expanding federal Canada Child Tax Benefit, whose increases are being phased in over several years, though a few provinces (British Columbia, Saskatchewan, Quebec and Newfoundland) have or are planning an integrated child benefit that will replace all or most social assistance child benefits with an income-tested program paying equal benefits to all low-income families, including the working poor. In those provinces, effective marginal tax rates on the movement from assistance to work have been or will be significantly reduced.

The American situation is quite different. In the US, a recipient's entitlement to state income assistance is time-limited and very conditional in any case. Nevertheless, the Earned Income Tax Credit at maximum levels likely more than fully replaces any child benefits which would have been available on assistance, although there may be a range of very low incomes (where the Credit phases in) where this is not the case.

Administration of the income test and the issue of responsiveness

In a fully integrated child benefit, there no longer should be child-related payments in the last resort social assistance system, nor in other income security programs such as unemployment insurance. But all families on social assistance and most on unemployment insurance then will need to receive the maximum amount of child benefits, since the amount they are paid by social assistance, unemployment insurance and other income security programs would be set on the assumption that the maximum child benefit is being paid. Consequently, an integrated child benefit program must be designed to deliver full benefits in as timely and responsive a fashion as possible for families that suffer a dramatic reduction in income and have little or no income of their own.

Traditional last resort income assistance programs have handled the need for responsiveness to income change by frequently testing recipients' incomes and by maintaining a delivery system that can respond rapidly to small changes in the circumstances that affect needs (e.g., reduced hours of part-time work, a change in rent). But the price for this responsiveness has been program administration that is highly intrusive in recipients' lives by requiring continual, detailed reporting and checking of income and other circumstances. In Canada and the US, the intrusive and investigative nature of social assistance administration has contributed to its highly stigmatizing nature.

Integrated child benefits are delivered to a much wider group of families than are last resort programs, so requiring such intrusive and frequent income testing of this population would be impractical for administrative and political reasons, as well as highly disagreeable. But there is a dilemma: Integrated child benefits demand a simple and non-intrusive means of determining income, in contradiction to the requirements of last resort programs – yet if integrated benefits are to function effectively for recipients of last resort programs, they must be able to deliver full payments immediately when required. So how have the four countries in this study solved this conundrum?

Australia, Canada and the United States employ the income tax system to test incomes for child benefit purposes. In Canada and the United States, the child benefit payment is based on income of the tax year being reported (i.e., the previous year). Consequently, the income upon which the amount of child benefit is calculated in both of these countries may be as much as a year or more out of date.

In the United States, the Earned Income Tax Credit does not act as an integrated child benefit; it is targeted only to low-income families in the workforce and last resort programs do not function the same way as in the other countries. The income tax system pays the Earned Income Tax Credit retrospectively, usually as a single lump sum payment (a few recipients opt for payment through their employer on their paycheque). This means that middle-income families that become working poor during the year must wait until the next year before receiving their Earned Income Tax Credit. Middle-income families whose circumstances change so radically that they have no earned income at all, and that would in other countries be entitled to social assistance, are not in any case entitled to the Earned Income Tax Credit, regardless of what the reporting period might be for income. The US 'solves' the responsiveness dilemma by not using the Earned Income Tax Credit to deliver child benefits to families with no income.

In Canada, the amount of the Canada Child Tax Benefit is determined on an annual basis according to family net income for the previous year as calculated on the annual income tax form, but the total entitlement is then divided by twelve and paid on a monthly basis – partly in order to integrate with social assistance, which is also paid on a monthly basis. The payment year is from July 1 of this year to June 30 next year.

As discussed in the Canada paper, the only provision for mid-year change in federal child benefits is when there is a change in family composition (e.g., separation of the parents or the birth of a child). For families whose income drops during the year to a level where they qualify for maximum payments for any reason other than family composition (e.g., loss of a job), the need for responsiveness is handled by having a provision in provincial social assistance to pay up to the equivalent of the maximum federal Canada Child Tax Benefit for families that are not getting full federal child benefits but are entitled to social assistance. In other words, provincial social assistance acts as a fallback system for the federal Canada Child Tax Benefit, but only for those families that experience such extremely difficult financial circumstances that they are entitled to social assistance. This arrangement means that families that suffer a drop in income but are not entitled to social assistance, and cannot apply mid-year for higher child benefits, must wait until they file their next tax return before getting full child benefits. The *quid pro quo* is that families with a rise in income during the year do not have their child benefits reduced. In the end, the Canada Child Tax Benefit 'catches up' to changes in income, even if it takes a year or longer.

Australia has the most fully integrated child benefit system of all the countries in this study, and has had it in place for some time. However, the nature of the income test for Family Tax Benefit Part A is being changed this year; there has not yet been an opportunity to experience a full cycle with the new system. Basically, for those families that want child benefit payments during the year, Australia will ask them to estimate *prospectively* their income for the coming year. Payments will be made on the basis of that estimate, and then reconciled on the tax form at the end of the year when actual income is reported. Periods when families are in receipt of social assistance are excluded from calculation of income for purposes of determining the entitlement to Family Tax Benefit.

Payments during the year can be delivered through a bi-weekly direct bank deposit, or through reduction of income taxes deducted from workers' paycheques. Alternatively, the benefits can be claimed as a lump sum at the end of the year on the tax return. To add to the range of choices, recipients may vary payment methods during the year. This means that a family with a precipitous drop in income can switch in-year to the bi-weekly system. Recipients of income support are required to use the bi-weekly payment mechanism. Anyone using the bi-weekly payment method may report any change in income, and the amount of Family Tax Benefit can be increased (or decreased).

Thus in Australia the responsiveness problem has been resolved by allowing the child benefits system to have a provision for some families to receive a bi-weekly payment based on current income, while others simply use the income tax system, as in Canada – although in Australia the tax system is used to estimate the coming year's income and then reconcile the following year. As the first cycle of the prospective income reporting system has not yet been completed, it is not known how this method of income assessment will perform. The problem of responsiveness is also reduced in Australia by the design of its system. As can be seen in the figures, for most income ranges, Australia pays a flat rate benefit and reduces benefits only over a comparatively narrow band of income.

The UK has not yet set up its system of income testing for the Integrated Child Credit and has still to decide what mechanism to use. Traditionally, the UK has relied upon frequent reporting of income; there appears to be less sense of stigmatization involved in such reporting than is the case in some other countries. The Working Families Tax Credit relies upon the submission of a special application form; payment is based on income over the previous time period (six weeks to three months) and benefits remain in pay at the established level for six months, regardless of change in circumstances. However, the Working Families Tax Credit is designed for families that are in work and not on income support, so it does not have to deal with the same need to be responsive as will the new Integrated Child Credit.

In Australia and Canada, the British have two types of solutions they could employ for their Integrated Child Credit: The Australian approach builds an optional arrangement of bi-weekly reporting into the child benefit program, while maintaining a less intrusive system for the majority. Alternatively, Canada uses a simple retrospective child benefit system, but continues to provide for temporary recourse through social assistance for some families that qualify for but do not yet receive the maximum federal benefit.

Conclusion

The national papers discuss the stated and unstated objectives of the child benefit system in each country. Of the many possible goals for child benefits, with regard to the two sometimes-competing fundamental objectives of 'vertical equity' (i.e., anti-poverty/income supplementation for lower-income families) and 'horizontal inequity' (i.e., fair treatment of families with children compared to those without children, at all income levels), how do the child benefit systems of the four countries compare?

The British system, if implemented as described in Figures 1 and 2, will address both vertical and horizontal equity objectives to some extent. The UK pays substantial benefits to low-income families and meaningful, though lower, payments for families at middle and higher incomes. However, the structure of the system, with its long plateaus and sharp slopes, weakens its performance in terms of vertical equity for non-poor families (since some similar-income families receive different amounts, while some different-income families get similar child benefits). With respect to single-earner families, Australia is also addressing both vertical and horizontal equity objectives. However, while Australia provides substantial payments to middle-income single-earner families, as can be seen in Figure 3, it pays none to higher-income dual-earner families. Australia therefore only partially meets horizontal equity objectives with regard to two-earner families.

The Canadian system resembles the Australian with respect to the horizontal equity objective in the case of lone-parent families, although it is less generous when it comes to the anti-poverty objective. However, for two-parent families, the Canadian system provides diminishing and relatively small payments to those in the middle-income range and little or nothing to those with high incomes, so it is not as successful in addressing the horizontal equity objective for non-poor families.

Australia and Canada treat single earners and lone parents, respectively, differently than dual-earner and two-parent families.

In both cases, this special treatment for a particular type of household is rooted in the history of the tax system, although the special tax benefits have now been fully 'cashed out' in Australia, to use the useful Australian term, and replaced with cash benefits in the child benefit system. The Canadian system retains its spousal equivalent nonrefundable credit in respect of the first child in one-parent families, with pro-horizontal equity results for one-parent families only, although the old children's tax exemption was effectively 'cashed out' as in Australia (i.e., the money that used to be spent on the children's tax exemption effectively was redirected to what is now the Canada Child Tax Benefit).

The American child benefit system is counter-redistributive, with large payments to upper-income families and nothing at all to those with no earned income. The US pays its largest child benefits to the working poor and to the wealthy, and less to others. To our knowledge, American commentators on child benefits almost always overlook the important role of their income tax system, perhaps assuming that tax preferences for families with children are not 'real' child benefits and not as tangible as the Earned Income Tax Credit – despite the experience in the other three countries in this study, which publicly debated the regressive effect of their old tax preferences for children and eventually replaced them with progressive income-tested benefits. In its unique design, the child benefit system in the US reflects a different philosophy of income security than the other countries: The American income security system is almost entirely focused on employment, and its child benefits system is designed mainly to strengthen families' ties to the labour market and to recognize the horizontal equity claims of taxpaying parents, virtually ignoring those with little or no earned income.

Despite all these differences among the four countries, there also are many similarities in the structures of their benefits. A glance at Figures 1 through 9 will show that there are several points where the child benefit structures converge. For example, all the countries end the first phase of their child benefits at around US $28,000 for lone-parent families with one child, give or take a few thousand dollars. There is a similar cluster around US$30,000 for two-parent families. Reflecting this pattern, there is a convergent cluster of high reduction rates prior to this income level.

The following papers provide detailed explanations of each child benefit system, how it works and the context in which it operates. The reader doubtless will spot many other similarities, and many other differences, among the four nations. It is our hope that we will be able to learn and to advance the development of child benefits in all four countries by better understanding both the similarities and the differences.

BENEFITS FOR CHILDREN: AUSTRALIA

Peter Whiteford[1]

INTRODUCTION

In common with other countries, the Australian system of support for families with children is intended to serve a range of objectives. These objectives include: contributing to the cost of raising children and redistributing resources over the life cycle; alleviating child poverty and boosting low family earnings; promoting equity within the tax system and redistributing income within families; and relieving unemployment and low income traps and increasing incentives to work, among other goals.

At different times the emphasis placed on different objectives has shifted, but it seems fair to say that Australia has gone further than many other countries in emphazising redistribution to low-income families, and also redistribution to mothers. Over the course of the last 25 years, successive Australian governments first 'cashed-out' the general tax assistance for families, so that most assistance is paid as benefits to mothers, then income tested this cash assistance while substantially increasing benefits to low-income families. While providing increased assistance to low-income families was part of an explicit anti-child poverty agenda, it also was intended to maintain and enhance incentives to work for low-income families in the workforce.

There also was a good deal of attention given to administrative issues, particularly in order to ensure satisfactory take-up of benefits, and to maximize work incentives. In addition, all payments for children in low-income families were administratively integrated and made separately payable to the mother, rather than as part of the beneficiary's income support payment. Subsequently, some of the remaining forms of tax assistance also were made available in the form of cash benefits, usually paid to mothers, and the basic income support system was partially individualized so that women received assistance in their own right rather than as dependants of a male 'breadwinner.'

However, as a consequence of these and other reforms, the system became more complex, and the higher effective marginal tax rates that are an unavoidable consequence of income testing became more salient over a wider range of private incomes. In combination with these policy concerns, a number of social and economic trends have raised further pressures. As in many other countries, the incidence of sole parenthood in Australia has increased over most of the past 25 years, so that currently around 20 percent of families with children are sole parents. Because sole parents in Australia have a comparatively high level of coverage of income support, and a relatively low level of employment, the growth in sole parenthood has been expensive in terms of government spending and has raised concerns about child poverty. These concerns have been heightened by the increase in unemployment among couples with children, first in the recession of the early 1980s and then in the recession of the early 1990s. While there have been falls in unemployment following these recessions, families with children do not appear to have benefited to the same extent as persons without responsibility for children. Recent studies by the OECD suggest that in the mid-1990s, Australia had one of the highest levels of non-employment among couples with children of any OECD country [Oxley et al. 1999].

In July 2000 the Australian system of assistance for families with children was again reformed as part of a broader program of reform of the taxation system. These reforms alleviated the high effective marginal tax rates facing many low-income families with children and simplified the system in some important respects. Part of the reforms also involved providing families with the choice of whether assistance is provided through cash payments or through the tax system.

In summary, the reforms introduced into assistance for families over the past 25 years provide ample illustration of the continuing tensions between the differing objectives of family assistance. The Australian experience illustrates the trade-off between universality and selectivity, the specific advantages and disadvantages of targeting, the alternative means of delivering family payments, and the problems of complexity and achieving simplicity.

Before turning to a detailed discussion of the current features of the Australian system of family assistance, there are a number of issues that should be noted. As is the case in many other countries, support for families with children in Australia is part of both the social security system and the taxation system. However, the Australian social security and taxation systems differ in important respects from those in most other OECD countries, including Canada, the United Kingdom and the United States.

Australia has never had a contributory social security system. (However, since 1992 there has been a mandatory private retirement savings plan with employer contributions that will rise to 9 percent. This system will not be mature for many years.) All benefits, including those for families with children, are financed from general taxation revenue. Maximum benefits are flat rate rather than earnings-related and generally are subject to income and assets tests. Income support payments for people of workforce age are of two main types – pensions, primarily for people with a disability, their carers and for widows and sole parents – and benefits or allowances, primarily for the unemployed and the short-term sick. Pension payments are generally more generous and have more relaxed income and assets tests. The unemployed are required to look actively for work, but sole parents with children under 16 and the disabled are not. Most payments apart from sickness allowance are available on an indefinite basis, so long as recipients continue to meet eligibility requirements.

The absence of contributory benefits means that the means-tested system has to perform the functions that in other countries are performed by social insurance. This means that the selective system in Australia must still encompass a majority of the population. A social security system that provided assistance only to the extremely poor would be politically unsustainable. Thus, the logic of means testing is very different in Australia even than in, for example, the United Kingdom. An illustration of the difference is that in the UK it is the poorest 20 percent (roughly) of the retired population that receives income support. In Australia, it is the richest 20 percent that is excluded from assistance.

For this reason, the income tests are relatively generous compared to those operating in the social assistance schemes of many other OECD countries [Eardley, Bradshaw, Ditch, Gough and Whiteford 1995]. In this context, the tests on assets are also comparatively very generous, being mainly designed to exclude those with very high levels of private wealth, rather than concentrate assistance on those with very low levels of wealth. In addition, the level of benefits tend to be higher relative to average earnings than is the case in the social assistance schemes in other English-speaking countries, and given the lower income test withdrawal rates, the cut-out points for benefits are further up the income distribution. The structure of assistance for families is significantly influenced by the design of income support payments. Because of the relatively high cut-out points, income support recipients can combine part-time work and receipt of benefits, and there are no 'hours rules' for benefit receipt as there are in the United Kingdom.

Correspondingly, because the benefit system is not contributory, there are no social security contributions as part of the taxation system. Income taxes take a relatively high proportion of all taxes, and the income tax system is comparatively progressive. In addition, there was no general broad-based consumption tax until July 2000.

A further point to note is that while Australia is a federal system, responsibility for income support policy – including assistance for families – rests predominantly at the federal level. There is some assistance for families provided by state government, mainly in the form of limited cash assistance with education costs, but these are so minor as not to warrant discussion. Moreover, income taxes are also collected only at the federal level, and there are no separate income taxes levied by any state. As a result of these features, the system of benefits and income taxes is uniform across Australia, which in this regard is more like the United Kingdom than Canada or the United States.

INCOME BENEFITS FOR CHILDREN

On 1 July 2000 the Australian government introduced major changes to the tax system including the introduction of a broad-based Goods and Service Tax (a VAT), substantial income tax cuts and changes to financial relationships between the States and the Commonwealth government. The personal income tax cuts cost about $12,000 million and in particular raise the level at which the top marginal rate cuts in, so that about 80 percent of taxpayers will be in the standard 30 percent range. (Details of the new tax scale are contained in Annex 1.) There also was an extensive compensation package for social security recipients, as well as major changes to assistance for families.

These changes to family assistance simplified payments by amalgamating a number of different forms of assistance, and also provided higher levels of assistance, with reductions in income test withdrawal rates. The new structure combined twelve of the pre-existing types of assistance into three new programs of assistance. This section deals with two of these – Family Tax Benefit Part A, which assists with the general costs of raising children, and Family Tax Benefit Part B, which is directed to single-income and sole-parent families. The third program, Child Care Benefit, is discussed later. Details of these programs are contained in Table 1.

Family Tax Benefit Part A

Family Tax Benefit Part A is paid for dependent children up to 20 years of age, and for dependent full-time students up to the age of 24 (who are not getting Youth Allowance or similar payments such as ABSTUDY and Veterans' Children Education Supplement). It is essentially a two-tier but integrated payment directed to most families with children, with a higher rate for lower-income families, including both those in work and those receiving income support. It replaced Minimum Family Allowance, Greater Than Minimum Rate Family Allowance, Family Tax Payment Part A and Family Tax Assistance Part A.

The maximum rate is paid up to family income of $28,200, and is then reduced by 30 cents for every extra dollar of income, until the minimum rate is reached. Part-payment at the minimum rate is available up to a family income of $73,000 (with an additional $3,000 for each dependent child after the first). Payments are then reduced by 30 cents in every dollar over that amount until the payment reaches nil.

To receive some Family Tax Benefit Part A, the maximum income levels are $76,256 a year for a family with one dependent child under 18 and $77,355 a year for a family with one dependant 18-24 years old. These thresholds are lifted by $6,257 for each additional dependent child under 18 and $7,356 for each additional dependent 18-24 years of age. There is also a separate income test applying to income from child maintenance payments.

Families receiving Family Tax Benefit Part A also may be eligible for extra payments, such as Rent Assistance if renting privately, the Large Family Supplement for four or more children, and Multiple Birth Allowance for three or more children born during the same birth.

Family Tax Benefit Part B

Family Tax Benefit Part B provides extra assistance to single-income families including sole parents – particularly families with children under 5 years of age. It replaced the Basic Parenting Payment, Guardian Allowance, Family Tax Payment Part B, Family Tax Assistance Part B, the Dependent Spouse Rebate (with children) and the Sole Parent Rebate.

In a couple, if the secondary earner's income is above $1,616 a year, payments are reduced by 30 cents for every extra dollar of income. Parents receive some Family Tax Benefit Part B if the secondary earner's income is below $10,416 a year if the youngest child is under 5 years of age, or $7,786 a year if the youngest child is between 5 and 18 years of age. There is no income test on the primary earner's income, so in the case of sole parents the payment is universal.

A late complication has been added to the system. In the replacement of Basic Parenting Payment by Family Tax Benefit (B), the change to the definition of income – from a fortnightly assessment of income to an annual (prospective) assessment for Family Tax Benefit (B) – means that some women who stop or start work at certain points of a financial year can lose, although many can also win. In order to ensure that there are no losers, a new top-up payment has been introduced. However, this top-up is not discussed further here.

Administrative issues

A new Family Assistance Office (FAO) has been set up in Centrelink (the agency that delivers Commonwealth benefits and some services), Medicare Offices (the public health insurance agency) and Australian Taxation Offices to allow families to claim all of their assistance from just one agency under one set of rules. The Family Assistance Office (FAO) is a 'one-stop shop' for integrated family assistance, operating through call centres from 15 March 2000 and as a "virtual office" from 3 July 2000. Further details can be found at http://www.familyassist.gov.au/.

The new system provides a wider range of choice of how family assistance can be paid. Families are able to choose to receive their Family Tax Benefit as a direct payment each fortnight or through the tax system. Fortnightly payments are paid into bank or credit union accounts. A lump sum through the tax system can be claimed when parents or their partner lodge a tax return and claim for Family Tax Benefit. Alternatively, parents will be able to choose to receive Family Tax Benefit periodically by employers reducing their tax installment deductions. If they choose this option, parents must lodge a claim for Family Tax Benefit when they or their partner lodge a tax return.

Families are able to change their method of payment at any time during the year. For example, they could get fortnightly payments for the first six months but decide to claim the remaining six months as a lump sum through the tax system. There are some exceptions. For people who receive Social Security and Veterans' Affairs Benefits, family payments are paid fortnightly into their bank or credit union account. Those claiming Rent Assistance also will have their Family Tax Benefit paid into their bank or credit union account because Rent Assistance cannot be paid through the tax system. (Other payments for families, such as the Maternity Allowance and the Maternity Immunization Allowance, also will be available only as direct payments into a bank or credit union account.) Health Care Card families also will receive their Family Tax Benefit paid fortnightly by direct deposit.

The definition of income for the purposes of the family income tests is the combined gross taxable income of both spouses (where relevant). In addition, income includes foreign income, certain employer-provided fringe benefits (over $1,000) and net losses from rental property ('negative gearing'), less any deductible child maintenance expenditure (50 percent of maintenance paid, increasing to 100 percent from July 2001).

Families are required to estimate their income. At the end of the financial year, payments will be assessed against actual income (and hours of child care actually used). If people have less income than they estimated, then they will receive extra payments. This is a change from current arrangements, where there is no adjustment if actual income is less than estimated income. Correspondingly, if actual income at the end of the year is more than estimated, people will have to repay any amounts they were overpaid. It is worth noting that this end-of-year reconciliation is a new feature of the system. Given the option to claim Family Tax Benefit through the tax system at the end of the year, and the need to ensure that people receive the same entitlement for each delivery option, reconciliation became necessary.

The reconciliation allows for either a top-up payment if income has been overestimated, or a debt if income has been underestimated. People will be able to overestimate their income to avoid an end-of-year debt and still receive a top-up payment based on actual income. The reconciliation also will allow for a Family Tax Benefit debt to be offset against a tax refund, and for a tax debt to be offset against a Family Tax Benefit entitlement. However, the Part A income test does not apply during any period that the person or partner is receiving income support (the maintenance income test still applies). Therefore the period on income support will be quarantined from the reconciliation.

IN-KIND BENEFITS FOR CHILDREN

Child care benefits and subsidies

Australia has an extensive program of assistance with child care costs, which was reformed as part of the July 2000 package. Child Care Benefit provides a maximum level of assistance for 50 hours of care of $120 per week per child (for approved care). Actual levels of assistance depend on the number of children in child care, the hours of care received, the type of service or care provided, and family income.

If family income is less than $28,200 (and approved care is used), families are eligible for the maximum rate of benefit, depending on hours of care paid for and whether a child goes to school. Above this income 'free area,' taper rates are 10 percent for one child in care, 15 percent and (above $66,000) 25 percent for 2 children in care, and 15 percent and (above $66,000) 35 percent for 3 or more children in care. The income test does not apply for incomes above $81,000. Families with income above this level are eligible only for the minimum rate of Child Care Benefit of $20.10 per week

Child Care Benefit is not available through the tax system. However, for 'approved' care (a formal child care service), there are two payment options. The first of these is direct payment to the child care service, so the child care fees are reduced by the amount of the Child Care Benefit and the parent pays only the difference between the full fee and the amount of benefit. Alternatively, families will be able to make lump sum claim from the Family Assistance Office after the end of the financial year, which will be paid directly into a bank or credit union account. To claim for 'registered' care (registered carers such as grandparents, relatives, friends or nannies), parents need to provide receipts to the Family Assistance Office. Money can be claimed at any time during the year, up to 12 months after the care was provided. Payments will be made directly into a bank or credit union account. If parents use a mix of approved and registered care, they will need to claim Child Care Benefit separately for each type of care.

Housing subsidies

Australia has two main forms of housing assistance. Income support recipients and families with children that are receiving the maximum rate of Family Tax Benefit Part A may be eligible for Rent Assistance, in addition to their pension, allowance or family payment. Rent Assistance is available to those in the private rental market who pay rent above certain specified levels. These eligible rent levels vary by type of family and numbers of children. Above these levels, Rent Assistance is paid at 75 percent of rent up to maximum amounts, which also vary by family type and number of dependent children.

For example, in order to receive the maximum Rent Assistance of $102.00 per fortnight, a family with 3 or more children would have to be paying private rents of $279.60 per fortnight. That is, the rent assistance would cover about 36 percent of their rental costs. If their rental costs were higher than this, there is no increase in assistance. In 1997-98, there were 911,000 benefit income units receiving rent assistance. Very roughly, this is equivalent to between 60 and 70 percent of all private renters in Australia (who, in turn, make up around 20 percent of household units).

The Commonwealth State Housing Agreement (CSHA) is an agreement between the Commonwealth and the States and Territories. Its purpose is to provide funding to assist those whose needs for appropriate housing cannot be met by the private market. The current Commonwealth State Housing Agreement provides more than $4 billion for housing assistance such as public and community housing, indigenous housing, crisis accommodation, home purchase assistance and private rental assistance. The most important component program in the Commonwealth State Housing Agreement is public rental housing assistance, which is available to individuals and families with incomes below specified thresholds. Eligibility requirements and administrative procedures vary among States and Territories. Around 5 percent of Australian households live in public rental housing (just under 400,000 households) and a further 0.5 percent in community housing. Rents for public housing are charged according to a household's assessable income until payments are equal to an established market rent. While arrangements differ across States, most households pay between 20 and 25 percent of their gross income in rent. The difference between the market rent and the rent actually paid is called the rent rebate.

Health care subsidies

Australia has a universal health care system, Medicare, although with user charges. For example, for a standard consultation with a general practitioner, an individual may be charged $35 and she then could claim a repayment from a Medicare office of around $23. However, doctors can choose to 'bulk-bill' the government directly and the patient would then not pay at all. Around 80 percent of services are bulk-billed.

Treatment in public hospitals is free of charge, but individuals can take out private health insurance to receive care from a doctor of their choice or to avoid waiting lists for non-urgent procedures. Many pharmaceuticals are subsidized, and social security recipients may be entitled to an additional payment that reimburses them for a minimum number of prescriptions in a year (although they have to pay up-front for those they receive). Above a certain level of expenditure in a year, pharmaceuticals are then free.

The health system is financed mainly through general taxation. Although there is a Medicare Levy of 1.5 percent of income that partly finances the health system, individuals do not need to pay the levy to receive health care. The government is concerned to increase private health insurance coverage, and there is a further 1 percent of income payable by higher-income earners who do not have private health care, as well as a tax rebate for private health insurance coverage, among other incentives.

INPUTS AND OUTCOMES

The level of support for children

As the new system of assistance for families was introduced only in July 2000, it is not possible to provide details of current levels of spending or of numbers of families assisted. Table 2 compares the new and old structures of family assistance, showing that 12 separate payments or tax measures have been collapsed into three new payments.

Table 3 compares actual expenses in 1999-2000 with Budget estimates for 2000-01. Spending on Family Allowances and Family Tax Payment is estimated to increase from around $7,200 million to nearly $9,900 million, an increase of 37 percent. Spending through the tax system is estimated at $860 million, or only around 8 percent of total spending on the major family payments. Spending on the relevant forms of Child Care assistance is projected to increase by around 25 percent from $840 million to $1,050 million.

Table 4 provides greater details on levels of spending and numbers of families and children assisted in 1998-99. As far as possible, the table attempts to separate out the previous payments into their new organizational structure, but this can be done only to a limited extent.

The largest single program for families with children in 1998-99 was the Family Allowance. Slightly more than half of the families and their children receiving Family Allowance were benefiting from the higher rate of assistance. Overall, more than 40 percent of Australian children under 16 were in families receiving the higher rate of Family Allowance. In total, spending on Family Allowance was around $6,400 million or roughly 1.1 percent of GDP. The Family Tax Payment Part A and the Family Tax Initiative Part A were essentially equivalent to Family Allowances, in being flat-rate assistance per child, except that the income test for the Family Tax Initiative Part A was slightly more liberal. However, published figures do not split either the cash benefits or the tax expenditures into their two components. The total tax expenditure spending on families (including the Family Tax Initiative, the Sole Parent rebate and the Dependent Spouse Rebate, for those with and without children) amounted to $1,257 million.

Figure 1 shows patterns of assistance for a single-income couple with one child under 5 and one between 5 and 12 years of age. Up until levels of income of $28,200 per year, this aggregate assistance is worth $11,240 a year, or nearly 40 percent of family earnings. This amount is made up of Family Tax Benefit Part B of $2,602 per year, Family Tax Benefit Part A for two children of $6,059 per year and Rent Assistance for a couple with two children of $2,579 per year. It can be seen that assistance stays stable for fairly long levels of gross family earnings, but with transition ranges between these plateaus, as first the higher rate of Family Tax Benefit Part A is withdrawn, then later the minimum rate of Family Tax Benefit Part A is income tested. The withdrawal of Rent Assistance occurs immediately after the withdrawal of the higher rate of Family Tax Benefit Part A. Income support recipients without children also are entitled to Rent Assistance, but working families or individuals without children are not.

Figure 1 Family assistance for single-earner couple, private renters, one child under 5 and one child 5-12, post-July 2000

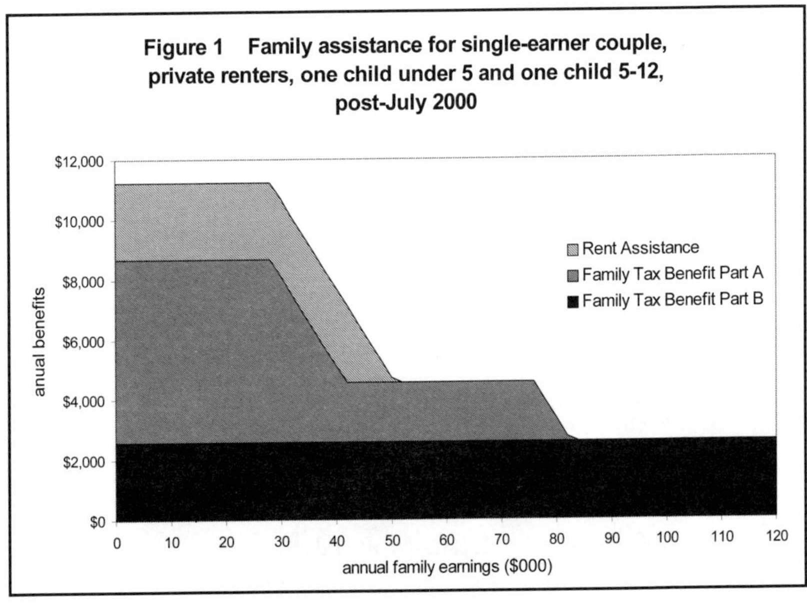

The Family Tax Benefit Part B of $2,602 per year is effectively a universal payment for single-income families, including sole parents. This payment would not be available for two-income families, except where the income of the second earner is very low. However, there is also a Dependent Spouse Rebate of $1,365 per year available through the income tax system for single-income couples without children, so the difference between this assistance is $1,237 per year for a couple with children.

Figure 2 shows levels of Family Assistance for a sole parent with one child less than 5 years of age, again with Rent Assistance. The total level of assistance is $8,211 per year, made up of $2,602 of Family Tax Benefit Part B, $3,029 of Family Tax Benefit Part B and $2,579 per year in Rent Assistance. These figures do not include the Parenting Payment Single that is received as income support by the majority of sole-parent families. The pattern is broadly similar to that for couples, although the level of assistance is lower because of the difference in the number of children.

Figures 3 and 4 show another way of presenting the value of assistance for families. This is calculated as the difference in assistance for different family types rather than as the level of payments directed to families. Figure 3 shows assistance for couples with two children. Figure 3 differs from Figure 1 in two respects. First, rather than Family Tax Benefit Part B being valued at $2,602, it is the difference of $1,237 between the assistance for couples with and without children that is shown. Second, the value of Rent Assistance is also shown as the difference in payments for couples with and without children. The difference in rent assistance is relatively low for income support recipients, but then increases where couples without children are no longer eligible

Figure 2 Family assistance for sole parent, one child under 5, post-July 2000

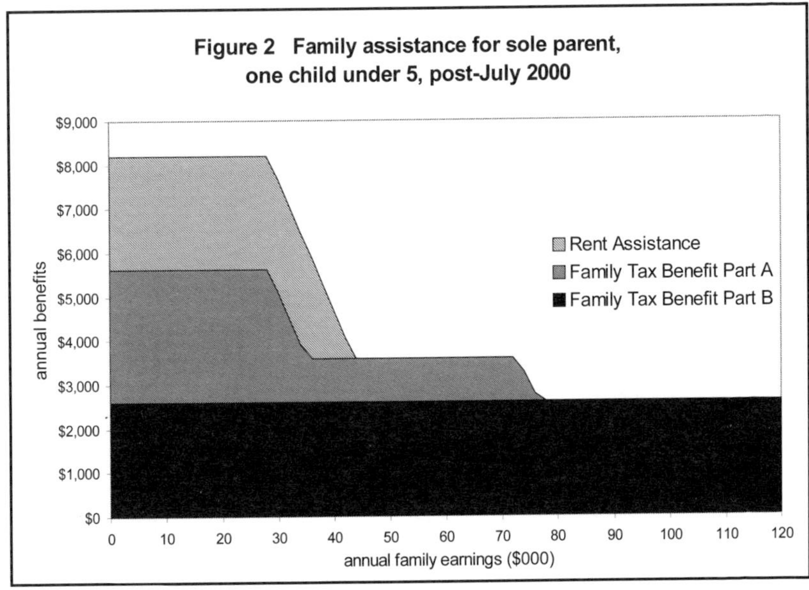

for income support. This larger difference reflects the fact that working couples without children are not entitled to assistance with housing costs. It is worth noting that there is no effect on the level of Family Tax Payment Part A, according to the difference measurement approach.

Figure 4 shows the 'difference' calculation for a sole parent with one child under 7. Here the point of comparison is a single person without children. In this case, the level of Family Tax Benefit Part B remains at $2,602, as there is no equivalent tax rebate for a single person (all individual taxpayers have the same basic tax threshold). The more marked initial pattern of increasing assistance with income reflects three effects. Sole parents are entitled to higher basic income support payments than single unemployed people, in addition to their payments for children. This advantage is compounded by the fact that the withdrawal rate on benefits is lower for sole parents than for unemployment beneficiaries, so sole parents keep this higher income support over a longer income range. There is a similar effect with Rent Assistance, which is only slightly higher for sole parents, but is not income tested until much higher income levels.

Finally, Figures 5 and 6 show total levels of assistance for these families, including the value of basic income support. In the case of a couple with two children, the figures include the family payments shown in Figure 1. To these are added the married rate of Newstart allowance for an unemployed person with a partner and the level of Parenting Allowance for a Partner with children. Each of these has a maximum value of $8,088 per year which, when combined with the other family payments, gives a total level

Figure 3 Family assistance for single-income couple using 'difference method,' private renters, one child under 5 and one child 5-12, post-July 2000

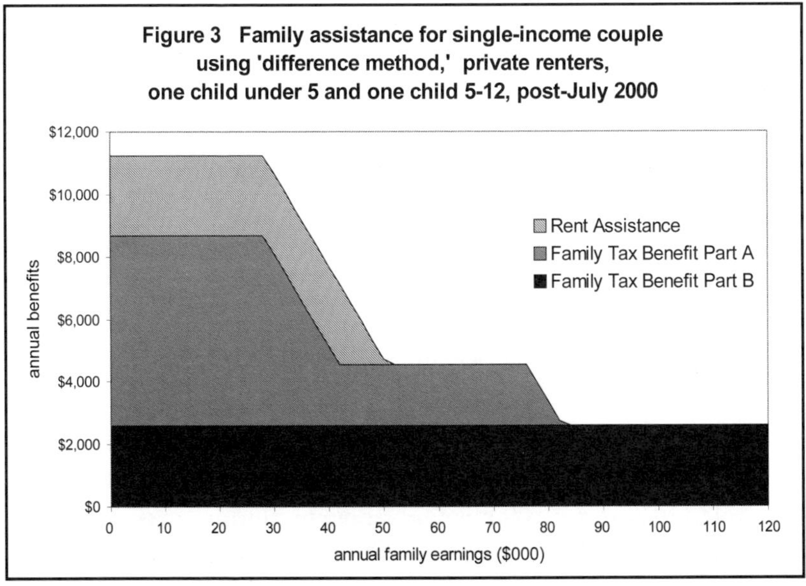

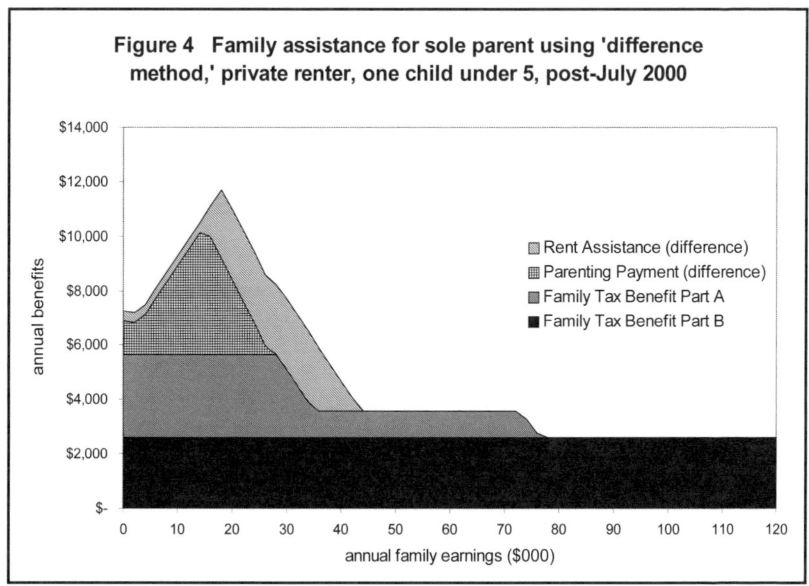

Figure 4 Family assistance for sole parent using 'difference method,' private renter, one child under 5, post-July 2000

of income support plus family payments of just over $27,400 per year. In the case of a sole parent in Figure 6, the level of income support for the adult is $10,205 per year.[2] In combination with the family payments received, this gives a total level of assistance for a sole parent with one child of just over $18,400 per year.

POLICY ISSUES

Delivery of benefits and assisting mothers

The ways in which payments are delivered has been a major focus of reforms to family assistance over the past 20 years. For much of this period, changes concentrated on making family assistance available as direct cash benefits rather than indirectly through the tax system. This approach was motivated by the objective of directing assistance to low-income families (which may not have benefited from tax rebates or deductions) and the desire to direct assistance to mothers. This direction of reform was partially reversed in 1996 with the introduction of the Family Tax Initiative, which was paid to middle-income families in the form of an increase in the basic tax threshold. It is important to note, however, that low-income families, including those on income support, were paid the same amount in the form of Family Tax Payment. This trend to providing further tax-based assistance was reinforced by the July 2000 changes, although the bulk of family assistance is still provided through cash benefits.

Reforms over many years also were designed to address the issue of the distribution of income within families. This thrust

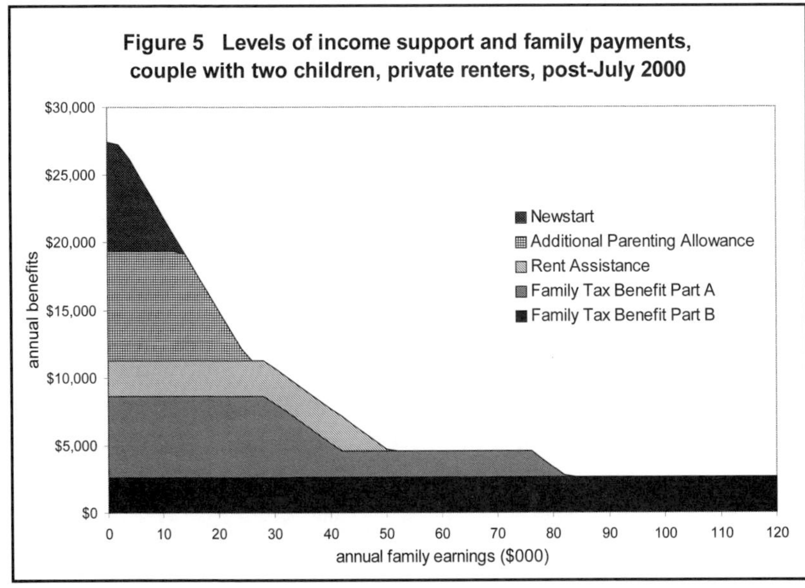

Figure 5 Levels of income support and family payments, couple with two children, private renters, post-July 2000

Figure 6 Levels of income support and family payments, sole parent with one child under 5, private renter, post-July 2000

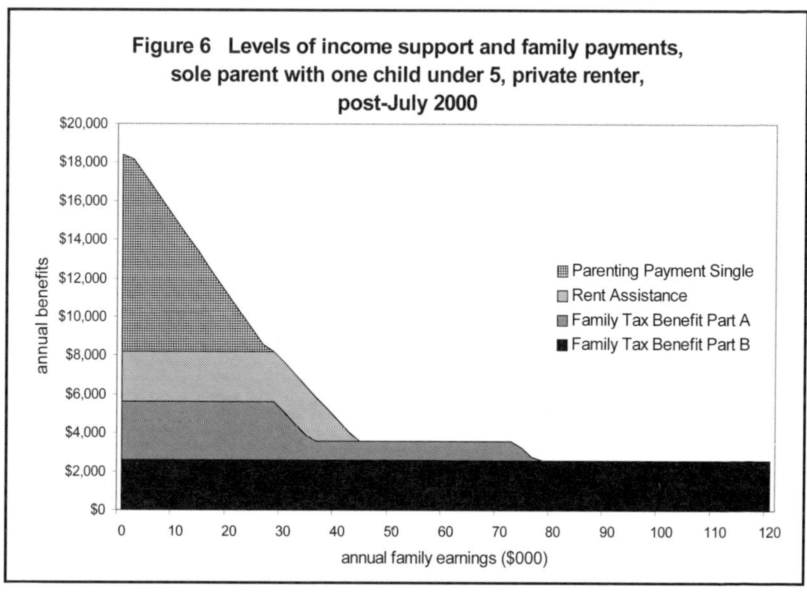

has applied both to supplementary benefits to families with children and more recently to income support benefits. Tax rebates for children, usually paid to the father, were replaced in 1976 by an increased level of universal cash benefits paid to mothers. In the second half of the 1980s, in-work income-tested family payments also were redirected to mothers, as were payments for children of unemployed couples and others on income support (previously the child-related payments had been made as part of the total payment to claimants, usually fathers rather than mothers). Subsequently, all payments for children in low-income families were administratively integrated and made separately payable to the mother, rather than as part of the (male) beneficiary's income support payment.

In the early 1990s, one of the remaining forms of tax assistance for single-earner couples with children also was made available in the form of a cash benefit paid to mothers (initially called the Home Child Care Allowance and later the Basic Parenting Payment). In 1995, the basic income support system was partially individualized so that women received assistance in their own right rather than as dependants of a male 'breadwinner.' For women with children, this change involved creating the Additional Parenting Allowance, which was not work tested where the youngest dependent child was under 16 years of age. Partner Allowance became available for those over 45 years of age, and also was not work tested. The provisions are gender neutral in the sense that men can also receive either Partner or Parenting Allowance, but just over 90 percent of recipients of both payments are women. Younger women without dependent children were then work tested and given payments as an individual entitlement. The income testing arrangements also were changed, so that a partner's payment is not affected until the private income of the earning spouse is sufficient to extinguish their own individual entitlement (i.e., the income testing is sequential rather than fully joint).

Take-up

A further focus of policy activity was to increase take-up of benefits for families in low-paid work. This included paying the income-tested supplement combined with the basic Family Allowance. Take-up initiatives included common claim forms for the two payments, mail-outs of application forms to families that ceased receiving income support and found work, and computer matching with income tax records to identify families that apparently were eligible and then inviting them to apply. Overall these initiatives appear to have been very successful. Whiteford and Doyle [1991] estimated that the take-up rate of the Family Income Supplement scheme in 1986 was only 13.6 percent of eligible families, although take-up of expenditure was around 16 percent. Bradbury, Doyle and Whiteford [1990] estimated that by 1989-90 take-up of expenditure was around 58 percent – that is, the amount of money actually spent on the program was consistent with all eligible families receiving 58 percent of their entitlements. In 1999 the number of families actually receiving the 'more than minimum rate of Family Allowance' was consistent with a take-up rate of 80 percent [Salma and Whiteford 1999].

It is interesting to note that take-up has never been regarded as a problem in the income support system. Because there are no social insurance benefits at all, it seems likely that the system is not regarded as stigmatizing and that take-up of income support payments is close to universal [Whiteford 2000]. Significantly, stigma and low take-up have never been regarded as problems by welfare agencies and lobby groups that represent benefit recipients

Responsiveness to income changes

Another issue in Australia has been concern with responding to changes in the income of recipients. In part, this issue has been seen as important in the context of containing the cost of the program, on the one hand, and providing effective incentives to work, on the other.

When the program was introduced in 1983, entitlement to Family Income Supplement was based on average joint parental taxable income in the four weeks preceding application. Entitlements were reviewed every six months. Recipients whose income fell could apply for reassessment at any time. Those whose income increased to more than 125 percent of previously assessed income (or more than 125 percent of the threshold for those receiving the maximum rate) were obliged to inform the then Department of Social Security so that entitlement could be reassessed.

In 1988-89, following the introduction of the more generous Family Allowance Supplement, these arrangements were changed so that entitlement was set for 12 months on the basis of joint parental taxable income in the financial year ending in the previous taxable year. (That is, assessments applied from January to December each year on the basis of taxable income between the previous 1 July and 30 June.) Entitlements could be reviewed during the year if the family experienced an increase or decrease of 25 percent or more in taxable income. Further refinements were introduced in 1990. This meant that Family Allowance Supplement payments would not be changed unless increases in income were greater than 25 percent; families could have their payments reassessed if the income drop was less than 25 percent, but they became entitled to the maximum rate of assistance; and families would retain their current entitlement, if this was more than under an assessment based on the previous year's income.

The responsiveness of the system to income changes was further altered in 1996. From January 1996, families whose eligibility and rates of payment had been determined could apply for reassessment on the basis of current income, no matter how small the reduction in income. Families whose income rose were obliged to have payments reassessed if income was 10 percent or more above their base year income and 10 percent above the income threshold. Changes in income of less than 10 percent would not incur an overpayment, but if incomes changed by more than this amount and payments were not reassessed, families then would incur a debt.

Before the 2000 reforms, around 140,000 to 150,000 'more than minimum rate' customers were paid on a current year estimate (around 60 percent of this sub-population). This figure included people who have reductions in income, which can be of more or less than 10 percent. Probably the more relevant number is how many have a debt at the end of the tax year (i.e., they should have provided an estimate of current income that was above the ceiling). In 1999-2000, there were 43,500 new Family Allowance debts attributed to estimates and a further 22,900 attributed to failure to report a notifiable event. This implies that around 3 to 4 percent of the total population (minimum and 'more than minimum' payments) incurred overpayments as a result of the 10 percent margin rules (since the 'failure to notify' debts would include those who should have changed from base year to current year following a change in circumstances).

The July 2000 reforms represent a further change in these arrangements. It is clearly premature to speculate about their impact, but it will be of interest to monitor this issue in the future.

Trends in child poverty

Concern with child poverty has been high on the policy agenda in Australia for many years, and many of the reforms to family assistance have been designed to alleviate these concerns.

In 1987 the Australian Prime Minister promised that by 1990 "no Australian child would need to be living in poverty." Subsequent initiatives included large increases in the real rates of child allowances for income support recipients and low-income working families, price indexation of these payments for the first time, and the extension of these higher payments to many more families in the workforce. Considerable effort was made to increase take-up of these allowances. Child support reforms increased maintenance payments received by sole parents, and a special program to assist sole parents to participate in the labour force was introduced.

When making the promise to abolish child poverty, the Australian government did not put forward an explicit poverty line in order to assess whether it had achieved its objective. However, it transpired that the implicit measure used were new 'benchmarks of adequacy.' These benchmarks were that the combined payments for children of income support recipients should be raised to 15 percent of the married rate of pension for children under 13 years of age, and 20 percent for children between 13 and 15 years of age. Because the married rate of pension was indexed, this also amounted to a commitment to maintain the real value of family payments for the first time. These figures were based on research on equivalence scales that suggested that these were more appropriate relativities for adequate family assistance [Whiteford 1985].

The most recent estimates of trends in child poverty have been prepared by Harding and Szukalska [1999]. They prepared four different estimates of trends in child poverty, using the Henderson poverty line as well as a range of poverty lines set at either 50 percent of mean or median equivalent family income (and with differing equivalence scales). However, their estimates compare levels of child poverty in 1982 and 1996, both well before and well after the initiatives of the 1987 to 1990 period. Because many other changes have taken place over this period, these estimates cannot be considered as guides to the impact of the policy reforms alone.

Using the Henderson poverty line, it is estimated that child poverty rose from around 20 to 24 percent between 1982 and 1996. However, all other measures find that poverty fell by roughly 30 to 40 percent, to between 8.0 and 12.5 percent of children. A recent study by the OECD [Oxley, Thai-Thanh, Förster and Pellizzari 1999] produces results similar to those of Harding and Szukalska [1999]. The OECD estimated that, between 1984 and 1994, poverty was nearly halved among non-working sole parents and reduced by 80 percent among non-working couples with children, so that the overall child poverty rate (with equivalent disposable income less than 50 percent of the median) fell from 15.5 to 10.9 percent.

In summary, there is a range of evidence to support the argument that policy changes in Australia have been effective at reducing income poverty among families with children, even if child poverty was not ended. However, the reduction in poverty comes at the price of greater income testing and consequently of high effective marginal tax rates for families with children.

Effective marginal tax rates, poverty traps and low income traps

As is well known, one disadvantage of targeting is that income testing necessarily produces higher effective marginal tax rates in the range of income over which benefits are with-drawn. As income testing was applied to the formerly universal family payments from 1987 onwards, and rates of assistance for low-income families were increased, this problem became more important. In essence, successive reforms were successful at reducing the salience of the 'poverty trap' and the 'unemployment trap,' but at the cost of creating 'low income traps.' These issues have been highlighted in Australian policy analysis and debate, most comprehensively by Ingles [1997]. They also have become the focus of government policy initiatives, particularly the July 2000 tax and benefit reforms.

Ingles [1997] calculated that over more than half of the total range of income up to $800 a week, effective marginal tax rates for a family with three children exceeded 80 percent, and for most of the balance they exceeded 60 percent. A family with three or more children would have to have an income over average earnings before its effective marginal tax rate was as 'low' as 40 percent. Put another way, a family with children that increased its private income from zero to $32,000 would have an increase in its disposable income of less than $9,000 per year.

The significance of these very high effective marginal tax rates for actual behaviour is debatable. Nevertheless, it is notable that while Australia has an overall level of joblessness that is one of the lowest in the OECD, it is among families with children – which face these high effective marginal tax rates – that joblessness is relatively high. In any case, high effective marginal tax rates do not have to change behaviour to be perceived as unfair. By definition, targeting imposes its heaviest burdens over the range of income where benefits are being withdrawn. More universal benefits financed by higher levels of general income taxation are likely to impose their costs somewhat further up the income distribution. 'Flattening' the effective marginal tax rates schedule necessarily spreads the tax rate further up the income distribution. Thus, it is families in the lower sectors of the earning distribution that feel the impact of targeting most severely.

CONCLUSION

The foregoing discussion shows that family assistance has been the focus of a great deal of policy activity in Australia for the past 25 years or more, and still remains at the center of social policy concerns. The Australian experience illustrates in practice many of the abstract issues often raised in academic discussion of family policy principles.

First, Australia is notable for the extent to which assistance for families was moved out of the tax system to achieve the objective of redistributing to those (mothers) with primary care and responsibility for children. However, this trend has now begun to be reversed, and the July 2000 changes to family assistance again will provide substantial assistance through tax mechanisms rather than direct cash payments. It remains to be seen how many families will choose this payment option.

The Australian system is also notable for the extent to which payments for low-income families not in work and those in employment have been integrated, so that families can move from welfare to work, with minimal disruption to their receipt of family payments. As earlier discussion has shown, Australia has taken income testing and selectivity to unrivalled heights (and back again). Assistance for middle- and high-income families has been redirected to low-income families through income testing of universal payments and substantially more generous payments for low-income families. These changes have been motivated both by concerns about how to control expenditure growth and about child poverty. There is evidence that increased assistance to low-income families has been effective at reducing income poverty [Harding and Szukalska 1999; Oxley, Thai-Thanh, Förster and Pellizzari 1999], but it appears that this has been at the cost of exposing many families to very high effective marginal tax rates [Ingles 1997].

The July 2000 reforms address these concerns to a very significant extent. However, while families currently in the range where their payments are withdrawn will have their effective marginal tax rates reduced from 80 to 60 percent, for those which become newly eligible, effective tax rates will increase from 30 to 60 percent. For some families receiving payments such as Youth Allowance[3] there are still possibilities for extremely high effective marginal tax rates, because of the interaction between the parental income test on Youth Allowance and the family income test on other payments.

The July 2000 reforms also simplified the system of family payments, reducing twelve payments to three. In many respects, this simplification appears to be considerable, although it can be noted that while administratively the previous system appeared complex, the structure of assistance has not been substantially changed. That is, the essence of the previous system involved a two-tier family payment, as does the new system. There is also the question of whether the system is simpler to understand for recipients. The success of simplification in this regard will be seen over the next few years. It will be worth monitoring, however, whether the change to a prospective statement of income and a reconciliation of entitlements at the end of the financial year is popular with the public.

ENDNOTES

1. This paper was written while the author worked with the Australian Department of Family and Community Services. The views expressed are my own and not those of the Department of Family and Community Services, nor the OECD.

2. Note that these are the annualized values of current fortnightly payments. Actual annual payments will differ, because basic rates of income support payments are increased twice a year. Family payments are increased once a year in line with inflation.

3. Youth Allowance is a payment made to young people who are either studying or training full time, or unemployed, or undertaking a combination of approved activities (e.g., part-time work and part-time study). Young people who are not independent are also subject to a Parental Means Test.

REFERENCES

Australian Bureau of Statistics. (2000). *Year Book Australia.* Catalogue No.1301.0. Canberra.

Australian Bureau of Statistics. (2000). *Australian Social Trends.* Catalogue No. 4102.0. Canberra.

Australian Bureau of Statistics. (1999). *Labour Force Status and Other Characteristics of Families.* Catalogue No. 6224.0. Canberra.

Australian Bureau of Statistics. (1999). *Income Distribution, Australia.* Catalogue No. 6523.0. Canberra.

Australian Bureau of Statistics. (1997). *Family Characteristics.* Catalogue No. 4442.0. Canberra.

Bradbury, B., J. Doyle and P. Whiteford. (1990). *Trends in the Disposable Incomes of Australian Families, 1982-83 to 1989-90.* Discussion Paper No. 16. Sydney: Social Policy Research Centre, University of New South Wales.

Harding, A. and A. Szukalska. (1999). *Trends in Child Poverty in Australia: 1982 to 1995-96.* Discussion Paper No. 42. Canberra: NATSEM, University of Canberra.

Ingles, D. (1997). *Low Income Traps for Working Families.* Discussion Paper No. 363. Canberra: Centre for Economic Policy Research, Australian National University.

Oxley, H., D. Thai-Thanh, M. Förster and M. Pellizzari. (1999). "Income Inequalities and Poverty among Children and Households with Children in Selected OECD Countries: Trends and Determinants." Paper given to the Conference on *Child Well-Being in Rich and Transition Countries: Are Children in Growing Danger of Social Exclusion?* Luxembourg.

Salma, U. and P. Whiteford. (1999). *Take-up of Family Allowance Supplement by Working Families.* Canberra: Department of Family and Community Services.

Stanton, D. and M. Fuery. (1995). "Developments in Family Payments Since 1983." *Social Security Journal.* December: 120-154.

Whiteford, P. (2000). *The Australian System of Social Protection – An Overview.* Policy Research Paper No. 1. Canberra: Department of Family and Community Services.

Whiteford, P. (1985). *A Family's Needs: Equivalence Scales, Poverty and Social Security.* Research Paper No. 27. Canberra: Development Division, Department of Social Security.

Whiteford, P. and J. Doyle, J. (1991). *Take-Up of Family Income Supplement in 1986: A Research Note.* Discussion Paper No. 29. Sydney: Social Policy Research Centre, University of New South Wales.

ANNEX 1: PERSONAL INCOME TAX SYSTEM, AUSTRALIA

Unit of taxation

The individual, although some rebates (tax credits) are based on joint family income tests of various sorts.

Pay-as-you-earn versus annual reconciliation

While the system is primarily based on a pay-as-you-earn basis, most taxpayers also submit annual tax returns. In 1997-98, 9.8 million individual taxpayers lodged tax returns. This is equivalent to 66 percent of the population aged 15 and over. However, more than three-quarters of taxpayers have tax instalments deducted from pay on a regular basis.

Federal/state/local mix

All income taxes are collected at the federal level. State governments have a range of revenue sources, including payroll taxes and various income taxes, but a good deal of their revenue comes from grants from the Commonwealth government. Revenue is shared with the states on the basis of tied and untied grants. Local property taxes (rates) are collected by local councils, which may provide discounts for low-income groups, but these vary. Owners, but not tenants, are liable for rates.

Progressivity

The tax scale has 5 rates – 0 percent, 20 percent, 34 percent, 43 percent and 47 percent in 1999-2000, as shown below. Rates have been cut and thresholds increased as part of the tax reform package. The zero rate applies to all income taxpayers – i.e., it is the same as a tax credit or rebate, not a tax deduction or allowance. All recognition for families also is provided through rebates or cash payments (i.e., the value is the same for all taxpayers irrespective of their marginal tax rate). There also are rebates for low-income earners and for recipients of social security benefits.

Income Tax Rates for 1999-2000 and 2000-01			
1999-2000		2000-01	
Annual taxable income range	Marginal tax rate	Annual taxable income range	Marginal tax rate
$0 - $5,400	0%	$0 - $6,000	0%
$5,401 - $20,700	20%	$6,001 - $20,000	17%
$20,701 - $38,000	34%	$20,001 - $50,000	30%
$38,001 - $50,000	43%	$50,001 - $60,000	42%
$50,000 - above	47%	$60,001 +	47%

Low Income Rebate for 1999-2000 and 2000-01	
Rebate amount	$150
Rebate threshold	$20,700
The rebate is withdrawn at the rate of 4 cents for every dollar of income above the threshold. The rebate is unchanged in 2001.	

Dependant Rebates for 1999-2000 and 2000-01			
1999-2000		2000-01	
Dependent Spouse (without children)	$1,340	Dependent Spouse (without children)	$1,365
Dependent Spouse (with children)	$1,452	Family Tax Benefit Part B (with children over 5)	$1,851
Sole Parent	$1,258	Family Tax Benefit Part B (with children under 5)	$2,640
The Dependent Spouse Rebate is withdrawn at the rate of 25 cents for every dollar of the dependent spouse's income that exceeds $282 per year.		In a couple, if the secondary earner's income is above $1,616 a year, payments are reduced by 30 cents for every extra dollar of income.	
To qualify for the Dependent Spouse Rebate (with children) or the Sole Parent Rebate, at least one child or student must have income less than $1,785 per year		To be dependent, a child must generally have an annual income of less than $7,662.	

Pensioner and Low Income Aged Persons Rebate for 1999-2000		
	Rebate	Threshold
Single	$1,358	$12,190
Married	$980	$10,300
Married, illness separated	$1,296	$11,880
The rebate is withdrawn at the rate of 12.5 cents for every dollar of taxable income above the threshold. Rates for 2000-2001 have not yet been announced.		

Beneficiary Rebate for 1999-2000
The rebate for recipients of allowances and benefits is calculated using the following formula: 02x (Allowance Received-Tax Free Threshold) If the total allowance received during the financial year is less than the tax free threshold, then no rebate is payable.

Family Tax Initiative (FTI) for 1999-2000

Family Tax Initiative is delivered in two ways: Family Tax Assistance through the Australian Taxation Office, and Family Tax Payment through Centrelink. Family Tax Assistance works by raising the tax free area for the main income earner. Family Tax Payment is paid to people who receive the higher rate of Family Allowance. There are two parts of the payment. Part A is for families with dependent children. Payment is made for each child as follows.

Number of dependent children	Family income threshold	Increase in tax free area
1	$70,000	$1,000
2	$73,000	$2,000
3	$76,000	$3,000
4	$79,000	$4,000
For each additional child, add	$3,000	$1,000

Part B is paid to families with at least one child under the age or five. To qualify, the main income earner's income needs to be below the threshold, and the partner's earnings less than $4,606 per annum. The threshold is $65,000 for one child, and it increases by $3,000 for each dependent child. Only one payment is made per family, irrespective of the number of children.

Medicare Low Income Thresholds for 1999-2000	
Individual	$ 13,550
Couple or Sole Parent	$ 22,865
for each child, after first	$ 2,100
Medicare Levy Surcharge Thresholds for 1999-2000	
Individual	$ 50,000
Couple or Sole Parent	$100,000
for each child, add	$ 1,500
A surcharge of 1 percent is added to the Medicare Levy for those with income above the Surcharge Threshold who do not have private health insurance.	

ANNEX B: BASIC NATIONAL STATISTICS, AUSTRALIA

GDP and population

The population at 30 June 1998 was 18.751 million.

Gross Domestic Product was $556,923 million. GDP per capita was $29,883.

Labour force

In 1998-99, there were 14.9 million people in the civilian population aged 15 years and over. There were 8.7 million people over 15 years of age employed (4.9 million men, 3.8 million women). There were 718,200 unemployed (ILO definition).

Children and families

Percentage of population under 15 (1999): 20.7 percent.

Families with children under 15 as a percent of all households (1999): 30.1 percent.

Average number of children: (1999): 1.95 per family with children (estimated)

	Couples	Lone parents	All families
1 child	32.9%	50.5%	37.7%
2 children	42.5%	33.2%	40.5%
3 children	18.3%	11.6%	16.9%
4+ children	6.2%	4.6%	5.9%

Lone-parent families as a percentage of all families with children under 15 (1999)

Total lone parents:	21.2 %
Lone mothers:	19.3 %
Lone fathers:	1.9 %

Percentage distribution of couples (1997-98)

Total couples with children	
No earners	9.7%
One earner	35.9%
Two earners	54.3%
Total sole parents	
Employed	47.4%

Distribution of children by labour force status of parents (1998)

Couples, two earners	44.9%
Couples, one earner	28.5%
Couple, no earners	7.4%
Sole parent, earning	8.1%
Sole parent not earning	11.1%

Child poverty

There are no official poverty estimates in Australia. Academic estimates for 1996 range between about 8 percent of children in poverty (half median current income) and 24 percent (the Henderson poverty line at 68 percent of median income).

Average incomes

Median income before tax ($ per week) by family type (1997-98)

Couple with children	$928
Couple without children	$605
Female Lone parent	$351
Male lone parent	$444
All lone parent	$362
Singles	$301
All income units	$499

Sources: *Australian Social Trends, 2000*, Australian Bureau of Statistics, Catalogue No: 4102.0; *Year Book Australia 2000*, Catalogue No. 1301.0.

TABLE 1
FAMILY BENEFITS, POST-JULY, 2000

	Family Tax Benefit Part A	Family Tax Benefit Part B	Child Care Assistance
Eligibility rules 1. Who is entitled to benefits	1. Family must have a dependent child under 21 or a qualifying dependent full-time student aged 21 to 24 years. A child or student cannot be a dependant if: they are receiving a Labour Market Program payment, pension or benefit such as Youth Allowance; or aged 5 to 15, not studying full time and their annual income is more than $7,662; or aged 16 to 24 and their annual income is more than $7,662 or they are receiving a Prescribed Education Scheme payment such as ABSTUDY. Residential qualifications: Parent/guardian must be an Australian resident. Child must be an Australian resident or dependent child of a	1. Family must have a dependent child under 16 or a qualifying dependent full-time student up to the age of 18 (who doesn't get Youth Allowance or a similar payment). Targets assistance to single income families, including sole parent families. Secondary earners must have income under a certain amount to qualify. Residential qualifications: As for Family Tax Benefit Part A, with the exception that Family Tax Benefit Part B can only be paid for up to 26 weeks of a temporary absence.	1. All families using "approved care" can get at least up to 20 hours of Child Care Benefit a week, no matter the reason. Families can claim up to 50 hours a week for each child in either "approved" or "registered" care, if working (including self-employment, paid leave, unpaid sick leave, paid or unpaid maternity leave or setting up business), actively looking for paid work, studying or training (including unpaid work to improve skills), have a disability, or are caring for a child or adult with a disability. People using "registered" care must satisfy one of the above conditions, irrespective of hours of Benefit

	Family Tax Benefit Part A	Family Tax Benefit Part B	Child Care Assistance
	resident and living with that person. More than the base rate of Family Tax Benefit Part A can be paid only for up to 26 weeks of a temporary absence. The base rate of Family Tax Benefit Part A can continue to be paid for up to three years of a temporary absence.		claimed. For couples, each partner must meet one of these requirements to claim up to 50 hours care a week. Child must be an Australian resident or dependent child of a resident. Claimant/partner must be a resident, or a Commonwealth-sponsored student, or a non-resident experiencing hardship or special circumstances.
2. Reciprocal responsibilities	2. To receive more than the base rate of Family Tax Benefit Part A for children of a previous relationship, reasonable action to obtain child support/maintenance must be taken. Blind pensioners are exempt from maintenance action test.		2. Children born on or after 1 January 1996 must have age appropriate immunisation, be on a catch-up schedule, or have an exemption. Both parents, or the sole parent, must meet the work/study/training test to receive any Benefit for registered care or Benefit for more than 20 hours per week of approved care.

	Family Tax Benefit Part A	Family Tax Benefit Part B	Child Care Assistance
3. Budget caps	3. Open-ended entitlement.	3. Open-ended entitlement.	3. Open-ended entitlement.
Benefits description			
1. Amounts per child	1. This is a two-tier payment, with a higher rate for lower income families, including both those in work and receiving social assistance. The basic payment (first tier in Canadian terms) is $974.55 per year per child under 18 and $1,306.70 per child 18-24 years (but very few 18-24 year olds would be eligible). An additional $208.05 per year per child is paid for the fourth and subsequent children. There is an additional payment for children born in multiple births until the children turn 6 years of age. For triplets this is $2,533.10 pa, and for quadruplets	This payment is made per family. Maximum rate of Family Tax Benefit Part B per year: Under 5 years $2,602.45. 5-15 years (or 16-18 years if a full-time student) $1,814.05. (Single income couples without children are entitled to a tax rebate of $1,340).	Approved care: Up to $122.00 per week for non-school child in 50 hours of care. Minimum rate of up to $20.50 per week for incomes over upper threshold. Rates for school children are 85 percent of the non-school rate. Registered care: Up to $20.50 per week for non-school child in 50 hours of work-related care. Rates for school children are 85 percent of the non-school rate.

	Family Tax Benefit Part A	Family Tax Benefit Part B	Child Care Assistance
	or more, it is $3,379.90 pa. The second tier is directed to low to low middle families with children. The additional assistance is $2,054.95 per year per child under 13 years, and $2,865.25 per year per child 13 to 15 years. The total combined payment per child is $3,029.50 per year for a child under 13 years of age, and $3,839.80 per year for a child 13 to 15 years of age.		
2. Income-related structure	2. The higher rate is paid up to a family income of $28,200, and is then reduced by 30 cents for every extra dollar of income, until the minimum rate is reached. Part-payment at the minimum rate is available up to a family income of $73,000 (plus an additional $3,000	2. There is no income test on the income of the primary income earner (including sole parents). The secondary earner in a partnered relationship can earn up to $1,616.00 each year before it affects their Family Tax Benefit Part B. Payments	2. Maximum rate payable for incomes under $28,200 or families on income support. Above this income 'free area', taper rates are 10 per cent for one child in care, 15 percent and (above $66,000) 25 percent for 2 children in care, and 15 percent and (above

	Family Tax Benefit Part A	Family Tax Benefit Part B	Child Care Assistance
	for each dependent child after the first). Payments are then reduced by 30 cents in every dollar over that amount until the payment reaches nil. To receive some Family Tax Benefit Part A, the maximum income levels are $76,256 a year for a family with one dependent child under 18 and $77,355 a year for a family with one dependent 18-24. These thresholds are lifted by $6,257 for each additional dependent child under 18 and $7,356 for each additional dependent 18-24 year old.	are reduced by 30 cents for each dollar of income earned of $1,616.00. A secondary earner can still get some Family Tax Payment Part B if their income is below: $10,291.00 a year if the youngest child is under 5; or $7,663.00 a year if the youngest child is between 5 and 18.	$66,000) 35 per cent for 3 or more children in care. Minimum rate payable over the following thresholds: (Number of children in care) 1 $80,980 2 $87,832 3+ $99,794+ $16,665 for each child after the third Assistance for registered care is not subject to an income test.
3. Definition of income	3. Combined income of both spouses (where relevant). Families are to provide their own estimates of their family income, and at the end of the financial year, there will be a reconciliation, which will mean that payments will be based on	3. Income for the second earner includes gross taxable income, foreign income, certain employer provided fringe benefits (over $1,000) and net losses from rental property (negative gearing), less any	3. Combined income of both spouses (where relevant). Income includes gross taxable income, foreign income, certain employer provided fringe benefits (over $1,000) and net

	Family Tax Benefit Part A	Family Tax Benefit Part B	Child Care Assistance
	the annual income for the financial year of payment. Income includes gross taxable income, foreign income, certain employer provided fringe benefits (over $1,000) and net losses from rental property (negative gearing), less any deductible child maintenance expenditure.	deductible child maintenance expenditure.	losses from rental property (negative gearing), less any deductible child maintenance expenditure.
4. Indexing	4. Indexed annually to consumer price index, and aggregate rates also tied to married rate of pension payments, which are also indexed to male average total weekly earnings (whichever higher).	4. Indexed to CPI.	4. No – benefit levels usually set in annual budget.
Delivery features 1. Administrative arrangements	1. Program administered by Commonwealth Department of Family and Community Services and the Australian Taxation Office, with benefits delivered by a new	1. See left.	1. See left.

	Family Tax Benefit Part A	Family Tax Benefit Part B	Child Care Assistance
	Family Assistance Office (FAO). The FAO has been set up in Centrelink (the agency that delivers Commonwealth benefits and some services), Medicare Offices (the public health insurance agency) and Australian Taxation Office. The Family Assistance Office (FAO) is a "one-stop shop" for integrated family assistance.		
2. How people get enrolled	2. Applicants must fill in special forms. Forms supplied at hospitals on birth of baby, and available from government offices,	2. See left.	2. See left.
3. Responsiveness	3. If Family Tax Benefit received as fortnightly payments required to advise the Family Assistance Office as soon as possible of any changes in circumstances. Payments recalcu-	3. See left.	3. Required to advise the Family Assistance Office as soon as possible of any changes in circumstances. Fee relief then recalculated.

	Family Tax Benefit Part A	Family Tax Benefit Part A	Child Care Assistance
	lated as soon as possible. If paid through the tax system recipients should keep a record of any changes to circumstances in order to correctly fill in the claim for lump sum payment at the end of the year. If paid through reduced withholdings necessary to submit a new withholding declaration to employer to reflect this change.		
4. Payment procedures	4. Direct fortnightly deposits payable to banks, building societies or credit unions. If through the tax system either as reduced income tax deductions or as refund cheque after the end of the financial year.	4. See left.	4. Paid through reduced fees payable to child care centres (government pays centres), or as refund to either parent on presentation of receipts.
5. Verification procedures	5. Extensive checking of identification papers on application (drivers license, passport, birth certificates etc.). Random audits	5. See left.	5. Extensive checking of identification papers on application (drivers license, passport, birth certificates

	Family Tax Benefit Part A	Family Tax Benefit Part B	Child Care Assistance
	of recipients and structured reviews of "high risk" categories.		etc.). Random audits of recipients.
6.Aboriginal peoples	6. Aboriginal people entitled on same basis as other families.	6. See left.	6. See left.
7. How program is delivered	7. Payments are made either fortnightly to a bank or credit union account, or through the tax system as a lump sum payment at the end of the financial year with the added option to reduce the amounts withheld from wages paid to claimant or partner.	7. See left.	7. For approved care, can be paid directly to child care services to reduce the fees charged, where entitlement is based on estimate of income, with end-of-year reconciliation. Alternatively, payment can be made as a lump sum to parents after end of financial year. For registered care, paid by direct credit on presentation of receipts
8. How program is financed	8. Financed from general government revenue.	8. See left.	8. See left.
9. National/state integration	9. Nationally administered program.	9. See left.	9. See left.

TABLE 2
SIMPLIFICATION OF FAMILY ASSISTANCE, JULY 2000

Pre-July 2000	Post-July 2000
Family Allowance Greater than Minimum Rate Minimum rate Family Tax Payment Part A Family Tax Initiative (Part A)	Family Tax Benefit Part A
Basic Parenting Payment Sole Parent Rebate Dependent Spouse Rebate (with children) Family Tax Payment Part B Family Tax Initiative Part B Guardian Allowance	Family Tax Benefit Part B
Childcare Assistance Childcare Rebate	Child Care Benefit

TABLE 3
ESTIMATED RESOURCES FOR FAMILY ASSISTANCE, 1999-2000 AND 2000-2001 ($ MILLION)

	1999-2000	2000-2001
Family Allowance	6,674.7	25.7
Family Tax Benefit	-	9,836.4
Family Tax Payment	529.1	10.0
Childcare Assistance	706.5	17.0
Childcare Rebate	135.0	50.0
Child Care Benefit	-	989.4

Source: Department of Family and Community Services, Portfolio Budget Statements, 2000-2001, http://www.facs.gov.au/

TABLE 4
SELECTED PROGRAMS AND POLICIES TO ASSIST FAMILIES, 1998-1999

Post-July 2000	Pre-July 2000	Estimated Cash Spending 1998-99	# of recipients (families)	Children affected
	Family Assistance	$7,145m	-	-
Family Tax Benefit Part A	Family Allowance	$6,412.6m	1,775,700	3,418,900
	Greater than Minimum Rate		909,200	1,799,400
	Minimum rate		866,400	1,619,400
	Family Tax Payment	$547.2m		
	Part A	-	479,300	919,900
	(Part B)	-	(364,200)	(797,300)
Family Tax Benefit Part B	Family Tax Initiative	$591m	706,000	-
	Parenting Payment	$5,375.8m	372,300 (single) 409,200 (partnered, basic) 236,600 (partnered, additional)	
	Sole Parent Rebate	$234m	275,000	-
	Dependent Spouse and related Rebates	$432m	451,000	-
Child Care Benefit	Childcare Assistance and Services	$868.8m	398,800	
	Childcare Rebate	$120.9m		
Other Family Assistance	Maternity Allowance	$165.6m	218,100	-
	Child Disability Allowance	$267m	90,800	101,400
	Child Support (1997-98)			
	CSA collections	$526m	{ 489,000	{ 753,500
	Private payments	$636m		

Note:

It is not possible to separately allocate expenditures on Family Tax Payment Part A and Part B, nor on the components of the Family Tax Initiative. Expenditure on Parenting Payment is mostly on the Single Rate of Parenting Payment and the Additional Rate of Parenting Payment (Partnered), but only the Basic Rate of Parenting Payment is included in the Family Tax Benefit Part B. The Dependent spouse and related rebates include tax rebates for persons without children.

BENEFITS FOR CHILDREN: CANADA

Ken Battle and Michael Mendelson

INTRODUCTION

Canada is undertaking a major restructuring of its principal federal and provincial[1] child benefit programs. This reform constitutes one of the most significant changes in the history of Canadian social policy: It has important implications not only for child benefits, but also for the future of income security policy generally and for the state of the 'Social Union' – the new term denoting the 'rules of the game' in Canada's highly decentralized federation in which the federal and provincial governments share power, virtually equally, over social policy. While the reform, known as the National Child Benefit, began only a few years ago (1998), it will complete a transformation of the philosophy and practice of Canadian child benefits policy that has occurred mainly incrementally over several decades.

In Canada, child benefits – meaning income payments on behalf of children, delivered either in the form of cheques or income tax reductions – historically have pursued two fundamental and related objectives, characterized as the 'anti-poverty' and 'horizontal equity' objectives. Under the anti-poverty objective, child benefits seek to help fill the gap between the earnings of low- and modest-wage parents and their families' income needs, based on the long-recognized and still highly relevant reality that a market economy does not vary wages and salaries to take into account the number of family members dependant on that income. The horizontal equity objective views child benefits as one way for society to provide some financial recompense for the fact that families at all income levels with children to support face costs that childless households at the same income level do not.

These twin objectives are interrelated. Both assume that society has an interest and obligation to help parents with their childrearing costs because children are viewed at least partially as a 'public good' or 'investment': Children grow up to become workers, taxpayers and citizens, and so it is in the interest of everyone – including those without children – that parents not face undue financial strain in the childrearing 'work' which they do, in effect, in part on behalf of everyone. The anti-poverty objective acknowledges that lower-income families have the least financial capacity and also seeks to mitigate the higher personal and societal risks of child poverty, in terms of children's immediate and long-term health, learning capacity and educational performance. For low-income families, the anti-poverty and horizontal equity objectives of child benefits effectively are the same. Concern about the horizontal equity objective typically has focussed on non-poor families, which have suffered a substantial decline (and, for some high-income families, disappearance) in their child benefits since the mid-1980s.

While the evolution of child benefits in Canada involves too many twists, turns and complexities to recount in any detail here, a proper understanding of the present reform requires situating it in the context of the long-term shift in the system's objectives and instruments. The overall trend has been toward greater 'targeting' – i.e., gearing child benefits to need as measured by family income. Since the late 1970s, the anti-poverty objective has been accorded greater weight at the expense of the horizontal equity objective. However, while it calculates the amount of payments on the basis of family income, Canada's child benefits system is not targeted narrowly to the poor in terms of eligibility: Rather, it is a broad-based system that covers the large majority (80 percent) of families. Indeed, in recognition of the need to seek to bolster the child benefit system's horizontal equity capacity, payments also are being increased for non-poor families and coverage will expand to more than 95 percent of all families with children within the next few years.

The history of Canadian child benefits can be divided into five main periods [Battle and Mendelson 1997]. The first phase, between the two world wars, can be characterized as 'regressive targeting': The personal income tax system provided a children's tax exemption that delivered its benefits in the form of income tax savings that increased with taxable income and excluded families that did not owe income tax – the majority, in those times of widespread poverty and low average incomes.

The arrival of universal, monthly Family Allowances in 1945 heralded the second phase, 'untargeted universality': While child benefits were extended to include low- and modest-income families, the better-off still got more (because they received both the children's tax exemption and Family Allowances).

The 1970s ushered in the third phase, 'progressive universality': Family Allowances were tripled, indexed to the cost of living and made taxable. A new 'income-tested' program administered through the personal income tax system – the refundable child tax credit – delivered its maximum payment to low-income families, a declining amount to middle-income families and nothing to the well-off.

The fourth phase, 'progressive targeting,' began in the 1980s. It evolved through a series of changes culminating in 1993 with a single, income-tested Child Tax Benefit program that increased payments for working poor families with children, maintained benefits for other low-income families, reduced amounts for middle-income families and excluded high-income families.

Canada recently entered a fifth phase, the 'integrated child benefit,' that broadens the scope of reform to include provincial child benefits and promises to strengthen both the anti-poverty and horizontal equity objectives. This large-scale reconstruction of child benefits is the primary topic of the paper.

INCOME BENEFITS FOR CHILDREN

The major child income benefit programs in Canada are the federal income-tested Canada Child Tax Benefit and two types of provincial child benefits – 'needs-tested' (i.e., income- and asset-tested) social assistance payments on behalf of children and income-tested child benefits and earnings supplements. These programs are the vehicles of the National Child Benefit reform – the main purpose of which is to replace needs-tested provincial child benefits with income-tested federal (and, if provinces so desire, provincial) child benefits, while providing equal payments to all low-income families (whether working or on Employment Insurance), as well as provincial health and social services for low-income families with children.

Canadian governments operate additional programs that either include a children's payment or benefit specific subgroups of children but typically are not included in the ambit of the child benefits system and are not part of the National Child Benefit reform. While these programs are not discussed in the text – with the exception of the spousal equivalent credit, which we include in the one-parent family example shown later – they are detailed in the tables. They include: the nonrefundable spousal equivalent tax credit for single-parent families (Table 1c), the refundable Goods and Services Tax/Harmonized Sales Tax credit for low-

and modest-income Canadians (Table 1c), several child-related disability tax provisions (Tables 1d and 1e), provincial/territorial refundable tax credits (Table 1e) and child benefits embedded in Canada's two major social insurance programs – Employment Insurance (the new name for Unemployment Insurance) and the Canada and Quebec Pension Plans (Table 3).

Canada Child Tax Benefit

In 1993 the federal government restructured its major child benefit programs by integrating the Family Allowance, refundable child tax credit and nonrefundable child tax credit into a single, income-tested Child Tax Benefit geared to low- and middle-income families, which comprise the large majority of Canadian families. The program also provided a new Working Income Supplement for working poor families.

In 1998, as its part of the federal-provincial National Child Benefit reform, the federal government reconfigured its Child Tax Benefit into the Canada Child Tax Benefit, in the process removing the Working Income Supplement in favour of a larger and equal benefit for all low-income families with children, regardless of employment status. Here, we focus on the benefit structure of the Canada Child Tax Benefit. Table 1a provides detailed information on the design parameters and delivery characteristics of the program, whose key characteristics are:

- an income-tested program that pays its maximum amount to lower-income families and a diminishing amount to non-poor families, excluding only the well-off

- a federal, nontaxable benefit paid monthly, on behalf of all eligible children under age 18 throughout Canada, to the parent considered to be primarily responsible for the care and upbringing of the child

- eligibility for and amount of benefit based on a simple test of family income (i.e., the income of both spouses if they live together, or of the spouse with whom the child lives in the case of divorced or separated couple) as calculated on the annual income tax return

- based on net family income, which allows for deduction of various employment-related expenses (e.g., contributions to occupational pension plans and individual retirement savings plans, child care expenses, union and professional dues)

The Canada Child Tax Benefit has a rather complex two-tiered structure whose parameters are changing annually as the National Child Benefit reform gradually is being implemented. Here, we describe the Canada Child Tax Benefit for the 12-month payment period July 2001-June 2002 (the payment year is from July 1 of one year to June 30 the next year), after the latest round of increases has been phased in.

The first tier of the Canada Child Tax Benefit, the 'basic Child Tax Benefit,' will pay a maximum $1,117 per child under age 18 per year from July 2001 through June 2002, delivered on a monthly basis. In addition, there is a small ($77 per year) supplement for larger families (for the third and each additional child) and up to $220 per year extra for each child under age 7 for whom the child care expenses deduction (a tax benefit for families with receipted child care) is not claimed. Provinces can vary these rates according to the age and/or number of children, within limits; only one province – Alberta – does so, varying its Canada Child Tax Benefit according to age. Alberta's estimated rates for July 2001-June 2001 are $1,031 for each child under 7, $1,101 for each child 7 to 11, $1,231 for each child between 12 and 15, and $1,304 for each child aged 16 or 17.

Maximum payments go to families with net incomes under $32,000 and are reduced gradually above this level at the rate of 2.5 percent for families with one child and 5 percent for those with two or more children. Eligibility for benefits ends at relatively high incomes – e.g., $76,680 in net family for families with one or two children (the majority of Canadian families with children are this size). Because the Canada Child Tax Benefit calculates its payment on the basis of net family income, a definition that allows substantial deductions (e.g., for child care expenses, private pension savings), families with gross incomes thousands of dollars above the $76,680 net family income level where eligibility for benefits ends typically still would qualify for some payment. Thus the Canada Child Tax Benefit is a broad-based social program that serves eight in ten families with children, excluding only the well-off.

Layered on top of the basic Child Tax Benefit is a second tier called the 'National Child Benefit Supplement' (NCBS) that goes to low-income families only. (The reason for the use of the term 'National Child Benefit' is that the increase to federal child benefits for low-income families constitutes the federal government's part of the federal-provincial National Child Benefit reform.) For the 12-month period July 2001-June 2002, the

National Child Benefit Supplement pays a maximum $1,255 for the first child, $1,055 for the second child and $980 for each additional child, phasing out above net family income of $21,744 at the rate of 11.1 percent for one child, 19.9 percent for two children and 27.8 percent for larger families, to end once net family income reaches $32,000 for families with one, two or three children (not coincidentally, the same level where the basic Child Tax Benefit begins to reduce its payments). Together, the basic Child Tax Benefit and the National Child Benefit Supplement amount to a maximum annual Canada Child Tax Benefit of $2,372 for one child, $2,172 for the second child and $2,175 for each additional child.

In the case of children in institutional care, a Children's Special Allowance is paid to the federal or provincial government department, child care agency or institution supporting that child. The payment also may be made to a foster parent. The Children's Special Allowance pays the same amount as the maximum Canada Child Tax Benefit for one child – for July 2001-June 2002, $2,372 per year.

The 2000 federal Budget announced several significant changes, foremost among them the restoration of full indexation. The Canada Child Tax Benefit and the personal income tax system's tax brackets and credits were fully indexed to the annual increase in the cost of living as of 2000. This change marks an important advance because federal child benefit programs and the income tax system (including its various child-related benefits) had been eroded steadily for a decade-and-a-half by partial deindexation. The Canada Child Tax Benefit's rates and income thresholds were adjusted by the amount of inflation over three percent a year, which in real terms meant that they fell by three percent if inflation ran over three percent or by the amount of inflation if the latter was under three percent. The same held for the personal income tax system's tax brackets and credits [Battle 1998, 1999].

The February 2000 Budget and the October 2000 Economic Statement and Budget Update announced further increases to the Canada Child Tax Benefit's rates and income thresholds (for both the basic Child Tax Benefit and the National Child Benefit Supplement). Moreover, the reduction rate on the basic Child Tax Benefit will be lowered in future (from 2.5 percent to 2.0 percent for one child and from 5 to 4 percent for two or more children by 2004). By July 2004, the maximum annual Canada Child Tax Benefit is slated to reach $2,520 for the first child, $2,308 for the second child and $2,311 for each additional child.

Figure 1 illustrates the Canada Child Tax Benefit for July 2001-June 2002. The dark area indicates the basic Child Tax Benefit that serves all but high-income families, while the grey area show the National Child Benefit Supplement targeted to low-income families.

It is not just low-income families that are seeing improvements in their federal child benefits. By increasing the basic Child Tax Benefit, raising its income threshold for maximum payments and eventually lowering the rates at which benefits are reduced, the federal government will boost payments to non-poor families and extend their reach even higher up the income ladder. As of July 2001, eligibility for benefits ends at net family income of $76, 680 for families with one or two children; this 'disappearing point' will rise to a projected $94,350 in net family income by July 2004. And because the Canada Child Tax Benefit is calculated on the basis of net family income, which allows the deduction of sev-

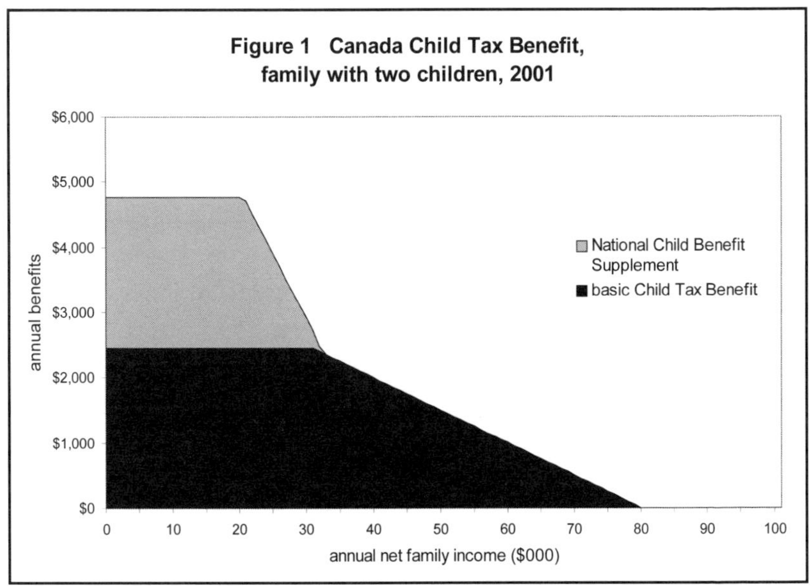

Figure 1 Canada Child Tax Benefit, family with two children, 2001

eral expenses typical to higher-income families (e.g., child care expenses, contributions to occupational pension plans and individual retirement savings plans), the actual disappearing point in terms of gross income would for most families be higher than $94,350 in 2004 – e.g., $109,350 for those contributing $15,000 to an individual retirement savings plan. Canada Child Tax Benefit coverage will increase to more than 95 percent of families with children by 2004.

Strictly speaking, these increases to the basic Child Tax Benefit are not part of the federal-provincial National Child Benefit. In reality, though, they constitute an important contribution to the overall reform of child benefits since they work toward restoring the horizontal equity objective and thereby reinforce the broad-based, non-stigmatizing and inclusive nature of the program.

Provincial income-tested child benefit programs

A key feature of the National Child Benefit reform is that the provincial and territorial governments are expected, although not required, to reduce their social assistance expenditures on behalf of children to take into account increasing federal expenditures on the National Child Benefit Supplement, provided that they 'reinvest' such savings in other programs and services for low-income families with children. The latter can include a wide range of programs to be determined by each province, such as income-tested child benefits and earnings supplements, child care, early childhood development services, and supplementary health care programs.

All provinces and territories, except Prince Edward Island, now offer income-tested child benefit programs and/or employment earnings supplements for families with children, most created under the National Child Benefit reform. Fully integrated child benefit programs – replacing most social assistance payments on behalf of children and extending provincial child benefits to the working poor and, in some instances, modest-income families – are now operating in British Columbia, Saskatchewan, Quebec and Newfoundland.

While their specific design parameters vary, all the provincial child benefit programs are aimed primarily at the anti-poverty objective and all utilize the same diminishing refundable tax credit model (i.e., maximum payments to low-income families, with declining benefits to non-poor families, that eventually disappear) of the federal Canada Child Tax Benefit. Indeed, most of the provincial benefits were designed to mesh with the federal system in terms of thresholds and reduction rates. However, Quebec also provides a nonrefundable child tax credit in support of the parental recognition and horizontal equity objectives for higher-income families.

One point of departure between the federal and provincial child benefit systems is that the former restored full indexation as of 2000. Whether the provincial benefits follow suit – they are not indexed at all – remains to be seen.

Table 1b gives details on provincial income-tested child benefit programs. Below is a description of British Columbia's program structure.

Launched in July of 1996, British Columbia's BC Family Bonus was Canada's first true integrated child benefit program, aimed at replacing most provincial needs-tested social assistance payments on behalf of children with an income-tested child benefit payable to all low-income families (including the working poor not in receipt of social assistance) and modest-income families with children. As of July 1, 2000, the maximum annual benefits are $305 for the first child, $505 for the second child and $580 for each additional child and are payable up to net family income of $18,000, above which payments are reduced at the rate of 8 percent for one child and 16 percent for two or more children, disappearing at levels that vary according to the number of children (e.g., $21,813 for families with one child and $23,063 for those with two children).

In 1998 the province added an employment earnings supplement, the BC Earned Income Benefit, though only for low-income families with children; the program does not serve childless couples and single workers. The maximum annual amount is \$605 for the first child, \$405 for the second child and \$330 for each additional child. Benefits phase in at the rate of 9.68 percent of work earnings over \$3,750 for families with one child, 16.16 percent for two children and 21.44 percent for three children, reaching their maximum amount at family earnings of \$10,000. Maximum benefits are reduced above net family income of \$20,921 at the rate of 12.1 percent for one child, 20.2 percent for two children and 26.8 percent for larger families, ending once income reaches \$25,921 for families with three or fewer children.

In terms of basic design characteristics (e.g., assessment and definition of income, eligible children, person to whom the cheque is paid) and delivery mechanisms, the BC Family Bonus and Earned Income Benefit are identical to the Canada Child Tax Benefit. Indeed, the federal government calculates and pays the BC Family Bonus and BC Earned Income Benefit on behalf of the provincial government along with the federal Canada Child Tax Benefit, the amounts combined into a single, monthly (federal-provincial) payment. Federal delivery through the Canada Customs and Revenue Agency confers provincial administrative savings, which in fact is one of the basic objectives of the National Child Benefit reform (to reduce duplication and overlap).

Provincial social assistance child benefits

Until recently, all provincial and territorial governments made payments on behalf of children through their social assistance systems at an estimated total cost in 1997 of $2 billion, or 40 percent of the $5 billion expenditure on the federal government's then major child benefit program, the Child Tax Benefit. Children constituted more than one-third (37 percent) of social assistance recipients as of March 1998.

The amount and design of social assistance benefits for children, as for adults, vary considerably from one jurisdiction to another. Just before the current reform began (1998), social assistance benefits for children ranged in most provinces from around $1,200 to $1,800 per child per year for basic needs (excluding shelter costs and the 'adult equivalent' benefit paid to the first child in single-parent families), though a few provinces paid below or above this range. In addition to cash payments, social assistance programs may pay special allowances (e.g., winter clothing allowances), in-kind benefits (e.g., supplementary health and dental care, prescription drugs) and housing subsidies on behalf of children.

Social assistance is Canada's income support program of last resort, available only to those who have exhausted almost all other sources of income (e.g., employment earnings, savings, social insurance benefits). To qualify for social assistance, applicants must undergo a comprehensive and intrusive 'needs test' (i.e., income and assets test) which scrutinizes their incomes, fixed and liquid assets, and budgetary needs (as determined according to regulations that take into account such factors as number and ages of children, family type and deemed employability of recipients). Changes in recipients' circumstances are monitored closely on a frequent (e.g., monthly) basis. Provincial welfare programs typically entail a considerable degree of administrative discretion. All systems have some form of appeal process.

As will be explained later, under the National Child Benefit, most provinces and territories are in the process of replacing their social assistance child benefits with increased federal child benefits and various provincial income-tested programs (both income and services) for lower-income families with children.

IN-KIND BENEFITS FOR CHILDREN

Child care benefits and subsidies

Most Canadian families – including the poor – pay for and obtain their child care on the open, unregulated, largely for-profit market, chiefly provided by neighbours or family members (e.g., grandparents). The most recent estimates, for 1998, show that only 10 percent of children aged 0 to 12 occupy a provincial government-regulated child care space, and of these only 31 percent receive a targeted-to-the-poor government subsidy (paid to the child care provider on behalf of eligible parents, not directly to the family).

Though most families pay for their child care out of their own pocket, they are potentially eligible for a partially offsetting federal and provincial income tax reduction in the form of a child care expense deduction (details of which are provided in Table 1e). However, the child care expense deduction only partly compensates for families' outlays on child care. In 1998, the median monthly fee for full-time, centre-based child care averaged $531 for infants (0-17 months), $477 for toddlers (18 months-3 years) and $455 for preschoolers (3-5 years), which for a year came to $6,372, $5,724 and $5,460, respectively. Currently, for families that qualify for the child care expense deduction, combined federal and average provincial income tax savings range from 25.5 percent of these expenses for claimants with taxable incomes under $30,004, 37.5 percent for those between $30,004 and $60,008, and 43.5 percent for those with taxable incomes over $60,008. While the majority of Canadians who claim the child care expense deduction are in the lower- and middle-income groups, simply because that is where most families are, parents in the upper income levels get a larger share of benefits than their numbers would warrant; they tend to claim larger amounts and also enjoy bigger tax savings because they are in a higher tax bracket.

Shelter subsidies

Canada uses the term 'social housing' to refer to a range of public housing, nonprofit housing, rent-geared-to-income assistance, and rural and native housing that is subsidized by government. Social housing is in short and – due to federal and provincial budget cuts – shrinking supply in Canada; waiting lists are long and getting longer. Most low-income families, including those on social assistance, get their housing in the private market and are unable to find subsidized housing.

Shelter subsidies for children accrue only indirectly. In some cases, families with children may receive higher priority for social housing. In most provinces, the rents paid by (the minority of) social assistance families that receive subsidized housing are negotiated between social assistance and housing officials, taking into account the social assistance benefits (including for children) paid for different kinds of households. For working poor recipients of social housing, rents are geared to income (generally 25-30 percent of gross income); there is a *de facto* children's component in the sense that larger units cost more but the rent is a fixed percentage of family income. Again, though, most families – the poor included – pay market rates for housing and receive no subsidy (though shelter allowances are part of provincial social assistance programs).

Food subsidies

As in the case of shelter, social assistance payments in Canada include amounts for food that take into account presence of children. But subsidized food programs are rare, especially public programs. Canada has no US-style food stamp programs. Some schools provide free or low-cost school breakfast and/or lunches. There are, however, many charitable organizations – called 'food banks' – that provide free surplus and donated food to people in need, including families with children.

Health care subsidies

Canada provides universal coverage without any point-of-service charges for essential medical services through its national health insurance system, commonly known as medicare. The medicare system is administered and funded by the provincial governments, with the federal government in turn providing some financing to the provinces. Federal funding is conditional on provinces' upholding the five principles of the federal Canada Health Act (universality, comprehensiveness, accessibility, portability and public administration) that provide a broad framework for the country's health care system. Medicare is Canada's most cherished public program, and one of the most important of all social programs for families with children – especially lower-income families, which face a higher risk of a wide range of health problems.

Canada's medicare system is not, however, comprehensive. Prescription drugs, dental care and eyeglasses, as well as some disability-related supports such as hearing aids, wheelchairs and prosthetic devices, are not covered. Provincial social assistance programs provide various supplementary health plans for some of these services, but the range of supplementary services varies considerably from one province to another. Children on social assistance generally are included in provincial supplementary health care plans and are covered for most of these services, but until recently other low-income children usually were not covered by the supplementary plans.

There have been various attempts to broaden the scope of supplementary health services to include low-income Canadians not on social assistance. Most provinces now extend some supplementary health care to social assistance recipients who move into the workforce, though this in-kind benefit is often limited both in terms of the range of services and the duration of coverage (e.g., up to one year), so that the absence of assured coverage for supplementary health remains a substantial barrier for many families on welfare that wish to return to work. However, some provinces are extending ongoing supplementary health care to the working poor under the National Child Benefit reform.

WHO GETS WHAT: DISTRIBUTION OF MAJOR INCOME BENEFITS FOR CHILDREN

We show the amount and distribution of major federal and provincial child-related benefits for two families living in the province of British Columbia in 2000 – a single parent with one child under age 7 and a two-earner couple with two children (one under

7 and one 7-17).[2] British Columbia is a good example because it pioneered the first replace-social assistance integrated child benefit (in 1996) whose concept lies at the heart of the current National Child Benefit reform.

The single-parent family potentially qualifies for five child benefits:

1. the federal Canada Child Tax Benefit

2. the federal Goods and Services Tax credit (intended to offset the increased tax burden imposed on lower-income families and individuals when the Goods and Services Tax was introduced in 1991)

3. the spousal equivalent nonrefundable tax credit (which provides federal and provincial income tax savings on behalf of the first child in a one-parent family equal to the spousal tax credit for one-income families in which the spouse does not work in the labour force)

4. the BC Family Bonus

5. the BC Earned Income Benefit

Figure 2 illustrates how the five programs distribute their benefits. The vertical sliver at the $0 point of the net family income axis represents the sum of two child-related benefits that remain in British Columbia's social assistance system – the child's portion of the basic support benefit and of the family's shelter allowance (calculated at its maximum amount). This one-parent family on social assistance receives $2,218 in support allowance on behalf of the first child (amounting to an adult equivalent benefit) and $2,340 in shelter allowance, for a total child-related benefit of $4,548 for the year. Note that these benefits typically go *only* to families on social assistance (i.e., families with children shown at the extreme left end of the graph). In this and the following example, we assume that social assistance families have no earned income.

The second-largest child benefit, depicted by the black area, is the federal Canada Child Tax Benefit, which we have calculated according to its forecast July 2001 configuration to incorporate the planned increase, but translated into 2000 dollars. It pays a maximum $2,440 and then declines above $21,214 in net family

Figure 2 Cumulative benefits for children, single parent with one child under 7, British Columbia

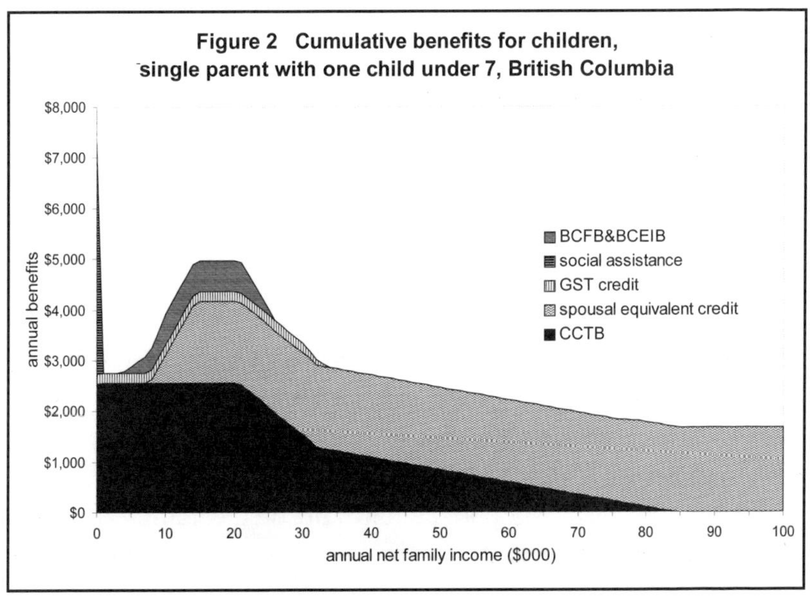

income to disappear over $83,000. The spousal equivalent tax credit (the large area with wavy lines) is worth up to $1,668 in federal and provincial income tax savings for families at $80,000 and above; note that it provides no benefit to the poorest families below the taxpaying threshold. The area with horizontal lines indicates the sum of the BC Family Bonus and the BC Earned Income Benefit, worth up to $610 annually. Finally, the thin area with vertical lines represents the children's portion of the federal refundable Goods and Services Tax credit, a maximum $202 per child per year.

As may be seen in Figure 2, the various child benefits add up to a less-than-perfect income-tested system overall that delivers its payments in a progressive fashion over much – but not all – of the income spectrum, namely between $18,000 and $84,000 in net family income. Despite British Columbia's and the National Child Benefit's shared core objective of fully removing children's benefits from social assistance, the province still pays a substantially larger child-related benefit through its needs-tested social assistance system than its new income-tested BC Family Bonus and BC Earned Income Benefit – in this example, $4,548 per year from social assistance child benefits as opposed to a maximum $610 from the new income-tested programs. As a result, child-related benefits still form part of the 'welfare wall' (this concept is explained in the following section) in this province, even though it has implemented a more integrated child benefit than almost any other province. For this family type and size, families on social assistance receive a total child benefit of $7,293 per year – 1.8 times the $4,165 for a working poor family with income of just $10,000. The upward slope between $1 and $14,000 results from the phase-in of the spousal equivalent tax credit and BC Earned Income Benefit.

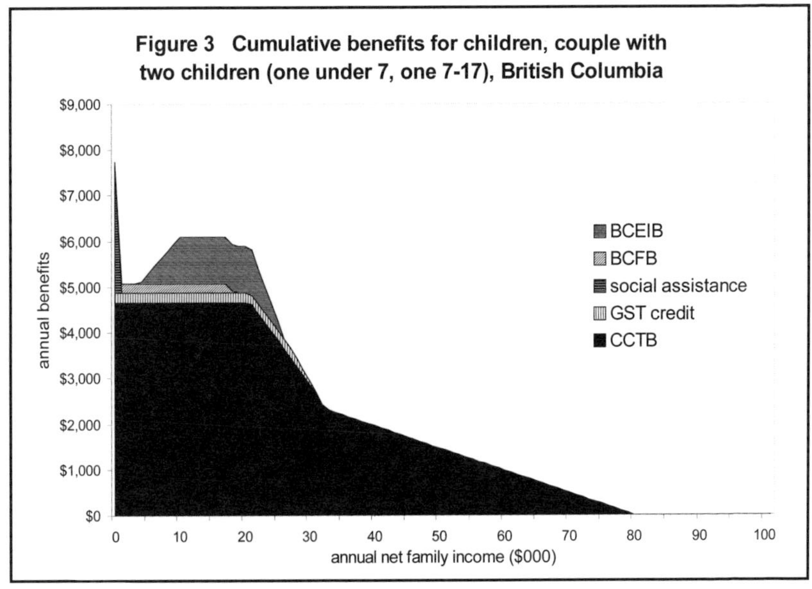

The picture is generally similar for couples with two children (one under 7, one 7-17), although they do not receive the spousal equivalent credit. Figure 3 shows the component programs and their cumulative effect. The amount of child benefits that remain embedded in the social assistance system is smaller than for single-parent families, since the latter's first child qualifies for what amount to an adult equivalent for the support allowance and a larger amount of the shelter allowance than for children in two-parent families. The social assistance child benefit is $2,664 per year for the two children together, as opposed to $4,548 for the first child in the one-parent family.[3] The other child benefit programs differ in amount (they are larger), but display the same distributional shape for two-parent families as for single-parent families. The overall picture shows that child benefits form a much smaller welfare wall for two-parent families because the amount of child-related benefits remaining in social assistance is much smaller than for one-parent families.

TOWARD AN INTEGRATED CHILD BENEFIT

Why reform?

To understand the rationale underlying Canada's unfolding National Child Benefit reform, it is helpful to explain briefly the major weaknesses of the child benefits system that it is in the process of replacing. To begin with, the old 'system' was not really a system in any rigorous sense of the word; rather, it was an uncoordinated group of programs operated by two levels of government.

The federal child benefits system, which throughout much if its history suffered from an irrational distribution of benefits, was rationalized in 1993 into a single, income-tested Child Tax Benefit (renamed Canada Child Tax Benefit effective July 1998, though the new program is very similar to the old) providing maximum payments to low-income families and diminishing benefits to non-poor families. While achieving vertical equity in its distribution of benefits, the federal program is not narrowly targeted to the poor in terms of reach. This 'broad based' characteristic – while no longer universal, the system is still extensive in coverage – advances the objective of social cohesion, since the large majority of families are served by the same program and no vulnerable group is excluded.

Among the Canada Child Tax Benefit's other virtues are its anonymous, non-stigmatizing and relatively efficient administration through the same income tax system that covers Canadians in all income groups and throughout the country. Families qualify and re-qualify for benefits based only on a simple test of their income; there is almost never any direct contact between recipients and administrators. Benefits are delivered on a frequent (monthly) basis.

Meanwhile, until very recently, all the provinces and territories delivered what amounted to cash child benefits through their social assistance systems, which provided benefits on behalf of children as well as adults. There was little if any explicit coordination with the federal child benefits system, and the two differed in terms of purpose, design and delivery.

Child benefits delivered through provincial and territorial social assistance systems pursue only the anti-poverty objective, and (along with adult benefits) are intended to provide sufficient funds for a family to meet basic necessities – i.e., to *replace* other sources of income. By contrast, federal child benefits are intended to *supplement* other sources of income.

Unlike income-tested child benefits' good performance in terms of social cohesion and inclusion, needs-tested social assistance in Canada has always been an exclusionary, socially marginalizing and divisive social program. The social assistance system is often highly discretionary and involves a relatively high degree of client-worker interaction. Social assistance imposes a significant social stigma on its recipients. It is a rules-and-regulations-ridden, highly complex system in which recipients typically are treated in a manner that tends to reinforce their economic powerlessness; employment skills and self-confidence may 'rust' and atrophy.

The scope of federal and provincial child benefits also differs significantly: Whereas federal child benefits have served all or almost all families with children, social assistance-delivered child benefits are restricted mainly to non-working poor families and exclude other low-income families such as those on Employment Insurance and the working poor. Social assistance programs have been politically vulnerable to cuts – either overt cuts from rate reductions or covert stealthy cuts from non-indexation or difficult-to-understand rule changes.

One of the major problems inherent in the uncoordinated non-system of federal income-tested child benefits and provincial needs-tested child benefits is that it never could deal effectively with the problem of persistent and extensive child poverty in Canada, because social assistance is so narrowly targeted and so unpopular. The blunt reality is that benefits offered by social assistance always will be extremely low, in addition to being stigmatized – perhaps *because* they are stigmatized.

Another significant problem with the two-tiered non-system has been characterized as 'the welfare wall' (recalling that social assistance in Canada is called 'welfare'). Social assistance families with children traditionally received child benefits from two sources – provincial social assistance benefits paid on behalf of children and federal child benefits. Other low-income families, notably the working poor and Employment Insurance poor, typically got federal child benefits only. Social assistance families thus enjoyed considerably larger – indeed, about double – child benefits than those paid to other low-income families, and this cash advantage does not count the value of the welfare system's income-in-kind benefits such as supplementary health and dental care, shelter allowances and special benefits such as winter clothing allowances.

Just before the introduction of the National Child Benefit in 1998, families on social assistance with one child under 7 and one child over 7 received on average $5,253 in total child benefits (about $3,000 on average from provincial social assistance[4] and $2,253 from the federal Child Tax Credit). Working poor families, by contrast, got only $2,753 (the basic Child Tax Benefit and a $500 per family maximum Working Income Supplement) – slightly more than half the amount of welfare families.

The term 'welfare wall' was coined by Sherri Torjman of the Caledon Institute of Social Policy to dramatize features of the tax/transfer system that can form barriers to moving from social assistance to the workforce [Battle and Torjman 1994] and Ken Battle applied it to child benefits [Department of Finance Canada 1997]. Families on social assistance received both cash and in-kind benefits on behalf of their children, over and above their federal child benefits. Parents on social assistance who managed to find paid work risked forfeiting thousands of dollars in social assistance-provided child benefits and in-kind benefits, on top of seeing their (typically low) wages reduced by federal and sometimes provincial income taxes as well as federal payroll taxes, and paying employment-related costs such as child care, clothing and transportation. In some cases, working poor families were worse off than welfare families in dollar terms, not even taking into account the heavier demands on their incomes from work-related costs. Even if working poor families managed to earn a better income than they got from social assistance, they still received only about half the amount of child benefits given to social assistance families.

Structural reform: the National Child Benefit

the formula

The reform of child benefits – known as the federal-provincial National Child Benefit – seeks to lower the welfare wall by creating an integrated, non-stigmatizing child benefit that treats all low-income families equally, whether they are working or not, while enabling the provinces to take additional actions to assist low-income families.

The main engine of reform is the new federal child benefit. As the federal government increases payments under the Canada Child Tax Benefit, the provinces are allowed to reduce their social assistance-provided child benefits by the amount of the federal child benefit increase, so long as the provinces 'reinvest' the resulting savings in other programs and services for low-income families with children. Over time, governments' objective is to raise the Canada Child Tax Benefit to the point where it alone, or in combination with provincial income-tested child benefits, displaces social assistance-delivered child benefits (estimated at a target of about $2,500 per child in 1998, about $2,600 in today's dollars). A $2,600 maximum Canada Child Tax Benefit pretty much would achieve the goal of an integrated child benefit:[5] All low-income families, regardless of their major source(s) of income, should receive the same level of child benefit, and the distinction between child benefits for the working poor and the non-working poor thereby be eliminated.

objectives

The federal and provincial governments have set three formal objectives for the National Child Benefit. It is intended: "to help prevent and reduce the depth of child poverty; to promote attachment to the workforce – resulting in fewer families having to rely on social assistance – by ensuring that families will always be better off as a result of finding work; and to reduce overlap and duplication through closer harmonization of program objectives and benefits and through simplified administration" [Department of Finance Canada 1997].

In a 1997 report of the Caledon Institute of Social Policy, the authors of this paper critically assessed the three objectives of the National Child Benefit [Battle and Mendelson 1997]. We supported the choice of *depth* of poverty (i.e., reducing the average distance of families below the poverty line) rather than *incidence* of child poverty as an objective. Progress in lowering incidence is a very poor indicator of the effective reduction in poverty. Were governments to employ reduction in incidence as a key indicator, a program that reduced substantially the depth of poverty of those who were least well off, but failed to bring them above the poverty line, would be judged as inferior to a program providing a few dollars to those who are best off among the poor, thereby bringing some people above the poverty line. Reduction in the depth of poverty is, on the other hand, a good indicator of the improvement of incomes for poor families.

We argued that it is unrealistic to set the prevention of child poverty as a formal objective of child benefits *per se*, though other programs (including some in the bundle of provincial 'reinvestments' under the National Child Benefit) can play a preventive role. We also endorsed the work incentive objective, with the caution that the National Child Benefit is no magic bullet but rather one among a range of initiatives required to dismantle the welfare wall. So too did we support the harmonization objective, which should underlie all intergovernmental relations.

We added some objectives to supplement governments' three: adequacy, fairness, dignity and independence, and economic stabilization.

The displace-social assistance target of $2,600 per child per year is only the first milestone. The Caledon Institute of Social Policy has argued that the Canada Child Tax Benefit should be raised higher within the first decade of the 21st century, to reach about $4,200 maximum per child annually, which is a rough and conservative estimate of the incremental cost of raising a child in a low-income family based on existing research. (We recommended that a new study be conducted to come up with more accurate and detailed estimates.) We also urged the federal government to improve child benefits for modest- and middle-income families – that have seen substantial losses since the 1980s – to better achieve the horizontal equity goal. Adequacy also requires full indexation; while the federal government did so as of 2000, the provinces have not yet followed suit.

The objectives of dignity and independence will be advanced through the broad-based, income-tested Canada Child Tax Benefit. Finally, resurrecting a traditional but long-lost objective of Canadian child benefits, Caledon recommended that the system also be seen as an important part of economic stabilization – an efficient vehicle to put cash into the hands of parents and thereby maintain consumer demand during a downturn and help cushion the effect of recessions.

progress

The National Child Benefit is unfolding according to plan, albeit too slowly and cautiously in our opinion. Over the past few years, the federal government has made a series of substantial increases to the Canada Child Tax Benefit that have boosted payments to low-income families and so enabled the provinces and territories to redirect social assistance savings into a range of income programs and social services for low-income families with children.

Provincial reinvestments to date total $305.2 million in 1998/99 and $498.2 million in 1999/2000. Child care took first place (39.4 percent in 1989/99 and 34.6 percent in 1999/2000), followed by income-tested child benefits and earnings supplements (31.1 percent both fiscal years), initiatives by Ontario municipalities and by Aboriginal communities (21.8 and 20.9 percent), early childhood development (4.5 and 9.3 percent) and supplementary health care (3.1 percent the first year and 4.1 percent the next year).

By 2004, Ottawa will spend a forecast $9 billion on the Canada Child Tax Benefit. This represents, in inflation-adjusted 2004 dollars, a $3.3 billion or 58 percent increase since the reform began. Low-income families will receive about $6 billion or two-thirds of the $9 billion total spending in 2004, while non-poor families will get the other $3 billion or one-third.

The federal government's target is to increase the maximum Canada Child Tax Benefit to an estimated $2,520 for one child and $2,308 for each additional child by 2004. These rates will come close to meeting the Caledon Institute's proposed $2,600 level (which in 2004 dollars will come to $2,800), which easily could be reached if not exceeded with one more increase in a forthcoming Budget.

The increase in federal cash child benefits for low-income families is striking over both the short and long term. In 2001, the Canada Child Tax Benefit will pay triple what Family Allowances delivered in 1946 for a low-income family with two children – $4,456 versus $1,451 (in inflation-adjusted 2002 dollars). Figure 4 illustrates the trend for a family with two children. Note that this figure looks only at cash benefits and does not include the value of two extinct tax-delivered programs (the children's tax exemption and its successor the non-refundable child credit, which provided little or no benefit to poor families) for which trend data are not available.

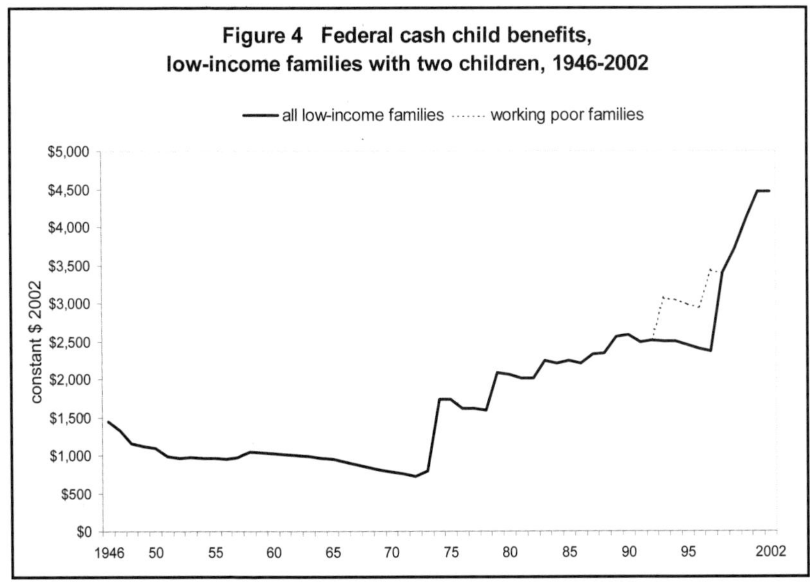

The other more modest but still crucial advance is that the federal government, in its 1999 and 2000 Budgets, began restoring child benefits for non-poor (mainly modest- and middle-income) families. In so doing, the federal government has broadened the scope of reform beyond the child benefit system's anti-poverty objective to begin bolstering its horizontal equity performance. Thus the two fundamental objectives of child benefits are being simultaneously strengthened.

criticisms

The complexity of Canada's child benefits system, together with the broad scope and rather complex nature of the federal-provincial National Child Benefit – extending as it does beyond income support to social and health services – have placed it beyond the understanding of the Canadian public, most journalists and, indeed, all but a handful of politicians. So the National Child Benefit debate has been confined largely to social advocacy organizations, anti-poverty groups and think tanks, most of which have been highly critical of the reform.

'discriminates against social assistance families'

The most damning allegation against the National Child Benefit is that it supposedly 'discriminates against social assistance families, the poorest of the poor.' Social assistance families will not get an increase in their net child benefits; rather they will see only an increase in the proportion coming from the federal Canada Child Tax Benefit and, in some provinces, new income-tested child benefits, and a concomitant decline in the share from provincial social assistance. By contrast, the working poor and other low-income families not on social assistance will enjoy an increase in their child benefits. To make matters worse, the National Child Benefit – touted by its supporters as a key advance in anti-poverty strategy – arrived after several years of overt or covert cuts to social assistance benefits in all provinces that have shrunk families' income, and amidst increasing efforts on the part of most provinces to require recipients to enter the workforce (e.g., workfare and tightened eligibility rules).

This criticism, parroted by a generally uninformed and uncritical media, misses (or rejects) the essential point of the National Child Benefit, which is to restructure income security policy for families by equalizing child benefits for all low-income families – raising payments for poor families not on social assistance to the level paid to social assistance families.

Social assistance families are receiving the same increase in their federal Canada Child Tax Benefit as other poor families, though their social assistance-delivered child benefits typically are being reduced accordingly. This has given rise to a great deal of confusion, not a little honest anxiety on the part of very vulnerable welfare recipients, and a field day for the critics. A key issue here is strategy: If Ottawa had gone with a big-bang approach (as proposed in a 1995 Caledon report) rather than an incremental, multi-year phased-in approach, and put enough money on the table for a quick (e.g., two-year) implementation, it could have fully displaced social assistance-delivered child benefits by raising the level of the new Canada Child Tax Benefit high enough to exceed the previous amount of combined federal and provincial child benefits payable to welfare families. While social assistance families still would have seen a smaller net increase in child benefits than the working poor, at least the former would have been a little better off than before. As well, the idea that one type of benefit was replacing another would have been apparent and easily explained. The painfully incremental strategy that was adopted instead has been a contributing factor to the criticism of the National Child Benefit.

However, even without a real increase in child benefits for social assistance families, it can be argued they will be better off under the National Child Benefit than they were before. Social assistance is a highly stigmatizing program prone to overt cuts or stealthy erosion on the part of the provinces. For example, a get-tough-on-social assistance plank was a prominent part of Ontario's Conservative government election platform, and it followed through with a 21.6 percent cut in social assistance for most recipients in October 1995. The reductions did not harm the party's fortunes, and indeed they may have helped. The Ontario Conservatives were subsequently handily re-elected, unlike the previous two provincial administrations, which had raised social assistance rates.

Income-tested social programs, by contrast with social assistance, have seen real and substantial increases in benefit rates for lower-income recipients, with broad public support. The Canada Child Tax Benefit, which was fully indexed as of 2000, is in a far better position than social assistance to enjoy further increases in the coming years. Thus if one is concerned about the adequacy of social assistance recipients' incomes, the best option is to provide a larger proportion of their incomes out of a politically popular and expanding program, such as the Canada Child Tax Benefit.

Moreover, it is critical to remember that the social assistance population is a dynamic, ever-changing group. Around half of welfare recipients leave for the workforce every year. Under the old system, these recipients lost all of their social assis-tance-delivered child benefits. By contrast, the Canada Child Tax Benefit is a 'portable' benefit (to borrow a concept from pension terminology) that accompanies families no matter what their primary income source: Welfare families no longer will lose child benefits if they move to the workforce, and working poor families will continue to receive their child benefits from the federal government even if they move to social assistance or Employment Insurance. If they improve their earnings, families will continue to receive the Canada Child Tax Benefit – though in a smaller amount if their income increases enough – far up the income scale.

As well, social assistance families receive the Canada Child Tax Benefit, without stigma, just like the large majority of Canadian families. Payment is automatic and painless, involving little or no contact with government officials. Moreover, some welfare families will benefit from some of the provincial reinvestments (not all of which are focussed on the working poor), though more so if they move into the workforce.

The National Child Benefit holds out the promise of more than just a restructuring and enhancement of child benefits. By removing a large group (children) from social assistance caseloads, it marks a major step forward in the essential task of dismantling the archaic welfare system and replacing it with more effective programs. In our view, the next challenge is to transform social assistance from its current conception as a last-ditch family income support program to a modernized role as a wage substitution program for adults, more suitable to a modern, active income security system.

'the welfare wall is more than child benefits'

Social advocates complain that the National Child Benefit does not deal with the variety of obstacles – more important, in their view, than the child benefits differential – that make it difficult for families to move from social assistance to the workforce. Chief among these barriers are lack of affordable and accessible child care and the fact that so many jobs typically available to low-income parents (when such jobs can, in fact, be found) do not pay a living wage and can leave families worse off financially than if they were on social assistance.

These are major problems, to be sure, but the National Child Benefit on its own cannot solve them. It is intended to lower the part of the welfare wall that results from differential child benefits and to reduce the depth of poverty. Under the National Child Benefit, some provinces are reinvesting social assistance savings in child care and extending supplementary health care to the working poor. But these initiatives cannot substitute for the range of reforms – such as a robust early childhood development system, supplementary health benefits, effective employment programs and decent adult income supports replacing traditional social assistance – that are needed to combat poverty.

marginal tax rage

Some economists claim that the National Child Benefit reform risks shooting itself in the foot, as it were, by imposing high effective marginal tax rates that supposedly sap the work ethic of the very families it is supposed to help. (By 'effective marginal tax rate,' we mean the percentage of additional income paid in income and payroll taxes or forgone due to income-tested programs' reduction rates.)

The Canada Child Tax Benefit has resulted in higher effective marginal tax rates for some working poor families (those in the $21,000-$30,000 net family income range) because of the decision to target (limited) new spending on low-income families. For example, an Ontario family with net income of $27,000 saw its effective marginal tax rate rise from 39.5 percent to 54.2 percent as a result of the higher reduction rate imposed on the National Child Benefit Supplement. At the same time, although more difficult to measure due to the complicated rules for social assistance, welfare recipients who moved into the labour market are enjoying a large decrease in their marginal tax rates.

The impact of this mix of higher and lower effective marginal tax rates on labour market behaviour remains an open question. The factors that can influence families' decisions regarding paid work (e.g., choice of full-time or part-time work, social assistance over work, overtime) are very complex and cannot simply be assumed as given according to the usual (and rather simplistic) interpretation of orthodox economic theory. Issues such as social expectations (e.g., Canadians' belief in the value of work, above and beyond its remuneration), opportunities and the perception of future opportunities, transportation and child care availability, employers' provision of family friendly policies, and many other variables fit into the equation – and it is not clear, nor does economic theory suggest, that the effective marginal tax rate is the most important of all these variables.

The National Child Benefit has objectives beyond the labour market, unlike 'pure' income supplements for the working poor. The National Child Benefit's impact on the depth of poverty and disposable income is equally as important – if not more so – than its effect on labour market behaviour.

POLICY ISSUES

Killing three birds with one stone: a larger, simpler and less steeply targeted child benefit?

Far and away the most important priority is to continue growing the new child benefit to create a strong income security system for Canadian families. So far, the federal government has not committed to moving beyond its $2,520 maximum target for 2004, which is a far cry from the $4,200 level proposed by the Caledon Institute and some other social policy groups.

As is evident to any reader of this report, the Canadian child benefit system is still very complex and difficult to understand. For better or worse, all programs must live and die in a political environment. In such an environment, a program is only as good as it is perceived. The ongoing reform of child benefits is difficult to explain, and consequently difficult to defend against criticisms. The structure and goals of the child benefit system must be easy to communicate, and to be easy to communicate that system must have a simpler and more straightforward structure.

This simplification could be achieved as part of the process of further increasing benefits for both poor- and non-poor families: The Canada Child Tax Benefit could be simplified from a two-tier to a single-tier program with a single (albeit significantly higher than at present) benefit, a single reduction rate and a single income threshold for maximum payments. Moreover, by getting rid of the upper tier (i.e., the National Child Benefit Supplement) and its higher reduction rate, working poor families no longer would face high effective marginal tax rates.

Figure 5 illustrates effective marginal tax rates for two-earner couples with two children in Ontario under the current Canada Child Tax Benefit and under a Caledon option that would pay a maximum $4,200 per child, using a $25,000 net family income threshold and reduction rates of 5 percent for one child and 10 percent for two or more children (i.e., double the current reduction rates for the basic Child Tax Benefit). Effective marginal tax rates are much lower for working poor families in the $20,000 to $30,000 net family income range, while non-poor families would receive substantial increases in child benefits in return for only modest (5 to 10 percentage point) increases in their effective marginal tax rates.

The downside of moving from a two-tier to a single-tier Canada Child Tax Benefit is cost. Two countries that pay much larger maximum child benefits than Canada (indeed, higher than the $4,200 'ultimate' target Caledon has proposed for Canada) – Australia and the UK – use multi-tier systems in which the distribution of child benefits resemble three tiers or plateaus with two sharp slopes. Such a 'stepped' shape is necessary to limit costs in systems that pay large benefits to lower-income families. If Australia and the UK were to use the current Canadian model, which reduces benefits gently for non-poor families and thus results in a smooth slope, the result would be a substantial increase in benefits for all families between $20,000 and $60,000. This doubtless would be very expensive due to the large percentage of families in that income range. Moving to a single-tier structure would be more costly still.

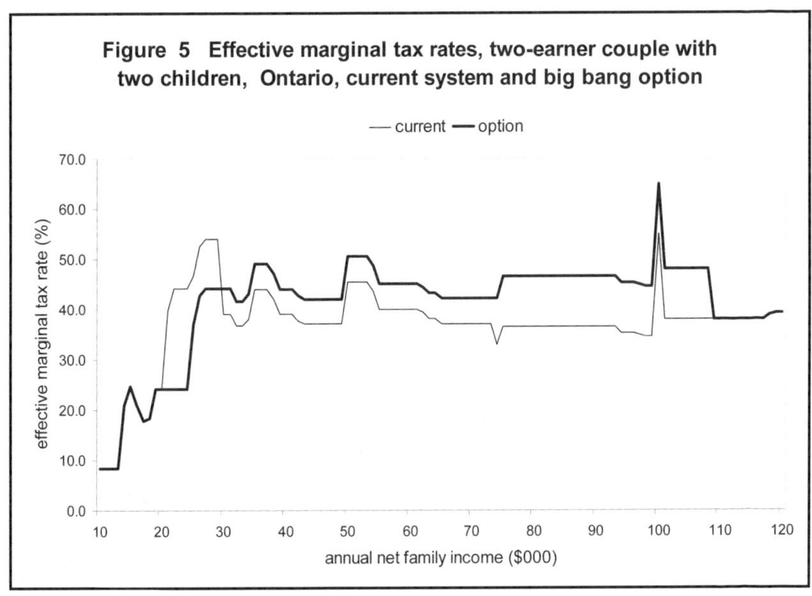

But it is important to grasp the advantages of a smooth as opposed to stepped structure. A smooth structure does not impose such high effective marginal tax rates on families that fall on the slopes. A smooth structure relates the amount of benefits progressively to the amount of income for non-poor families, whereas stepped structures result in vertical inequities (families at the end of one plateau and the beginning of the next plateau get very different amounts of child benefit even though their incomes are not as different, while families at either end of each plateau receive similar amounts even though their incomes are very different).

Thus the design of child benefits involves trade-offs between equity and efficiency objectives and the ever-dominant constraint of cost. Whatever particular design that Canada ends up using in future, the most pressing issue is to go beyond the current commitment to a larger but still relatively modest maximum Canada Child Tax Benefit and build a strong family income security system that serves the needs of poor and non-poor families alike.

The income definition issue

The federal Canada Child Tax Benefit and provincial income-tested child benefits use net rather than gross income to calculate eligibility for and amount of payments. This information (e.g., deductions for private pension contributions and child care expenses) is provided by all taxfilers as a matter of course when they fill out their annual income tax return. The federal government defends this definition on the grounds that child benefits should be allocated on the basis of families' income after taking into account employment-related expenses required to earn that income. However, the net family income definition gives rise to both horizontal and vertical inequities.

Horizontal inequity can arise because families with the same total (gross) income receive different amounts of child benefits depending on how much they are able to deduct to reduce their net income for child benefit purposes. Vertical inequities can occur when upper-income families end up with similar amounts of child benefit as middle-income families, and when some middle-income poor families qualify for the same benefits as low-income families. The use of net family income results in a systematic bias in favour of higher-income families, because they are more likely to be able to deduct sizable amounts for such commonplace items as contributions to occupational pension and individual retirement savings plans and for child care expenses.

This is not a trivial matter: The distribution of the Canada Child Tax Benefit across the income range looks very different when gross rather than net income is used. The Canada Child Tax Benefit currently pays out an estimated $2.7 billion or 35 percent of its total $7.6 billion to non-poor families over $30,000 on the basis of net family income. But in terms of actual (gross) income, it spends fully 63 percent or $4.8 billion on over-$30,000 families. Higher-income families in the select $70,000-plus group get $137 million or just 1.8 percent of Canada Child Tax Benefit payouts on the basis of net income but, in terms of actual (gross income), account for $917 million or 12.1 percent of benefits.

The Canada Child Tax Benefit should be based on gross family income and the program's parameters readjusted upwards on an equitable basis with the savings. Self-employed families, which may incur significant business losses, will require a new definition of income.

Lack of responsiveness

One of the enduring concerns about using the income tax system to deliver social benefits is its lack of responsiveness to changes in income. There can be a considerable lag – up to 18 months – between assessment of income and calculation of the Canada Child Tax Benefit. While the program can adjust quickly to change in family composition, such as marriage breakdown or death of a spouse, it is not designed to do so in response to changes in income due to getting or losing a job.

Interestingly, despite the substantial amount of agonizing over the issue of responsiveness in theoretical discussions of social benefits design, the lack of responsiveness of the Canadian child benefits system appears to be a non-issue in practice. So far as we know, there has never been a complaint about this problem from a social advocacy group or reported in the media, though federal officials say they have received some complaints from individual taxpayers. Indeed, if anything, the case might be the opposite. In a focus group with recipients of the BC Family Bonus held by the authors, the response to the possibility of some form of more regular (e.g., monthly) income testing to improve responsiveness was uniformly one of horror, as this was seen as reintroducing the much-reviled social assistance monthly reporting requirements. Recipients were more than willing to give up any potential benefit of improved responsiveness in return for lack of intrusiveness.

One of the reasons for responsiveness being a 'non-issue' in the Canadian system might be its design. There is a significant range of income before there is any reduction in benefits – a long stretch (up to about 41 percent of average family income) in which the Canada Child Tax Benefit effectively acts as a flat-rate demogrant. Many people with low incomes always will receive the maximum amount, whether in work or out of work, and so the issue of responsiveness does not arise for them. Aside from change in family composition (usually due to marriage breakdown or birth of a child, to which the system can adjust soon after notification), there could well be relatively few families that drop in one year from a comfortable income to a low income and thus need maximum child benefits as fast as possible. Unfortunately, this empirical question has not yet been investigated.

Nevertheless, an income-tested child benefit program must have a fall-back for the few exceptional cases who do need a full child benefit immediately. In the Canadian system, this requirement is handled simply enough through the long-established social assistance system, as a kind of emergency back up for this and other contingencies in which income-tested social programs cannot respond quickly to need. Employment Insurance also can respond quite rapidly to income loss due to unemployment, and is more generous for low-income families with children since they can receive up to 80 percent of their average weekly earnings (as opposed to 55 percent for other recipients); unfortunately, only a minority of unemployed Canadians now qualify for Employment Insurance because eligibility rules have been tightened.

A more fully integrated reform

The National Child Benefit has not reached its goal of fully replacing all social assistance-embedded child benefits throughout Canada. Families on social assistance still receive some child-related benefits in most or all provinces.

Getting from where we are today to a fully integrated child benefit will not be easy. If future federal governments were to raise the Canada Child Tax Benefit towards the $4,200 level Caledon and some other groups has suggested, then getting rid of all remaining social assistance benefits for children would help pay for such a costly program (assuming Ottawa could benefit from provincial savings). Other cost-shifting changes beyond the scope of this paper, such as the reform of the shelter allowance component of social assistance and the elimination of one or more of the secondary child benefit programs, also must be considered.

CONCLUSION

If the issue of child poverty is ever to be effectively addressed, solutions must be found that are consistent with the values and aspirations of Canadians. Most Canadians want to do more to fight poverty, but not through the discredited traditional mechanism of social assistance that tends to marginalize the poor and perpetuate poverty. Presumably even social advocacy groups that have opposed the National Child Benefit would admit its advantages over traditional social assistance, so long as the new system extended real child benefit increases to families on social assistance. While the National Child Benefit cannot by itself resolve the challenge of child poverty, it is a relatively efficient and politically legitimate vehicle through which to deliver better income benefits to Canada's children, poor and non-poor alike – thus strengthening both the anti-poverty and horizontal equity objectives of child benefits and the goal of social inclusion that is key to a modern social security system for the new century.

ENDNOTES

1. We include the three territories – Yukon, Northwest Territories and Nunavut – that have the same social policy responsibilities as the 10 provinces.

2. Calculations for the Canada Child Tax Benefit, refundable GST credit, BC Family Bonus and BC Earned Income Benefit are straightforward and simply follow the set formula for each program. The child-related portion of social assistance was estimated using the 'difference method' employed in this study: We subtracted the amount of social assistance for a single person from the amount for a one-parent family with one child, and the amount of social assistance for a childless couple from that for a couple with two children.

3. Using the 'difference method,' for the one-parent family with one child we subtracted the annual amount of social assistance benefits for a single employable adult ($2,100 in support allowance and $3,900 in maximum shelter allowance, for a total $6,000) from the amount for a single parent with one child ($4,308 in support allowance and $6,240 in maximum shelter allowance, for a total of $11,808), which produced a figure of $4,548 for child benefits still embedded in the social assistance system. For the couple with two children, we subtracted social assistance benefits for a childless couple ($3,492 in support allowance and $6,240 in maximum shelter allowance, for a total $9,732) from the amount for a couple with two children ($4,596 in support allowance and $7,800 for maximum shelter allowances, for a total $14,916), which resulted in a figure of $2,664 for child-related social assistance payments.

4. In most provinces, social assistance benefits for children ranged between $1,200 and $1,800 per child, not counting child-related shelter allowances or the adult equivalent welfare benefits generally paid on behalf of the first child in one-parent families.

5. Because social assistance rates vary from one province to another, a single amount – e.g., $2,600 – would exceed benefits in some provinces but not fully displace them in another. Moreover, the $2,600 target is not intended to displace the adult equivalent benefit for the first child in social assistance families. Nor would it replace shelter assistance for children in social assistance families.

REFERENCES

Battle, K. (1999). *Credit Corrosion: Bracket Creep's Evil Twin.* Ottawa: Caledon Institute of Social Policy.

Battle, K. (1998). *No Taxation Without Indexation.* Ottawa: Caledon Institute of Social Policy.

Battle, K. (1997). *The National Child Benefit: Best Thing Since Medicare or New Poor Law*? Ottawa: Caledon Institute of Social Policy.

Battle, K. (1991). "Child Benefits Reform." Appendix to *Children in Poverty: Toward a Better Future.* Ottawa: Standing Senate Committee on Social Affairs, Science and Technology.

Battle, K. and M. Mendelson. (1997). *Child Benefit Reform in Canada: An Evaluative Framework and Future Directions.* Ottawa: Caledon Institute of Social Policy.

Battle, K. and L. Muszynski. (1995). *One Way to Fight Child Poverty.* Ottawa: Caledon Institute of Social Policy.

Battle, K. and S. Torjman. (1994). "The Welfare Wall: An Analysis of the Welfare/Tax System in Ontario." In A. Maslove ed. *Taxation and the Distribution of Income.* Toronto: University of Toronto Press.

Caledon Institute of Social Policy. (1993). *The Welfare Wall: The Interaction of the Welfare and Tax Systems.* Ottawa.

Canada. (1994). *Improving Social Security in Canada: A Discussion Paper.* Ottawa: Department of Human Resources Development Canada.

Canadian Council on Social Development. (1997a). "Integrating children's benefits: what will result?" Ottawa: January.

Canadian Council on Social Development. (1997b). "CCSD's Response to the 1997 Federal Budget." Ottawa: March.

Collins, Stephanie Baker. (1997). "Child poverty and the federal budget: Is this the best we could do?" *The Catalyst*, Volume 20, No. 1, February-March 1997. Toronto: Citizens for Public Justice.

Department of Finance Canada. (1997). *Working Together Towards a National Child Benefit System.* Ottawa: Her Majesty the Queen in Right of Canada.

Durst, D. ed. (1999). *Canada's National Child Benefit: Phoenix or Fizzle?* Halifax, Nova Scotia: Fernwood Publishing.

Federal/provincial/territorial governments. (2000). *National Child Benefit Reinvestment Report.* http://socialunion.gc.ca

Federal/provincial/territorial governments. (1999). *National Child Benefit Progress Report.* http://socialunion.gc.ca

Federal/provincial/territorial governments. (1999). *National Child Benefit Progress Report: Supplementary Statistical Information.* http://social union.gc.ca

Federal/provincial/territorial governments. (1997). *The National Child Benefit: Building a Better Future for Canadian Children.* http://socialunion.gc.ca

Freiler, C. and J. Cerny. (1998). *Benefiting Canada's Children: Perspectives on Gender and Social Responsibility.* Ottawa: Status of Women Canada.

Human Resources Development Canada. (1995). *Income Security for Canada's Children: A Supplementary Paper.* Ottawa: Minister of Supply and Services Canada.

Mendelson, M. (1997). *A Preliminary Analysis of the Impact of the BC Family Bonus on Poverty and on Social Assistance Caseloads.* KPMG.

Ministerial Council on Social Policy Reform and Renewal. (1995). *Report to Premiers.*

Naylor, N. (1995). "Assessing the Possibility of a National Child Benefit Program." In M. Dooley et al. eds. *Family Matters: New Policies for Divorce, Lone Mothers, and Child Poverty.* Toronto: C.D. Howe Institute.

National Anti-Poverty Organization. (1997). "Martin Does Nothing to Address "Third World Poverty" in Canada." Ottawa: February.

National Council of Welfare. (1998). *Child Benefits: Kids Are Still Hungry.* Ottawa: Minister of Public Works and Government Services Canada.

National Council of Welfare. (1997). *Child Benefits: A Small Step Forward.* Ottawa: Minister of Supply and Services Canada.

Naylor, N. (1995). "Assessing the Possibility of a National Child Benefit Program." In M. Dooley et al. eds. *Family Matters: New Policies for Divorce, Lone Mothers, and Child Poverty.* Toronto: C.D. Howe Institute.

Naylor, N., R. Abbott and E. Hewner. (1994). *The Design of the Ontario Child Income Program.* Ottawa: Caledon Institute of Social Policy.

Novick, M. and R. Shillington. (1997). *Mission for the Millennium: A Comprehensive Strategy for Children and Youth.* Toronto: Campaign 2000.

Ontario Coalition for Better Child Care. (1997). "Ottawa fiddles with child poverty as social programs burn." Toronto: February.

Poschmann, F. (1999). *Growing Child Benefit, Growing Tax Rates.* Toronto: C.D. Howe Institute.

Pulkingham, J., G. Ternowetsky and D. Hay. (1997). "The New Canada Child Tax Benefit: Eradicating poverty or victimizing the poorest?" *CCPA Monito*r, Vol. 4, No. 1, May.

Sayeed, A. (1999). *Improving the National Child Benefit: Matching Deeds with Intentions.* Toronto: C.D.Howe Institute.

Statistics Canada. (2000a). *Income in Canada 1998.* Catalogue No. 75-202-XPE. Ottawa: Minister of Industry.

Statistics Canada. (2000b). *Income in Canada 1998.* Catalogue No. 75-202-XIE. Ottawa: Minister of Industry.

ANNEX 1: PERSONAL INCOME TAX SYSTEM, CANADA

Unit of taxation

The unit of taxation is the individual. However, federal and provincial refundable tax credits (including the federal Canada Child Tax Benefit and refundable Goods and Services Tax credit, provincial income-tested child benefits and employment earnings supplements, and other refundable provincial tax credits) are based on net family income (i.e., the combined income of both spouses, minus various specified deductions).

Pay-as-you-earn versus annual reconciliation

Employees have their income taxes withheld at source (paycheque) by their employers. Self-employed Canadians and those with significant amounts of unearned taxable income file quarterly. Annual reconciliation is completed for calendar years, with the return due by April 30 for employees and June 15 for the self-employed.

Who is responsible for submitting tax returns

All individuals are required to fill out an annual income tax return if they pay contributions (i.e., premiums) to the Canada Pension Plan (i.e., because they had employment earnings above $3,500), have a balance of income tax owing from the precious year, were sent a request to file a return, had a taxable capital gain or sold capital property, had to repay any Old Age Security or Employment Insurance benefits, or have not repaid amounts they withdrew from their Registered Retirement Savings Plan (i.e., individual retirement savings plan) in order to buy a house or use the money to go to school.

Even if they do not meet any of the above legal requirements, Canadians are encouraged to file income tax returns if it potentially could be to their or their family's advantage – e.g., want to claim an income tax refund, to apply for the Goods and Services and Harmonized Services Tax credits, to continue receiving Canada Child Tax Benefit payments (both parents must file, even if they have no income), to carry forward unused portions of the tuition and education nonrefundable tax credits, or receive income for which they could contribute to a Registered Retirement Savings Plan.

Federal/state/local

The federal and all provincial and territorial governments levy personal income taxes. With the exception of Quebec, which operates its income tax system itself, all provinces have the federal government collect their income taxes on their behalf, using the common tax return. Until recently, again with the exception of Quebec, provincial income tax systems were closely integrated with the federal income tax system; provinces simply calculated their income tax as a percentage of basic federal tax, and thus used the same tax thresholds, tax rates, income definition and nonrefundable credits and deductions. However, several provinces are now altering their income tax systems (e.g., Alberta and Manitoba) or are considering doing so, though they will continue to have the federal government administer their systems on their behalf.

Progressivity

The federal (and almost all provincial) income tax systems have three broad tax brackets: 17 percent of taxable income up to $30,003 in 2000, 24 percent of taxable income (it is being lowered from the previous 26 percent to 24 percent as of July 1 2000, which means an effective rate of 25 percent for 2000) between $30,004 and $60,008, and 29 percent of taxable income $60,009 and over. Effective January 2001, the bottom tax rate will be lowered from 17 to 16 percent and the middle rate from 24 to 22 percent; the old top tax rate of 29 percent will fall to 26 percent on incomes between about $60,000 and $100,000 and the top tax rate will be the same as before (29 percent) though only above $100,000. Also, the high-income surtax (5 percent of basic federal tax above $15,500) will be eliminated in 2001. There are a number of personal non-refundable credits that reduce income tax (including the basic personal, spousal, spousal equivalent, aged, disabled, Employment Insurance premiums, Canada Pension Plan contributions, medical expense, and education and tuition fees) and a child care expense deduction that lowers taxable income. Between 1986 and 1999, tax thresholds, credits and deductions were only partly indexed, which had an overall regressive impact, but they were fully reindexed as of 2000.

Quebec also has a progressive income tax system. The province of Alberta is introducing a single rate income tax system with larger personal credits.

Percentage of taxfilers owing income tax

The latest available statistics, for the 1996 taxation year, show that of 20.8 million Canadian who filed income tax returns, 14.2 million (68.3 percent) owed income tax.

Administrative body

The federal Canada Customs and Revenue Agency administers federal and, on their behalf, provincial and territorial income taxes (with the exception of Quebec, which runs its own provincial income tax system).

ANNEX 2: BASIC NATIONAL STATISTICS, CANADA

GDP and population

GDP: $1,052.0 billion (3rd quarter 2000)

Population: 30.5 million (1999)

Labour force

Unemployment rate: 6.9 percent (November 2000)

Participation rate: 66.2 percent (November 2000)

Children and families

Number of children under 18: 6,804,000 (1998)

Percentage of children under 18: 22.6 percent (1998)

Families with children under 18: 3,750,000 (1998)
as percentage of all households: 29.9 percent

Average number of children per family: 1.8 (1998)

Among families with head under 65 and children under 18 (1998)

a. number of single-parent families: 688,000

female head	580,000
male head	109,000

as percentage of all families with children:

all single-parent families	18.3 percent
female head	15.5 percent
male head	2.9 percent

b. families with no earner as percentage of total:
8.3 percent

families with one earner as percentage of total:
25.2 percent

families with two or more earners
as percentage of total: 66.5 percent

c. mother-only families employed as % of all mother-only families: 87.0 percent

Child poverty

Statistics for 1998 (using Statistics Canada's low income cut-offs, income before income tax)

number all poor children under 18: 1,274,000
poverty rate: 18.8 percent

number poor children in two-parent families: 700,000
poverty rate: 12.3 percent

number of children in single-mother families: 529,000
poverty rate: 56.3 percent

Average incomes (head under 65), 1998

a. pre-transfer income (i.e., market income)

two-parent families:	$65,766
single-parent families:	$22,290
mother-only:	$19,242
father-only:	$38,790
childless couples:	$60,300

b. post-transfer income (i.e., total income)

two-parent families:	$70,043
single-parent families:	$29,887
mother-only:	$27,195
father-only:	$44,253
childless couples:	$63,961

c. post-tax income (i.e., total income less income tax)

two-parent families:	$55,074
single-parent families:	$26,279
mother-only:	$24,424
father-only:	$36,180
childless couples:	$49,769

TABLE 1a
INCOME-RELATED BENEFITS

	Canada Child Tax Benefit
Eligibility rules	
1. Who is entitled to benefits	1. Those with dependent children under age 18, natural born, adopted or being cared for by the family. Open to Canadian citizens and families with landed immigrant status or Convention refugee status. No requirement for type of income (e.g., not restricted to families with employment earnings), hours of work, disability status or other conditions. No time limits.
2. Reciprocal responsibilities	2. Recipients must apply for benefits at birth of child; each parent must file an income tax form (even if they have no income) in order to track family income.
3. Budget caps	3. Open-ended entitlement.
Benefits description	
1. Amounts per child	1. First tier: Basic Child Tax Benefit of maximum $1,117 per child annually (July 2001-June 2002), plus an additional $221 for each child under age 7 for whom child care expenses deduction not received and an extra $78 for the third and each additional child. (Maximum amounts for July 2000-June 2001 are $1,104 per child plus $219 for each child under 7 for whom child care expenses not claimed and extra $77 for third and each additional child). One province – Alberta – varies the federal benefit by age of child (for 2001, an estimated $1,031 for each child under 7, $1,1018 for each child 7 to 11, $1,231 for each child between 12 and 15, and $1,304 for each child aged 16 or 17). Second tier: National Child Benefit Supplement (restricted to low-income families) of forecast maximum $1,255 for the first child ($977 for July 2000-June 2001), $1,055 for the second child ($771 in 2000) and $980 ($694 in 2000) for each additional child. Together, the basic Child Tax Benefit and National Child Benefit Supplement amount to a forecast maxi-

	Canada Child Tax Benefit
	mum annual payment of $2,372 for one child ($2,081 previous year), $2,172 for a second child ($1,875 previous year) and $2,175 for the third and each additional child ($1,875 previous year). Age (except in Alberta), order of children and family structure irrelevant.
2. Income-related structure	2. First tier: Maximum basic Child Tax Benefit payable up to net family income of $32,000 for July 2001-June 2002 ($30,004 previous year), above which payments are reduced by 2.5 percent of net family income for families with one child and 5.0 percent for those with two or more children. No minimum benefit: Child Tax Benefit disappears at net family income of $76,680 for families with one or two children ($74,164 previous year). Second tier: Maximum National Child Benefit Supplement goes to families with net income under $21,744 ($21,214 previous year) and reduces at rate of 11.1 percent for one child, 19.9 percent for two children and 27.8 percent for larger families, to end once net family income reaches $32,000 ($30,004 for July 2000-June 2001).
3. Definition of income	3. Net family income: Combined income of both spouses from all sources (e.g., employment, investments, social programs other than the Canada Child Tax Benefit itself) net of child care expenses, contributions to Registered Pension Plans (i.e., occupational pension plans) and Registered Retirement Savings Plans (i.e., individual private retirement savings plans), union and professional dues, attendant care expenses, certain employment expenses, carrying charges and interest expenses, business investment losses, moving expenses, and investments in oil, gas and mining ventures.
4. Indexing	4. As of 2000, CCTB amounts and net family income thresholds (for both basic Child Tax Benefit and National Child Benefit Supplement) are fully indexed annually according to change in Consumer Price Index (used to be partially indexed to inflation over 3 percent).

	Canada Child Tax Benefit
Delivery features 1. Administrative arrangements	1. The Canada Customs and Revenue Agency administers the program under the Canadian Income Tax Act.
2. How people get enrolled	2. Applying parent must fill out a special form and each year each parent must file an income tax return.
3. Responsiveness	3. Eligibility for and amount of benefit based on net family income as assessed through the income tax return. Benefits are paid monthly, and the payment period is July 1 of one year to June 30 of next year. No reconciliation of income reported during the accounting period with income as of the end of the accounting period, so there can be a considerable lag – up to 18 months – between assessment of income and calculation of amount of benefit. No allowance for ongoing reporting of income changes (e.g., a significant rise or fall due to employment or unemployment), but does allow for recalculation in the case of change of family composition (i.e., marriage or marriage breakdown, birth or adoption of a new child). Retroactive payments can be paid for up to 11 months from the month that the federal government receives the application.
4. Payment procedures	4. Payment to the parent considered to be primarily responsible for the care and upbringing of the child (usually the mother, but can also be father, grandparent or guardian).
5. Verification procedures	5. In addition to auditing of financial information provided on income tax returns, non-financial information (e.g., marital status, children and residence) subject to review through payment validation and control programs.
6. Aboriginal peoples	6. Paid to Aboriginal families on same conditions as all others, although some Aboriginal people object to

	Canada Child Tax Benefit
	filling out income tax form. Although income earned on reserve by Status Indians under certain conditions specified by the Indian Act and by the courts in tax exempt, tax returns still have been filed by individuals who have only tax exempt income to ensure that benefits for children are received.
7. How program is delivered	7. Monthly payments by federal Canada Customs and Revenue Agency in form of cheques or direct deposit to bank accounts.
8. How program is financed	8. Financed through federal general revenue; counted as tax expenditure (i.e., tax revenue loss) rather than direct program expenditure.
9. National/state integration	9. Federal government administers and delivers most provincial/territorial income-tested child benefits on behalf of provincial/territorial governments. Where authorized by legislation, federal government makes available Canada Child Tax Benefit client information to support other child-related benefit programs, such as Quebec Family Allowance, Ontario Child Care Supplement for Working Families and Employment Insurance Family Supplement.

TABLE 1b
INCOME-RELATED BENEFITS

	Provincial and Territorial Child Benefits
Eligibility rules 1.Who is entitled to benefits	1. Those with dependent children under age 18, natural born, adopted or being cared for by the family. Open to Canadian citizens and families with landed immigrant status or Convention refugee status. With exception of employment earnings supplements, which require eligible families to have employment income, no requirement for type of income, hours of work, disability status or other conditions. No time limits.
2. Reciprocal responsibilities	2. Recipients must apply for benefits and each year each parent must file an income tax form (even if they have no income) in order to track family income.
3. Budget caps	3. Open-ended entitlement.
Benefits description 1. Amounts per child 2. Income-related structure	1&2. *BC (British Columbia) Family Bonus*: Maximum amount July 2000-June 2001 is $305 for first child, $505 for second child and $580 for each additional child. Maximum payments up to net family income of $18,000, above which benefits are reduced at the rate of 8 percent for one child and 16 percent for two or more children, disappearing at $21,813 for one child and $23,063 for two children. *BC (British Columbia) Earned Income Benefit*: Maximum benefit is $605 for the first child, $405 for the second child and $330 for each additional child. Benefits phase in at the rate of 9.68 percent of work earnings over $3,750 for families with one child, 16.16 percent for two children and 21.44 percent for three children, reaching their maximum amount at family earnings of $10,000. Maximum benefits are reduced

	Provincial and Territorial Child Benefits
	at the rate of 12.1 percent of net family income above $20,921 for one child, 20.2 percent for two children and 26.8 percent for families with three or more children, ending at $25,921 for families with one, two or three children. *Alberta Family Employment Tax Credit:* Maximum benefit is $500 per child and $1,000 per family. Phases in at the rate of 8 percent of employment earnings above $6,500 and is reduced at the rate of 4 percent of net family income above $25,000. Eligibility ends once net family income exceeds $37,500 for families with one child and $50,000 for those with two or more children. *Saskatchewan Child Benefit*: Maximum $528 a year for first child, $738 for second child and $812 for each additional child. Maximum payments go to families with net family income under $15,921, and are reduced at the rate of 15.05 percent for one child (30.14 percent for two and 45.2 percent for three) of net family income between $15,921 and $20,921 and 2.95 percent for one child (9.94 percent for two and 18.4 percent for three) above the latter threshold. *Saskatchewan Employment Supplement:* Maximum $2,100 for the first child and $420 for each additional child, with a family limit of $3,780 (i.e., families with five or more children). Benefit phases in at the rate of 25 percent of employment earnings above $1,500, reaching the maximum payment at $7,500. The benefit is reduced by 25 percent of net family income above $12,900, disappearing at $21,300. *Manitoba Child Related Income Support Program*: Maximum $360 per child to families with income (from employment and the Canada Child Tax Benefit, less

	Provincial and Territorial Child Benefits
	certain deductions – $1,052 per child under 9 and $952 for those 9 to 17, plus 6 percent of income) up to $12,384, above which payments are reduced by 25 percent to end at $13,824, which amounts to employment earnings of about $10,000. Social assistance recipients are not eligible for the program. Benefits and income thresholds have been frozen for many years, so it has become progressively targeted down the income scale and has a low take-up rate. *Ontario Child Care Supplement for Working Families*: Targetted to working poor and modest-income families with children under age 7. Maximum payment of $1,100 per child under 7 is phased in at the rate of 21 percent of family work earnings above $5,000 for one child, 42 percent for two children and 63 percent for larger families. Single parents receive a supplement of up to $210 per child under age 7. Maximum benefits are payable once family earnings reach $10,238 and phase out at the rate of 8 percent of net family income above $20,000, disappearing at $33,750. Families in receipt of social assistance are not eligible for the program. (Eligibility is *not* dependent upon families' having child care expenditures.) *Quebec Family Allowances*: For two-parent families, pays maximum $795 per child up to net family income of $21,825; benefits are reduced by 25 percent of net family income between $21,825 and $50,000 but pay minimum $131 for the first child, $174 for the second child and $975 for the third and each additional child up to $50,000 (the latter much larger amount reflects Quebec's attempt to introduce a pronatalist element into its child benefit system, since the province's birth rate is low). Above $50,000 net family income, benefits are reduced by 5 percent of net family income above $50,000, disappearing at $52,620 for families with one

	Provincial and Territorial Child Benefits
	child, $56,120 for families with two children and $75,600 for those with three children. Single-parent families also receive a supplement of up to $1,300 per family, reduced by 35 percent of net family income between $15,332 and $20,921 and by 25 percent of net family income between $20,921 and $50,000, with the same minimum payments as for two-parent families up to $50,000, above which bene-fits decline by 5 percent until they disappear at the same points as for two-parent families. *Quebec nonrefundable child tax credit*: Maximum $598 for the first child and $552 for each additional child. Because it reduces provincial income tax payable, the child tax credit does not help low-income families that fall below the provincial taxpaying threshold – i.e., the credit is income-tested for taxpaying families in terms of eligibility, though the amount of the benefit (in the form of a provincial income tax break) is the same for virtually all recipients. *Quebec Parental Wage Assistance Program*: Benefits phase in at the rate of 28.5 cents for each dollar of employment earnings above $1,200. Maximum supplement is $3,534 for two-parent families and $2,422 for single-parent families, payable up to $13,600 for couples and $9,700 for one-parent families. Benefits are reduced by 43 cents per dollar above the thresholds, disappearing at $21,825 for two-parent families and $15,332 for single-parent families. *de facto universal child benefit system in Quebec*: Because higher-income families not eligible for Quebec Family Allowances receive the nonrefundable child tax credit, while low-income families not eligible for the tax credit get Quebec Family Allowances, then the two income-tested programs together form a universal system of child benefits.

	Provincial and Territorial Child Benefits
	New Brunswick Child Tax Benefit: Maximum $250 per child per year to families with net incomes up to $20,000, above which benefits are reduced by 2.5 percent of net family income for one child and 5 percent for two or more children (the same reduction rates as the federal Canada Child Tax Benefit) and disappear at $30,000 for families with one or two children (the threshold increases by $5,000 for the third and each additional child). *New Brunswick Working Income Supplement:* Maximum $250 per family per year and phases in at the rate of 4 percent of family earnings above $3,750, reaching the maximum amount at earnings of $10,000 and then diminishing at the rate of 5 percent of net family income above $20,921 to disappear at $25,921. *Nova Scotia Child Benefit:* maximum $403 per year for the first child, $319 for the second child and $286 for each additional child. Benefits decline over net family income of $16,000 at rates that increase per child to end eligibility at family income of $20,921. *Newfoundland and Labrador Child Benefit:* Maximum $204 for the first child, $312 for the second child, $336 for the third child and $360 for the fourth and each additional child. Benefits diminish above net family income of $15,921 at the rates of 4.08 percent for one child, 10.32 percent for two children, 17.04 percent for three children and an additional 7.2 percent for each additional child, disappearing at $20,921. *Northwest Territories Child Benefit*: Maximum basic benefit of $330 per child per year. Families with employment income over $3,750 may qualify for Territorial Workers' Supplement of maximum $275 for one child and $350 for two or more children. Benefits are reduced above net family income of $20,921

	Provincial and Territorial Child Benefits
	at the rate of 3 percent for one child and 5 percent for two or more children. *Nunavut Child Benefit:* Same parameters as Northwest Territories Child Benefit that preceded it (Nunavut territory split off eastern Arctic from Northwest Territories in 1999). *Yukon Child Benefit.* Maximum $300 per child per year to families with net family income up to $16,700, above which benefits decline at the rate of 2.5 percent for one child and 5 percent for two or more children to end once net family income reaches $28,700 for one or two children, $34,700 for three children, and an additional $6,000 higher for each additional child.
3. Definition of income	3. Net family income: Combined income of both spouses from all sources (e.g., employment, investments, social programs other than the Canada Child Tax Benefit itself) net of child care expenses, contributions to Registered Pension Plans (i.e., occupational pension plans) and Registered Retirement Savings Plans (i.e., individual private retirement savings plans), union and professional dues, attendant care expenses, certain employment expenses, carrying charges and interest expenses, business investment losses, moving expenses, and investments in oil, gas and mining ventures.
4. Indexing	4. Provincial/territorial child benefits and employment earnings supplements are not indexed.
Delivery features 1. Administrative arrangements	1. The Canada Customs and Revenue Agency administers provincial/territorial child benefit and earnings supplement programs under the Canadian Income Tax Act (exceptions: Saskatchewan Employment Supplement is delivered by the provincial government using a telephone call centre; Quebec delivers its own programs).

	Provincial and Territorial Child Benefits
2. How people get enrolled	2. In case of programs delivered by Canada Customs and Revenue Agency on behalf of provinces, people are automatically enrolled using net family income assessment for Canada Child Tax Benefit, and each year each parent must file an income tax return. Provincially delivered programs use own application forms and/or telephone call centers.
3. Responsiveness	3. Eligibility for and amount of benefit based on net family income as assessed through the income tax return. Benefits are paid monthly in British Columbia, Saskatchewan, Manitoba, Ontario, New Brunswick, Nova Scotia, Newfoundland, Northwest Territories, Nunavut and Yukon. Quebec pays monthly for direct deposits to bank and quarterly for cheques paid directly to recipients, unless otherwise requested. Twice-yearly payment in Alberta (January and July). Payment period is July 1 of one year to June 30 of next year. No reconciliation of income reported during the accounting period with income as of the end of the accounting period, so there can be a considerable lag – up to 18 months – between assessment of income and calculation of amount of benefit. No allowance for ongoing reporting of income changes (e.g., a significant rise or fall due to employment or unemployment), but does allow for recalculation in the case of change of family composition (i.e., marriage or marriage breakdown, birth or adoption of a new child). Retroactive payments can be paid for up to 11 months from the month that the federal government receives the application. (Exception: the Saskatchewan Employment Supplement is based on monthly reporting of income.)
4. Payment procedures	4. Cheque or direct deposit to the parent considered to be primarily responsible for the care and upbringing of the child (usually the mother, but can also be father, grandparent or guardian).

	Provincial and Territorial Child Benefits
5. Verification procedures	5. In addition to auditing of financial information provided on income tax returns, non-financial information (e.g., marital status, children and residence) subject to review through payment validation and control programs.
6. Aboriginal peoples	6. Paid to Aboriginal families on same conditions as all others, although some Aboriginal people object to filling out income tax form. Although income earned on reserve by Status Indians under certain conditions specified by the Indian Act and by the courts in tax exempt, tax returns still have been filed by individuals who have only tax exempt income to ensure that benefits for children are received.
7. How program is delivered	7. For most programs, provincial child benefits combined with federal Canada Child Tax Benefit by federal Canada Customs and Revenue Agency in form of single cheques or direct deposit. Alberta Family Employment Tax Credit, Saskatchewan Employment Supplement, Manitoba Child Related Income Support Program and Quebec child benefit programs are delivered by their respective provincial governments.
8. How program is financed	8. Financed through provincial general revenue.
9. National/state integration	9. Federal government administers and delivers most (eight of 12 jurisdictions which offer such programs) provincial/territorial income-tested child benefits on behalf of provincial/territorial governments. Where authorized by legislation, federal government makes available Canada Child Tax Benefit client information to support other child-related benefit programs, such as Quebec Family Allowance, Ontario Child Care Supplement for Working Families and Employment Insurance Family Supplement.

TABLE 1c
INCOME-RELATED BENEFITS

	Nonrefundable Spousal Equivalent Tax Credit	Children's Portion of Refundable Goods and Services/Harmonized Sales Tax Credit
Eligibility 1. Who is entitled to benefits	1. Single parents with dependent child under age 18, natural born, adopted or being cared for by the family. Open to Canadian citizens and families with landed immigrant status or Convention refugee status. Parent must have taxable income, but no requirement for type of income, hours of work, disability status or other conditions. No time limits.	1. Families with dependent child under age 19, natural born, adopted or being cared for by the family. Open to Canadian citizens and families with landed immigrant status or Convention refugee status. No requirement for type of income, hours of work, disability status or other conditions. No time limits.
2. Reciprocal responsibilities	2. Single parent must file an income tax form.	2. Both parents must file an income tax form.
3. Budget caps	3. Open-ended entitlement.	3. Open-ended entitlement.
Benefits description 1. Amounts per child	1. Single parents can claim same tax credit in respect of one child as one-earner taxpayers can in respect of a spouse with little or no income. In 2000, the spousal equivalent is worth $1,044 in	1. As of July 2000, maximum credit is $205 per adult, $205 for one child in a single-parent family (i.e., a form of adult equivalent), $107 per child and a single-person supplement of $107 for single parents and

	Nonrefundable Spousal Equivalent Tax Credit	Children's Portion of Refundable Goods and Services/Harmonized Sales Tax Credit
	federal income tax savings and a combined federal-average provincial income tax reduction of $1,566 (provincial income taxes vary from one province to another as a percentage of basic federal tax).	single adults (latter phases in above earnings of $6,546).
2. Income-related structure	2. Because the credit is nonrefundable, it provides little or no assistance to low-income single parents with little or no tax liability.	2. Maximum amounts are reduced at the rate of 5 percent of net family income above $26,284. For a couple or single parent with one child, for example, the maximum GST credit amounts to $517 ($205 plus $205 plus $107) and disappears at net family income of $36,624.
3. Definition of income	3. Taxable income of single parent: a. income from employment, investments, private pensions, rents and other private sources plus most social programs (except Canada Child Tax Benefit, refundable Goods and Services/Harmonized Goods and Services Tax Credits, provincial/territorial child benefits, compensation received from	3. Net family income: Combined income of both spouses from all sources (e.g., employment, investments, social programs other than the Canada Child Tax Benefit itself) net of child care expenses, contributions to Registered Pension Plans (i.e., occupational pension plans) and Registered Retirement Savings Plans (i.e., indi-

	Nonrefundable Spousal Equivalent Tax Credit	Children's Portion of Refundable Goods and Services/Harmonized Sales Tax Credit
	province or territory if victim of crime or motor vehicle accident, veterans pensions, life insurance death benefit) b. minus contributions to Registered Pension Plans and Registered Retirement Savings Plans, union and professional dues, child care expenses, attendant care expenses, business investment loss, moving expenses, carrying charges and interest expenses, exploration and Development expenses, other employment expenses.	vidual private retirement savings plans), union and professional dues, attendant care expenses, certain employment expenses, carrying charges and interest expenses, business investment losses, moving expenses, and investments in oil, gas and mining ventures.
4. Indexing	4. Fully indexed as of 2000 (partially indexed from 1986-1999).	4. Fully indexed as of 2000 (partially indexed from program's creation in 1991 to 1999).
Delivery features		
1. Administrative arrangements	1. The Canada Customs and Revenue Agency administers the tax credit under the Canadian Income Tax Act.	1. See left.
2. How people get enrolled	2. By filing annual income tax return and claiming the credit.	2. One spouse or single parent files income tax return and claims the credit on behalf of family.

	Nonrefundable Spousal Equivalent Tax Credit	**Children's Portion of Refundable Goods and Services/Harmonized Sales Tax Credit**
3. Responsiveness	3. Because based on last year's income, not responsive to changes in income or eligibility (i.e., becoming a single parent) in current year.	3. See left. But efforts are under way to improve responsiveness of the credit to changes in family and personal circumstance and streamline its administration.
4. Payment procedures	4. Reduces federal and provincial income taxes, so results in annual tax reduction or tax refund.	4. Most recipients receive quarterly payments. Newfoundland Harmonized Sales Tax Credit is paid in October installment of GST credit
5. Verification procedures	5. In addition to auditing of financial information provided on income tax returns, non-financial information (e.g., marital status, children and residence) subject to review through payment validation and control programs.	5. See left.
6. Aboriginal peoples	6. Same as for all others.	6. See left.
7. How program is delivered	7. Federal income tax system.	7. See left.
8. How program is financed	8. Federal and provincial general revenues (as revenue loss).	8. Federal general revenues (as revenue loss).

	Nonrefundable Spousal Equivalent Tax Credit	Children's Portion of Refundable Goods and Services/Harmonized Sales Tax Credit
9. National/ state integration	9. Federal government administers provincial incomes taxes (and thus the provincial portion of the spousal equivalent tax credit) on behalf of all provinces except Quebec, which has its own income tax system (with a provincial spousal equivalent credit).	9. Federal government administers GST/HST Credit and administers the Harmonized Sales Tax (which combines federal and provincial sales taxes in three provinces) on behalf of New Brunswick, Nova Scotia and Newfoundland.

TABLE 1d
INCOME-RELATED BENEFITS

	Nonrefundable Medical Expense Tax Credit	Nonrefundable Disability Tax Credit
Eligibility rules 1. Who is entitled to benefits	1. Helps offset cost of a designated list of health-related goods and services, and disability supports. Credit may be claimed in respect of the medical expenses of a taxfiler, spouse or dependants. Its provisions apply to all Canadians and not just to persons with disabilities. Total medical expenses must be more than $1,637 or three percent of net income, whichever is less. For Canadian citizens and families with landed immigrant status or Convention refugee status. Claimants must have taxable income, but no requirement for type of income, hours of work, disability status or other conditions. No time limits.	1. Helps offset additional – but often hidden and indirect – costs of disability (e.g., higher utility costs, additional transportation costs, higher prices for goods because of fewer shopping choices and many hidden costs related directly to the care of children – e.g., a trained caregiver rather than a babysitter, even at an age when a child typically would not require such supervision, dietary supplements, special toys, adapted equipment, tailor-made clothing or other items, such as diapers. Person for whom credit is claimed must have physical or mental disability that is severe and prolonged and markedly restricts their ability to perform one or more activities of daily living all or almost all of the time. Claimants must have taxable income, but no requirement for type of income, hours of work, disability status or other conditions. No time limits

	Nonrefundable Medical Expense Tax Credit	Nonrefundable Disability Tax Credit
2. Reciprocal responsibilities	2. Claimant must file an income tax form.	2. Claimant must file an income tax form.
3. Budget caps	3. Open-ended entitlement.	3. Open-ended entitlement.
Benefits description		
1. Amounts per child	1. Average federal income tax savings from the medical expense tax credit was $282 in 1997, the most recent year for which data are available. The average provincial income tax savings was $141, for a total federal/ average provincial tax savings of $423 in 1997.	1. Worth a maximum $730 in federal income tax savings or $1,095 in combined federal/average provincial tax savings.
2. Income-related structure	2. Because the credit is nonrefundable, it provides little or no assistance to low-income single parents with little or no tax liability.	2. Because credit is nonrefundable, it is of no value to persons too poor to pay income tax. But In cases where an individual pays no income tax or not enough to benefit from the entire credit, the unused portion can be transferred to ano-ther family member (e.g., parents).
3. Definition of income	3. Taxable income of applicant (i.e., parent who credit on behalf of child): a. income from employment, investments,	3. See left.

	Nonrefundable Medical Expense Tax Credit	**Nonrefundable Disability Tax Credit**
	private pensions, rents and other private sources plus most social programs (except Canada Child Tax Benefit, refundable Goods and Services/Harmonized Goods and Services Tax Credits, provincial/terri-torial child benefits, compensation received from province or territory if victim of crime or motor vehi-cle accident, veterans pensions, life insurance death benefit) b. minus contributions to Registered Pension Plans and Registered Retirement Savings Plans, union and professional dues, child care expenses, attendant care expenses, business investment loss, moving expenses, carrying charges and interest expenses, exploration and Development expenses, other employment expenses	
4. Indexing	4. Fully indexed as of 2000 (partially indexed from 1986-1999).	4. See left.
Delivery features 1. Administrative arrangements	1. The Canada Customs and Revenue Agency administers the tax credit under the Canadian Income Tax Act.	1. See left.

	Nonrefundable Medical Expense Tax Credit	Nonrefundable Disability Tax Credit
2. How people get enrolled	2. By filing annual income tax return and claiming the credit.	2. See left.
3. Responsiveness	3. Because based on last year's income, not responsive to changes in income or eligibility (i.e., becoming disabled or facing higher medical expenses) in current year.	3. Because based on last year's income, not responsive to changes in income or eligibility (i.e., becoming disabled) in current year.
4. Payment procedures	4. Lowers federal and provincial income taxes, so results in annual tax reduction or tax refund.	4. See left.
5. Verification procedures	5. Financial and nonfinancial information provided on income tax returns subject to review through payment validation and control programs.	5. See left.
6. Aboriginal peoples	6. Same as all others.	6. See left.
7. How program is delivered	7. Federal income tax system.	7. See left.
8. How program is financed	8. Federal and provincial general revenues (as revenue loss).	8. See left.

	Nonrefundable Medical Expense Tax Credit	**Nonrefundable Disability Tax Credit**
9. National/state integration	9. Federal government administers provincial incomes taxes (and thus the provincial income tax credit) on behalf of all provinces except Quebec (has own tax system and child care tax credit).	9. See left.

TABLE 1e
INCOME-RELATED BENEFITS

	Refundable Medical Expense Tax Credit	Child Care Expense Deduction
Eligibility rules 1. Who is entitled to benefits	1. Helps offset cost of a designated list of health-related goods and services, and disability supports. Credit may be claimed in respect of the medical expenses of a taxfiler, spouse or dependants. Its provisions apply to all Canadians and not just to persons with disabilities. Total medical expenses must be more than $1,637 or three percent of net income, whichever is less. For Canadian citizens and families with landed immigrant status or Convention refugee status. Based on level of employment income, but no requirement for type of income, hours of work, disability status or other conditions. No time limits.	1. Parents (lower-income parents for couples) who work or study can claim income tax deduction of up to $7,000 for each child under age 7 and up to $4,000 for each child aged 7-15 in respect of receipted child care expenses. Parents whose children have severe disabilities and are eligible for the disability tax credit can claim up to $7,000 in child care expenses regardless of the child's age. Up to $4,000 can be claimed in child care expenses for a child who does not qualify for the disability tax credit but who is considered mentally or physically 'infirm.' Claim may be made regardless of child's age: Not imposing an age limit is intended to recognize the fact that many families care for an adult child who is disabled. Claimant must have taxable income (before deducting child care expenses).

	Refundable Medical Expense Tax Credit	Child Care Expense Deduction
2. Reciprocal responsibilities	2. Claimant must file an income tax form.	2. Claimant must file an income tax form.
3. Budget caps	3. Open-ended entitlement.	3. Open-ended entitlement.
Benefits description		
1. Amounts per child	1. Maximum credit is the lesser of $507 and 25 percent of eligible medical expenses.	1. & 2. Maximum deduction of $7,000 for each eligible child translates into a combined federal/average provincial tax savings of $1,785 for claimants with taxable income under $30,004; $2,625 for taxfilers with taxable income between $30,004 and $60,008; and $3,045 for claimants with taxable income over $60,008. The $4,000 deduction provides a combined federal/average provincial tax savings of $1,020 for taxpayers with taxable income under $30,004; $1,500 for those between $30,004 and $60,008; and $1,740 for taxpayers with taxable income over $60,008.
2. Income-related structure	2. Taxfilers must earn at least $2,535. Credit reduced by 5 percent of net family income above $17,664.	
3. Definition of income	3. Net family income: Combined income of both spouses from all sources (e.g., employment, investments, social programs other than the	3. Taxable income: total income, minus contributions to Registered Pension Plans and Registered Retirement Savings Plans, union and professional dues, child care ex-

	Refundable Medical Expense Tax Credit	Child Care Expense Deduction
	Canada Child Tax Benefit itself) net of child care expenses, contributions to Registered Pension Plans (i.e., occupational pension plans) and Registered Retirement Savings Plans (i.e., individual private retirement savings plans), union and professional dues, attendant care expenses, certain employment expenses, carrying charges and interest expenses, business investment losses, moving expenses, and investments in oil, gas and mining ventures.	penses, attendant care expenses, business investment loss, moving expenses, carrying charges and interest expenses, exploration and Development expenses, other employment expenses
4. Indexing	4. Fully indexed as of 2000 (partially indexed from 1986-1999)	4. See left.
Delivery features 1. Administrative arrangements	1. The Canada Customs and Revenue Agency administers the tax credit under the Canadian Income Tax Act.	1. See left.
2. How people get enrolled	2. By filing annual income tax return and claiming the credit.	2. See left.
3. Responsiveness	3. Because based on last year's income, not respon-	3. See left.

	Refundable Medical Expense Tax Credit	Child Care Expense Deducton
	sive to changes in income or eligibility (i.e., becoming disabled or facing higher medical expenses) in current year.	
4. Payment procedures	4. Reduces federal income tax, so results in annual tax reduction or tax refund.	4. See left.
5. Verification procedures	5. Financial and non-financial information provided on income tax returns subject to review through payment validation and control programs.	5. See left.
6. Aboriginal peoples	6. Same as all others.	6. See left
7. How program is delivered	7. Federal income tax system.	7. See left.
8. How program is financed	8. Out of federal general revenues (as revenue loss).	8. Out of federal and provincial general revenues (as revenue loss).
9. National/state integration	9. None (federal only benefit).	9. Federal government administers provincial incomes taxes (and thus the provincial portion of the child care expense deduction) on behalf of all provinces except Quebec (which has its own income tax system).

TABLE 1f
INCOME-RELATED BENEFITS

	Children's Portion of Refundable Provincial Tax Credits
Eligibility rules 1. Who is entitled to benefits 2. Reciprocal responsibilities 3. Budget caps	 1. Those with dependent children under age 18, natural born, adopted or being cared for by the family. Open to Canadian citizens and families with landed immigrant status or Convention refugee status. With exception of employment earnings supplements, which require eligible families to have employment income, no requirement for type of income, hours of work, disability status or other conditions. No time limits. 2. Recipients must apply for benefits and each year each parent must file an income tax form (even if they have no income) in order to track family income. 3. Open-ended entitlement.
Benefits description 1. Amounts per child 2. Income-related structure	 1&2. The federal government administers on behalf of the Newfoundland government the *Newfoundland Harmonized Sales Tax Credit* worth a maximum $40 per adult and $60 per child annually to families and individuals with net family incomes under $15,000. Benefits are reduced at the rate of 5 percent of net family income above $15,000, disappearing at $17,000 for a single parent with one child and $19,000 for a couple with two children. *Ontario* offers *a provincial refundable sales tax credit* worth up to $100 per adult and $50 per child, reduced at the rate of 2 percent of net family income minus $4,000; for a couple with two children, for example, eligibility ends once net family income reaches $19,000.

	Children's Portion of Refundable Provincial Tax Credits
	Manitoba provides a *refundable cost of living tax credit* that pays up to $190 per adult, $190 for the first child in a single-parent family and $25 per child, reduced at the rate of 1 percent of net family income; benefits disappear at net family income of $43,000 for a family with two children. A new *Saskatchewan Sales Tax Credit* will be available to lower-income families and seniors as of April 2000, payable in October 2000. Benefits are up to $77 per person or $264 per family per year.
3. Definition of income	3. Net family income: Combined income of both spouses from all sources (e.g., employment, investments, social programs other than the Canada Child Tax Benefit and provincial child benefits) net of child care expenses, contributions to Registered Pension Plans (i.e., occupational pension plans) and Registered Retirement Savings Plans (i.e., individual private retirement savings plans), union and professional dues, attendant care expenses, certain employment expenses, carrying charges and interest expenses, business investment losses, moving expenses, and investments in oil, gas and mining ventures.
4. Indexing	4. Not indexed.
Delivery features 1. Administrative arrangements	1. The Canada Customs and Revenue Agency administers on behalf of provinces.
2. How people get enrolled	2. File annual income tax return.
3. Responsiveness	3. Not responsive to changes affecting eligibility for current year because based on previous year's income.

	Children's Portion of Refundable Provincial Tax Credits
4. Payment procedures	4. Quarterly payments for new Saskatchewan Sales Tax Credit, annual for others.
5. Verification procedures	5. Financial and non-financial information provided on income tax returns subject to review through payment validation and control programs.
6. Aboriginal peoples	6. Same as all others.
7. How program is delivered	7. Federal income tax system.
8. How program is financed	8. Financed through provincial general revenue.
9. National/state integration	9. Federal government delivers these refundable tax credits on behalf of provincial governments.

TABLE 2
INCOME- AND ASSET-TESTED BENEFITS

	Children's benefits from provincial social assistance
Eligibility rules	
1.Who is entitled to benefits	1. Families that qualify for social assistance on basis of 'needs test' (see below) with dependent children under age 18, natural born, adopted or being cared for by the family. Open to Canadian citizens and families with landed immigrant status or Convention refugee status. No time limits. Note that children's benefits through social assistance largely have disappeared or are in process of doing so in almost all provinces as they switch to income-tested programs and services for low-income families under the National Child Benefit reform.
2. Reciprocal responsibilities	2. Parents must report any changes in circumstances (e.g., employment, new child, marital status) track family income and, where required, must show active job search. In some provinces, some or all recipients must take part in community or other work (workfare).
3. Budget caps	3. Open-ended entitlement.
Benefits description	
1. Amounts per child	1. Just before the current reform began (1998), welfare benefits for children ranged in most provinces from around $1,200 to $1,800 per child per year for basic needs (excluding shelter costs), though a few provinces paid below or above this range. Benefits typically varied by such factors as age and number of children. Social assistance also may pay on behalf of children special allowances (e.g., winter clothing allowances), in-kind benefits (e.g., supplementary health and dental care, and prescription drugs) and housing subsidies.

	Children's benefits from provincial social assistance
2. Income-related structure 3. Definition of income	2. & 3. Canada's income support program of last resort, available only to those who have exhausted all other sources of income (e.g., employment earnings, savings, social insurance benefits). To qualify for social assistance, applicants must undergo a comprehensive and intrusive 'needs test' (i.e., income and assets test) which scrutinizes their incomes, fixed and liquid assets, and budgetary needs (as determined according to regulations that take into account such factors as number and ages of children, family type, deemed employability of recipients).
4. Indexing	4. Not indexed.
Delivery features	
1. Administrative arrangements	1. Monthly by provincial/territorial social assistance departments and, in Ontario, municipal governments.
2. How people get enrolled	2. Must apply in person and undergo intrusive need test.
3. Responsiveness	3. Very responsive to changes affecting eligibility and amount of benefits.
4. Payment procedures	4. Monthly payments by cheques or direct deposit.
5. Verification procedures	5. Social assistance authorities can investigate applicants' and recipients' personal circumstances to verify information they give (e.g., bank accounts, talk to neighbours).
6. Aboriginal peoples	6. Delivered by local band governments to on-reserve recipients under federal program.
7. How program is delivered	7. By provincial, municipal or Aboriginal band government.

	Children's benefits from provincial social assistance
8. How program is financed	8. Provincial general revenues, theoretically with (undeterminable) federal financial transfer (practically speaking, no federal support any longer).
9. National/state integration	9. Federal-provincial National Child Benefit is removing child benefits from most provincial social assistance systems. Provincial social assistance systems vary considerably in terms of rates and regulations, though all based on needs-tested model.

TABLE 3
CONTRIBUTORY SOCIAL INSURANCE ENTITLEMENTS

	Employment Insurance Family Supplement	**Canada and Quebec Pension Plan Children's Benefits**
Eligibility		
1. Who is entitled to benefits	1. Low-income families eligible for Canada Child Tax Benefit whose heads are in receipt of Employment Insurance (Canada's new name for its federal unemployment insurance system)	1. Natural or adopted child of a deceased plan member, or a child in the care and control of the deceased member at the time of death. The child must be under 18 or 18-25 and attending postsecondary education on a full-time basis. No time limits.
2. Reciprocal responsibilities	2. Family head must actively search for employment, must apply for Canada Child Tax Benefit and must file income tax return each year.	2. None.
3. Budget caps	3. Open-ended entitlement.	3. Open-ended entitlement
Benefits description		
1. Amounts per child 2. Income-related structure 3. Definition of income	1., 2. &3. Employment Insurance replaces 55 percent of recipients' average insurable earnings up to maximum $413 per week for up to 45 weeks (with penalties for previous users in the form of a lower replacement rate, which can be as low as 50 percent).	1., 2. &3. The Canada Pension Plan children's benefit is a flat rate $174.07 per month and is normally paid to the person with whom the child is living, although directly to the child in the case of those 18-25. The Quebec Pension Plan pays $55.27 a month.

	Employment Insurance Family Supplement	Canada and Quebec Pension Plan Children's Benefits
	The Family Supplement increases an Employment Insurance recipient's benefits to as high as 80 percent of average insurable earnings for recipients with net family income [defined in previous tables] below $20,921 (i.e., the same threshold as for the maximum base Canada Child Tax Benefit as of 1999), above which payments are reduced until they disappear at $25,921 (i.e., above that level, the EI recipient no longer qualifies for the Family Supplement and receives benefits at the regular rate of 55 percent of insurable earnings). EI covers employees only.	All recipients receive same amount. Children of Canada Pension Plan and Quebec Pension Plan disability beneficiaries also qualify for the same amounts as the children of deceased contributors (i.e., $174.07 per month for CPP beneficiaries and $55.27 per month for QPP beneficiaries. All recipients receive same amount. CPP and QPP cover all employees and self-employed.
4. Indexing	4. Employment Insurance benefits effectively are not indexed.	4. Canada and Quebec Pension Plan benefits are indexed to change in average earnings.
Delivery features 1. Administrative arrangements	1. Delivered by federal Human Resources Development Canada under Employment Insurance Act.	1. Canada Pension Plan benefits are delivered by federal Human Resources Development Canada under Canada Pension Plan Act. Quebec delivers Quebec Pension Plan.
2. How people get enrolled	2. Apply at Human Resources Development Canada local office.	2. See left.

	Employment Insurance Family Supplement	Canada and Quebec Pension Plan Children's Benefits
3. Responsiveness	3. Because Family Income benefit is based on last year's net family income, not responsive to changes in income in current year. Employment Insurance benefit upon which the Family Income benefit is based calculated on average weekly insurable earnings.	3. Not an issue.
4. Payment procedures	4. Monthly cheques.	4. See left.
5. Verification procedures	5. Program audit procedures.	5. See left.
6. Aboriginal peoples	6. Same as others.	6. See left.
7. How program is delivered	7. Human Resources Development Canada.	7. See left. In Quebec, by Régie de rente de Québec.
8. How program is financed	8. Premiums levied on employees and employers.	8. Premiums (called 'contributions') levied on employees, self-employed and employers.
9. National/ state integration	9. None: federal program only.	9. Canada Pension Plan and Quebec Pension Plan virtually identical in terms of benefit structure and financing.

BENEFITS FOR CHILDREN: THE UNITED KINGDOM

Jane Millar

INTRODUCTION

Support for children is in the middle of major reform in the UK. This is a turning point, when important decisions are being taken about the future. The changes, some already made and some proposed for the future, are about both the *level* of financial support offered and the *structure* of that support. More money will be transferred to families and it will be transferred in different ways.

Families, and children, are increasingly at the centre of the policy agenda. Over the past two decades there has been a significant growth in child poverty in the UK, which now has the highest rate of child poverty in the European Union [Micklewright and Stewart 2000] and one of the highest rates in the developed world [Unicef 2000]. The number of children in relative poverty in the UK has increased threefold over the past 25 or so years and the latest figures (for 1998/99) show that 4.4 million children – one-third of all children – are living in households with incomes of less than half the average after meeting housing costs [DSS 2000a]. Using a measure of 'socially perceived necessities,' Gordon et al. [2000] found that 34 percent of children lacked at least one of these items and 18 percent lacked two or more. Some children stay poor for long periods, and there is increasing concern about both the short-term and long-term consequences of this problem [Gregg et al. 1999]. The government has made a pledge to end child poverty within twenty years and to reduce child poverty by half within the next decade. Progress towards this goal is being measured by an annual poverty audit, two of which have now been published [CM 4445 1999; DSS 2000b; see also Howarth et al. 1999; Rahman et al. 2000].

This rise in child poverty has taken place in the context of major changes in family structure and employment:

- Family structure: About one-quarter of families with children in the UK are headed by a lone parent. About 2.7 million children live in these families, or one-quarter of all children. Children in lone-parent families have a particularly high risk of poverty [Ford and Millar 1998].

- Labour market: Rising inequalities in earnings and the growth of low pay, persistent unemployment for certain groups/regions and a growing polarization between households that are 'work-rich' (with two or more earners) and those that are 'work poor' (with no earners). Children in workless households have a particularly high risk of poverty [Gregg et al. 1999].

The policy agenda is increasingly focused upon reforming the welfare state to adapt to these family and labour market changes. The argument goes broadly as follows: The post-war Beveridge welfare state was designed to deal with a particular set of social and economic circumstances, including full employment, stable families and a gendered division of labour. These conditions no longer apply and so it is necessary to create a new welfare state that is adapted to current needs.

The government has argued that the welfare state should be reconstructed around the goal of supporting employment, of creating the conditions under which all working-age people can support themselves through the labour market. This objective involves both helping people get into employment and ensuring that they have adequate incomes in work. The Beveridge welfare state *replaced* wages for people unable to work. The modern welfare state increasingly must concentrate upon *supplementing* wages for people who are in work.

Philosophy and goals of current policy

The above policy analysis is clearly reflected in statements about the goals of current income maintenance policy. The Treasury (increasingly the policy leader in the area) has summarized these as: helping parents to find work; reforming tax and benefits in order to reward work; and providing direct financial support to all families, while targeting extra resources on those who need it most [HM Treasury 1999]. A later Treasury paper, on the 2000 Budget, sets out the principles underpinning tax and benefit reform for families with children as:

- providing financial support for all families with children, through the foundation of universal Child Benefit, recognising the additional costs and responsibilities that all parents face when their children are growing up; and

- providing help in the fairest way, and targeting extra financial support on those *who* need it most *when* they need it most, such as mothers with young children, particularly around childbirth, or those on lower or middle incomes … [HM Treasury 2000a:3, emphases in original].

The government's policy of support for children thus pursues both horizontal and vertical equity aims through a mixture of universal and selective benefits.

The historical context

Taxes and benefits have been used variously for supporting families in the UK at different times and in different combinations. Child tax allowances were first introduced in 1909, mainly for reasons of horizontal equity between taxpayers with children and those without. Family Allowances were introduced in 1946, for second and subsequent children. This program was intended as a contribution to the costs of raising children, and it was assumed that wages would cover the costs of the first child. Benefits for child dependants also were included in National Insurance (the contributory benefit programs) and National Assistance (the 'last resort' program for those with no other means of support, renamed Supplementary Benefit in 1966 and Income Support in 1988), which meant that non-working parents received additional support for their children.

This system remained intact until the 1970s, when some significant changes were made. By that time, Family Allowances had not been increased for many years and there was increasing concern that the existing measures did little to target child poverty [Brown 1988]. The child tax allowance did nothing to help families too poor to pay tax and provided more help to richer than to poorer families. The *1975 Child Benefit Act* created a new system of universal support. Both Family Allowances and child tax allowances were abolished and Child Benefit was introduced (from April 1977) as a universal cash payment for all children, including the first.

Child Benefit has remained much the same since then, with just two major changes. In 1977 a supplement for lone-parent families was introduced, paid per family not per child, and abolished in July 1998 (though existing claimants can continue to receive it). A higher rate of Child Benefit has been payable for the first child since 1991 – a differential justified originally as an affordable way of transferring extra resources to families with children [Ditch et al. 1992].

The 1970s also saw the start of additional income-tested benefits for families in low-paid employment. Income-tested help with housing costs was introduced early in the decade and has grown substantially since then. Family Income Supplement was introduced in 1972 for families with children, where one of the parents was working for at least 30 hours per week, with wages below a certain level, taking family size into account. Family Credit replaced Family Income Supplement in 1988. Family Credit had the same structure, but was available to those working 24 or more hours per week (reduced in 1992 to 16 hours).

The system inherited by the Labour government in 1997, after its first general election victory in 18 years, thus consisted of universal Child Benefit, contributory and income-tested benefits for non-working families, and income-tested benefits for poor working families.

INCOME BENEFITS FOR CHILDREN

There are three main types of support for children in the UK: universal (for all children), income-tested (dependent upon family income and excluding those with capital above a certain level) and other benefits (including both contributory and non-contributory benefits). The income-tested benefits are the most complex, so we describe the universal and other benefits first. As a general point, it should be noted that benefits in the UK are usually expressed as a weekly figure, but the figures given here have been converted to annual amounts to be consistent with the other countries' reports.

Universal/contributory/other benefits for children: rates, rules and administration

Tables 1 and 2 summarize the rules for these benefits, which are all administered by the Benefits Agency (the delivery agency of the Department of Social Security, which is responsible for policy) with the Contributions Agency (part of the Inland Revenue) responsible for maintaining National Insurance records. Child Benefit is claimed by post, with families usually coming into the system with the birth of the child. Very few families fail to receive this benefit, which is generally paid to the mother (although families can opt otherwise) in cash or directly into bank accounts. The first child receives a higher rate than subsequent children.

Child Dependency Increases (i.e., additional amounts in respect of children) were abolished for short-term National Insurance benefits in 1983, but are still payable with most long-term National Insurance benefits, including widows' benefits. The amount does not vary with income or family circumstances, but Child Dependency Increases are not paid if a partner is earning above a certain level, so for a couple they are, in effect, both contributory and income-tested. In contrast to Child Benefit, the payment is lower for the first than for subsequent children (dating from when the higher Child Benefit rate for first children was introduced). The Guardians Allowance is paid at the same rate as the National Insurance additions, to people bringing up orphaned children. There is also a very small Child's Special Allowance paid where a divorced parent has subsequently died (received by only 12 families in 1998). Disability Living Allowance goes to people in need of extra care or with mobility needs, including children aged over five (for mobility) and from birth (for care).

Income-tested benefits for children: rates, rules and administration

Although these programs potentially serve everyone and not just families with children, income-tested benefits are also child-related benefits, in that amounts paid usually vary with the number (and sometimes age) of children. The rules for the main income-tested benefits are summarized in Table 3, but should be treated with caution because complex and detailed rules apply and the table of necessity gives a simplified overview. It should be noted that, in general, income-tested benefits in the UK are nationally applied with little local or individual discretion (with the partial exception of Housing Benefit). In addition, there is a substantial degree of harmonization in the system, with similar rules and rates applying to various benefits.

These benefits can be subdivided into three main groups, according to the employment status of the claimant:

i. For 'non-working' people: Income Support and income-tested Jobseekers Allowance (contributory Jobseekers Allowance does not include additions for children). People working 16 hours and above per week, or with working partners, are not eligible to claim these benefits. Those claiming Jobseekers Allowance must be available for work, but this is not necessarily the case for Income Support. In effect this means unemployed couples with children receive Jobseekers Allowance and disabled parents and lone-parent families receive Income Support (lone parents are not required to register for work until their youngest child is 16 years of age). The income and asset tests are the same for both benefits. The amount paid varies with family size (number of adults and children). Disabled children receive a higher level of benefit.

ii. For 'working' people: Working Families Tax Credit and Disabled Person's Tax Credit. To claim these, at least one adult in the family must be working for 16 or more hours a week, and a higher rate is received by those working 30 hours or more. The Working Families Tax Credit is only for those with children, the Disabled Person's Tax Credit is for those receiving certain disability benefits (so may include childless people and those with children). The amount received varies with the number of children and the level of net income. The Working Families Tax Credit includes a Child Care Tax Credit that pays up to 70 percent of registered child care costs (up to a ceiling).

iii. For both 'working' and 'non-working' people: Housing Benefit and Council Tax Benefit. These benefits reduce rent payments and local taxes for low-income people, usually meeting the full costs for non-working people and part of the costs for others. The amount received varies with family income, family size (number of adults and children) and the level of rent/council tax.

In all cases, the income test is based on the income of the family (cohabiting adults and dependent children). Income is always based on net earnings (i.e., after tax and National Insurance contributions) plus other sources of income. However, the definition of net income varies somewhat across the benefits because various sources of income – for example, benefits and child maintenance – are treated in slightly different ways. One important point to note is that because Child Benefit counts as income for Income Support/Jobseekers Allowance purposes, the 'scale rates' shown in Table 3 are in effect reduced by the amount of Child Benefit. Receipt of Income Support/Jobseekers Allowance also gives access to some 'passported' benefits for children (e.g., free school meals and free welfare food, described below). Recipients also can apply to the 'Social Fund' which includes regulated payments (e.g., maternity grants) and discretionary grants (e.g., to help people leaving residential care in setting up a new home) and budgeting loans. Anyone who has been on benefit for at least 26 weeks can apply for a budgeting loan, and interest-free repayments are then deducted from benefits.

The benefits for non-working people (Income Support/ Jobseekers Allowance) are intended to identify and meet current needs. They are based, therefore, on an assessment of current weekly income from information given on a standard form completed in a personal interview at a local Benefits Agency office. The weekly amount is calculated by adding up the adult rates, child rates and family premium and reducing this total by the amount of any non-disregarded income. The benefit is then paid either weekly or fortnightly in arrears, to the main claimant on behalf of the family as a whole. Entitlement continues as long as eligibility is maintained, but claimants are required to notify any changes in circumstances immediately. If overpayments are made as a result of failure to report such changes, these will be retrieved back from claimants, and such claimants can be disqualified from benefits and/or prosecuted if deliberate fraud is suspected.

The benefits for working people (Working Families Tax Credit/Disabled Person's Tax Credit) are intended as additions to wages and are designed to be simpler in structure and administration. Claims are made by post to a special unit in the Inland Revenue, less detailed information is required and they are awarded for a fixed period of time. Earnings are averaged over six weeks (or three months) in order to even out fluctuations caused, for example, by irregular overtime working. Once awarded, Working Families Tax Credit remains in payment for 26 weeks, regardless of changes in income or circumstances. It is paid by employers, alongside wages, and so may be paid weekly or monthly, in cash or by bank transfer, depending on the method the employer uses. Couples can opt to have Working Families Tax Credit claimed by the non-earning partner.

As noted above, the Working Families Tax Credit includes a contribution to the costs of child care in the form of a Child Care Tax Credit that meets up to 70 percent of the cost of care, up to a ceiling. It is payable to lone parents and couples where both partners are in work of more than 16 hours per week (or one is in work and the other is receiving incapacity or disability benefits). The Child Care Tax Credit is paid only in respect of registered care and so does not include care by family, friend or neighbours. Such formal care accounts for only about a quarter of the child care used by families with pre-school children [Dilnot and McRae 1999].

Housing Benefit/Council Tax Benefit claimants who live in social housing (i.e., rented from a Local Authority or Housing

Association) receive support in the form of a reduction in rent/council tax, rather than as a cash benefit. Private tenants get a cash payment, although this can be paid direct to their landlord. For those receiving Income Support/Jobseekers Allowance, entitlement to these housing-related benefits is based on the information supplied for the Income Support/Jobseekers Allowance claim, although it must be separately claimed. For those in work, Housing Benefit and Council Tax Benefit are awarded for up to 60 weeks, but claimants are required to notify any changes in income or circumstances immediately (unlike Working Families Tax Credit).

New benefits/tax credits

As noted above, there has been no recognition of the costs of children through tax allowances since the 1970s. However, a Children's Tax Credit is to be introduced in April 2001. This new program replaces the Married Couples Tax Allowance (abolished from April 2000) and will reduce the tax bill for families with earnings above the tax threshold. The Children's Tax Credit will be worth a maximum of £442 per family for standard rate taxpayers. Higher rate taxpayers will have payments reduced by £52 for every £780 of income liable for the higher rate of tax (at 2000-01 rates, the higher tax rate is applicable to earnings of above £32,785, as detailed in Annex 1). About 1.5 million claims for the Children's Tax Credit have been made so far, and it is expected that about 5 million families will claim in total. Couples can choose which partner claims the credit or can share it equally, unless one or both are higher rate taxpayers, in which case the partner with the higher income must claim.

However, the Children's Tax Credit will be in place for only two years because there is to be another major change in the system in 2003 when a new Integrated Child Credit is to be introduced [HM Treasury 2000b]. This reform will bring together the child components of Income Support/Jobseekers Allowance with the child components of Working Families Tax Credit and the Children's Tax Credit, to create a single system of support for children, regardless of the working status of their parents. The new Integrated Child Credit will be paid in addition to the existing Child Benefit, and also to the main carer. Thus much of the present system will disappear in favour of this single benefit for all poor and many middle-income children, discussed in more detail below.

IN-KIND BENEFITS FOR CHILDREN

Cash payments and services are generally kept separate in the UK. All children are entitled to free health care (free at point of use) and free education (from age four in pre-school nurseries, from four or five in schools). There is some income-tested support for child care costs, as described above. Children in families receiving Income Support/Jobseekers Allowance are also entitled to free school meals (lunches), worth about £210 per child per annum. Babies and young children in low-income families also may be entitled to free milk and vitamins, worth £138 per child per annum.

The government also has been increasing expenditure on educational provision and introducing a range of new measures for the support of children and families. The most recent spending plans propose an increase in education spending of 5.4 percent per year in real terms over the next three years [HM Treasury 2000c].

Table 4 summarizes some of the new family policy initiatives introduced over the past three years. For children, the most important of these are the Sure Start program for pre-school children, the National Child Care Strategy and the Educational Maintenance Allowances. Sure Start is based in 250 areas around the country and is locally developed and organized. It can include a range of services such as health care and special needs provision and it is intended "to improve the life chances of very young children in deprived areas by making sure they are ready to learn when they get to school" [HM Treasury 2000c: 8]. About one-fifth of all poor pre-school children are living in Sure Start areas. The National Child Care Strategy has been established in order to expand child care services for pre-school children and after-school and holiday care for older children. It is being developed by Local Authorities in partnership with private and voluntary organisations. The Educational Maintenance Allowances are income-tested payments aimed at encouraging children from poor families to stay on at school after 16. There also are policies to help parents combine employment and family life, and a number of locally based programs aimed at the most deprived areas in the country.

INPUTS AND OUTCOMES

Children are the focus of this report, but much of the information available about expenditure and receipt relates to families and/or to the benefits as a whole, not just to the portion that is paid for children. Here we show child statistics as far as possible and broader statistics where these are the only figures available.

Table 5 provides an overview of the main benefits for children, showing the numbers in receipt in late 1998/early 1999 (predating the introduction of the Working Families Tax Credit, so some basic statistics about the first year of operation are included). Total expenditure also is shown, but note that for Income Support/ Housing Benefit/Council Tax Benefit this amount includes spending on childless people as well as children and families.

The table shows the number of families and children receiving these benefits. In 1998 there were about 12.6 million children for whom Child Benefit was being received, including 1.6 million children with the one-parent addition (this number will fall over time, as no new families have been able to claim this since 1998). There were almost 1.6 million children in families receiving Family Credit, and similar numbers in families receiving Housing Benefit and Council Tax Benefit. It is not possible to identify the number of children for whom child dependency increases to National Insurance benefits were being received, but is possible to identify the number of children in families receiving Widow's Benefits (about 73,000), Guardians Allowance (about 3,000) and Disability Living Allowance (203,000 children under 16).

Lone-parent families form a significant proportion of families receiving income-tested benefits. Such families make up about 24 percent of all families with children but 51 percent of family credit recipients, 63/66 percent of Housing Benefit/Council Tax Benefit families and 77 percent of Income Support/Jobseekers Allowance families. The take-up of these benefits is generally estimated to be in the 85-95 percent range, with Family Credit having a slightly lower estimated take-up than the other benefits.

In some cases, families will be receiving more than one benefit, so it is not possible simply to add up these figures to arrive at total receipt. However, Table 6 shows 'cross-benefit' receipt of seven key benefits in August 1999, mainly income-tested and disability-related benefits, but not including Child Benefit (which is paid for all children). About 4.0 million children under 16 in families – 34 percent of all children under 16 – received one or more of these seven benefits. Of these, about 1.5 million were in couple families and 2.4 million in lone-parent families. Almost all children in lone-parent families are likely to be receiving some form of benefit support (in addition to Child Benefit). About half of the children in couple families receiving benefit were in working families, compared with only about a quarter of those in lone-parent families receiving benefit. About 1.2 million children aged under five were in families receiving one or more of these benefits, including about 0.5 million pre-school children in lone-parent families.

Table 7 and Figures 1 and 2 show expenditures on children and families based on the definitions used by the Department of Social Security in its recent review of social security expenditure [DSS 2000c]. The 'children's' expenditure, totalling £7,297 million in 1998-99, is accounted for mainly by Child Benefit, plus the one-parent addition and the small amounts on Guardians Allowance. The 'family' expenditure, which includes maternity benefits and Family Credit/Working Families Tax Credit, consists largely of spending on lone-parent families and not couples with children (e.g., it does not include Jobseekers Allowance spending on unemployed families with children). The £10,139 million spent on families in 1998-99, then, is an underestimate of the total. The total for children and families is £17,436 million, or about one-fifth of all benefit expenditure.

These figures also show trends in real spending since the late 1980s and projections forward over the next few years.

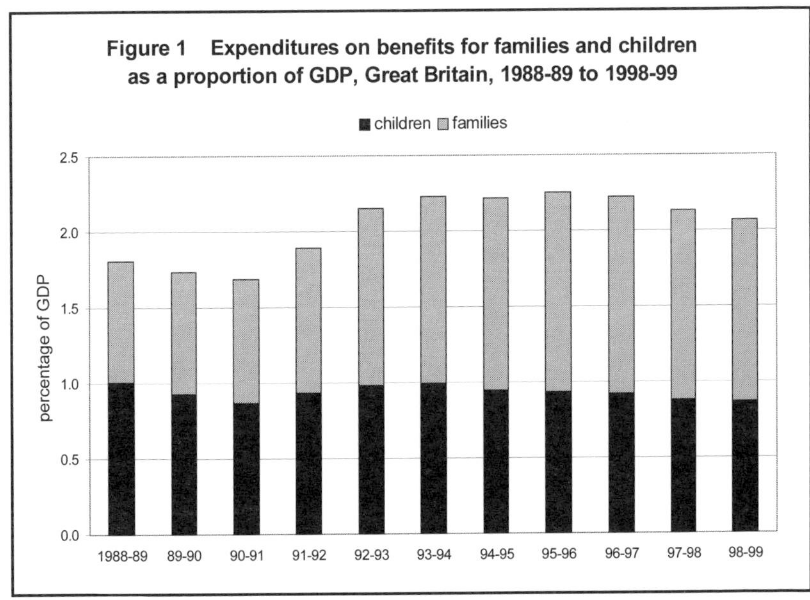
Figure 1 Expenditures on benefits for families and children as a proportion of GDP, Great Britain, 1988-89 to 1998-99
children
families
percentage of GDP
0.0
0.5
1.0
1.5
2.0
2.5
1988-89
89-90
90-91
91-92
92-93
93-94
94-95
95-96
96-97
97-98
98-99

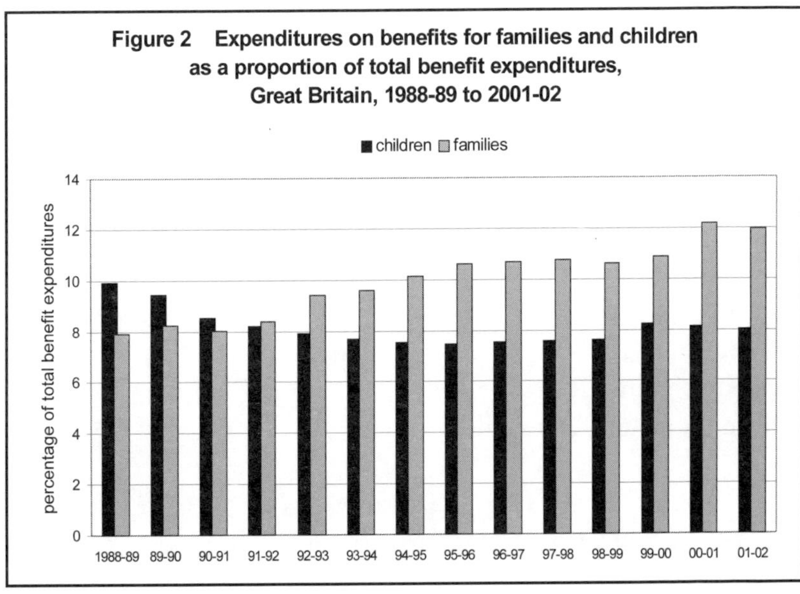
Figure 2 Expenditures on benefits for families and children as a proportion of total benefit expenditures, Great Britain, 1988-89 to 2001-02
children
families
percentage of total benefit expenditures
0
2
4
6
8
10
12
14
1988-89
89-90
90-91
91-92
92-93
93-94
94-95
95-96
96-97
97-98
98-99
99-00
00-01
01-02

Throughout the 1990s, spending on children and families has fluctuated at around 2 percent of GDP. In real terms (set by 1998-99 prices), spending on children rose from about £6,900 million to around £7,300 million in the ten years up to 1998-99, and spending on families almost doubled. The total will continue to increase, particularly with additional expenditure planned on tax credits that will come to make up about one-third of the spending on families and children by 2001-2002. Further measures announced in the 2000 Budget (i.e., not included in Table 7) mean that the government is planning to spend an extra £7,000 million each year on children and families by 2002. This amount is divided into £2,700 million on Working Families Tax Credit, £1,800 million on Children's Tax Allowance, £2,500 million on Child Benefit and income-related benefits, and £200 million in other expenditure [HM Treasury 2000a].

The level of support for children

Turning from total expenditure to the level of support offered to individual children and families also highlights the significant benefit increases that have been introduced over the past few years. Table 8 shows the level of support available to the first child in four different types of family in 1997 and 2001 (when the Children's Tax Credit comes into effect): non-working and receiving Income Support or Jobseekers Allowance, low-paid working and receiving Working Families Tax Credit, working and paying standard rate tax, and working and paying higher rate tax. There are substantial increases for all these types of family, but in particular for families in low-paid employment, where maximum amounts of benefit have more than doubled (from about £1,250 to about £2,600 per annum) over these four years. The children's rates in Income Support/Jobseekers Allowance have been reduced from three age bands (0-10, 11-15, 16-17) to two (0-15, 16-17), resulting in particularly large increases for younger children. For a first child aged under 10, Income Support has been increased from about £880 in 1997-98 to about £1,610 from October 2000.[1]

By 2001 the range of support offered to first children will run from a minimum of about £806 (for a higher rate taxpayer) to a maximum of about £2,600 (for a low-paid worker). Second and subsequent children receive lower amounts, with a range between about £538 and about £1,890. From April 2001, a family with one wage earner, working for at least 30 hours per week at the National Minimum Wage and claiming full tax and benefit entitlements, will have a 'minimum income guarantee' of £214 net per week (just over £11,000 per annum) [HM Treasury 2000b].

To give some idea of the support offered at different levels of gross earnings, we examine the situation of two 'model' family types: a lone parent with one pre-school child and a couple with two children, one pre-school and one of school age. Figures 3 through 6[2] show the amount that would be received from the various benefits by these model families at different levels of gross earnings. This is a very simplified picture, assuming no capital and no income other than from earnings (no child maintenance payments, for example). The families are assumed to live alone in Local Authority accommodation, paying rent of £2,283 and council tax of £499. They are assumed to have just one earner, who earns the National Minimum Wage (£3.60 per hour) and who moves from Income Support to Working Families Tax Credit at 16 hours of work per week. The lone parent is assumed to have become a lone parent after 1998, and so is not eligible for the extra benefits that were abolished for new claimants in that year. The calcula-

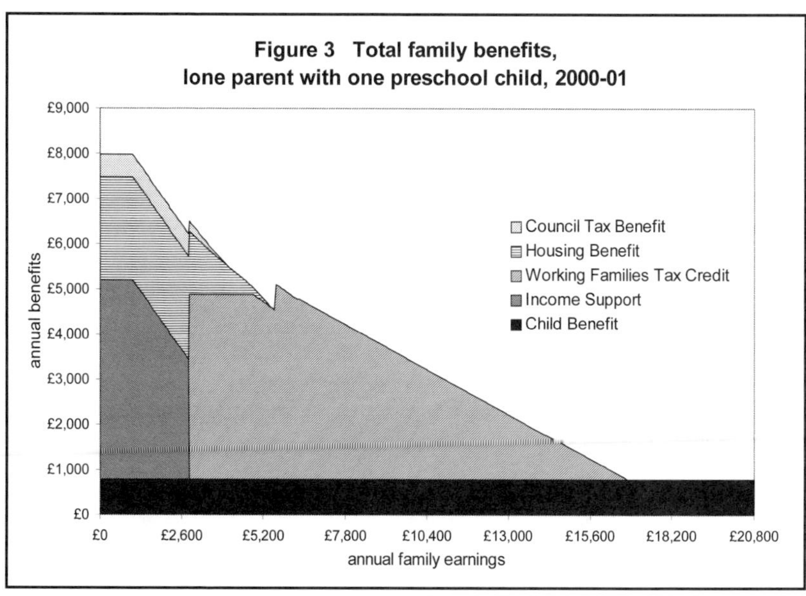
Figure 3 Total family benefits,
lone parent with one preschool child, 2000-01
£9,000
£8,000
£7,000
£6,000
£5,000
£4,000
£3,000
£2,000
£1,000
£0
annual benefits
Council Tax Benefit
Housing Benefit
Working Families Tax Credit
Income Support
Child Benefit
£0
£2,600
£5,200
£7,800
£10,400
£13,000
£15,600
£18,200
£20,800
annual family earnings

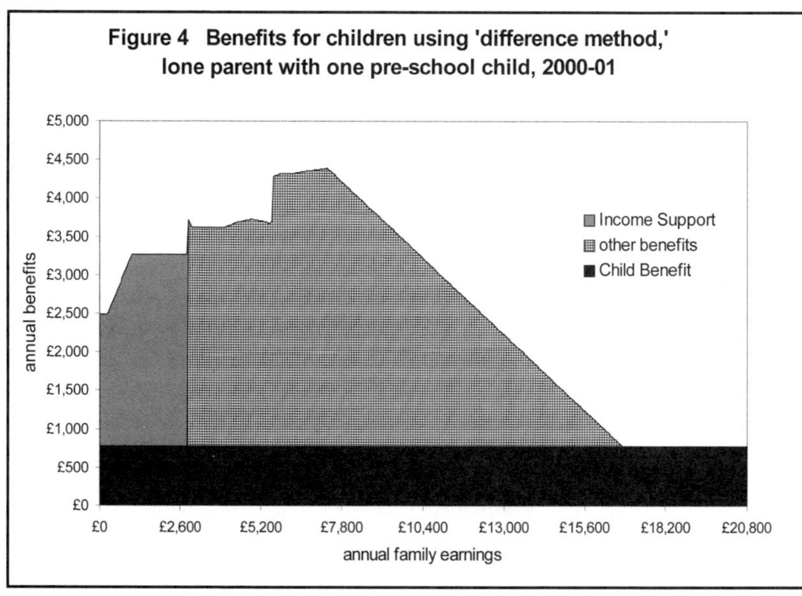
Figure 4 Benefits for children using 'difference method,'
lone parent with one pre-school child, 2000-01
£5,000
£4,500
£4,000
£3,500
£3,000
£2,500
£2,000
£1,500
£1,000
£500
£0
annual benefits
Income Support
other benefits
Child Benefit
£0
£2,600
£5,200
£7,800
£10,400
£13,000
£15,600
£18,200
£20,800
annual family earnings

tions are made for Child Benefit, Income Support, Working Families Tax Credit, Housing Benefit and Council Tax Benefit, based on benefit rates applying during the financial year 2000-01 (mainly from April 2000, though some children's increases come into effect from October). The Children's Tax Credit, which does not come into operation until April 2001, is not included; nor are the tax payments such families would make.[3]

These are, of course, hypothetical examples and the picture would vary for families in different circumstances. In particular, owner-occupiers with mortgages receive much more limited help with housing costs. Families paying for child care would receive some help with the costs of this item. Lone-parent families receiving child support maintenance would gain more from this source if they were working than if they were not working, because of the different treatment of child support in the Income Support and Working Families Tax Credit income tests (it is partly counted in the former and not counted in the latter). These figures assume 100 percent take-up of all benefits, although in practice families with higher incomes tend to have lower take-up rates. However, despite the limitations, the analysis does provide a useful picture of the type and level of direct financial support offered to families with children.

Figure 3 shows the current benefit 'package' for the lone-parent family with one pre-school child. The amounts shown are the total benefits that would be received for the family as a whole and not just the amounts for children. A lone parent with one child who has no other income would receive just under £8,000 per year from a combination of Child Benefit, Income Support, Housing Benefit and Council Tax Benefit. Income Support is reduced for any earnings above £1,040 per year. Once in work at

16 hours per week, the family would receive about £6,200 in benefits, but this falls quite steeply until the 30 hour bonus comes into effect and provides a small boost. Income-tested benefits run out at gross wages of about £17,000 for this family type, which is above median female full-time earnings of £14,700 in April 1999 [Office for National Statistics 1999].

To try and separate out the specific support for children, and to provide a way of making cross-national comparisons, Figure 4 shows the difference between the benefits that this lone-parent family would receive and benefits that would be received by a single childless person.

Non-working lone parents with one child would get about £2,500 more than a single person on Income Support, rising to about £3,200 if the lone parent has some part-time earnings, because lone parents are able to retain more of their earnings from part-time work than are single people. The working lone parent starts off by being about £3,500 better off than the working childless person, but there is some fluctuation in the 'difference' measure at these lower wage levels arising, in part, from the operations of the income tests for Working Families Tax Credit and Housing Benefit/Council Tax Benefit. Working Families Tax Credit is counted as part of income for Housing Benefit and Council Tax Benefit assessment purposes, which means that once a family starts to receive Working Families Tax Credit, housing-related benefits are reduced. This does not happen for the childless person (who has no entitlement to Working Families Tax Credit), so childless people receive more housing-related assistance than those with children. For families with children, then, Working Families Tax Credit is designed to be the main source of in-work support, although in practice families may be claiming one or the other.

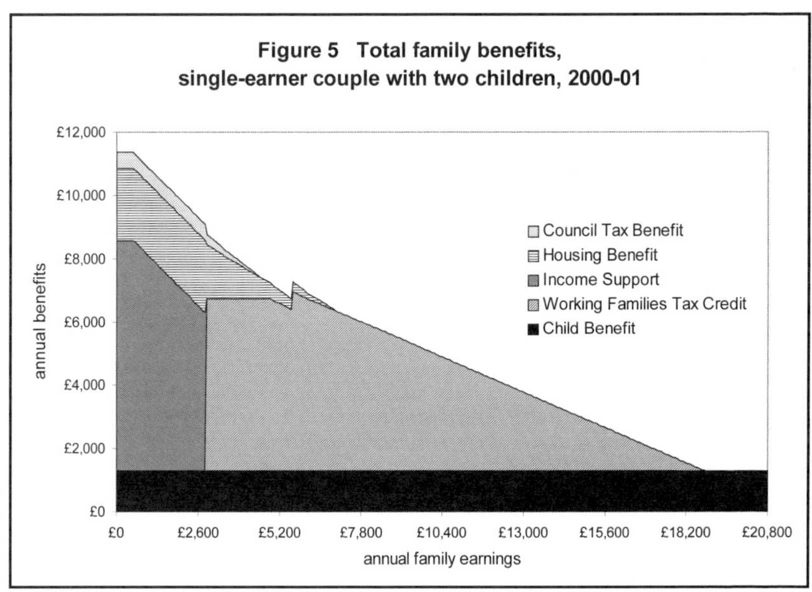
Figure 5 Total family benefits,
single-earner couple with two children, 2000-01
£12,000
£10,000
£8,000
£6,000
£4,000
£2,000
£0
annual benefits
Council Tax Benefit
Housing Benefit
Income Support
Working Families Tax Credit
Child Benefit
£0
£2,600
£5,200
£7,800
£10,400
£13,000
£15,600
£18,200
£20,800
annual family earnings

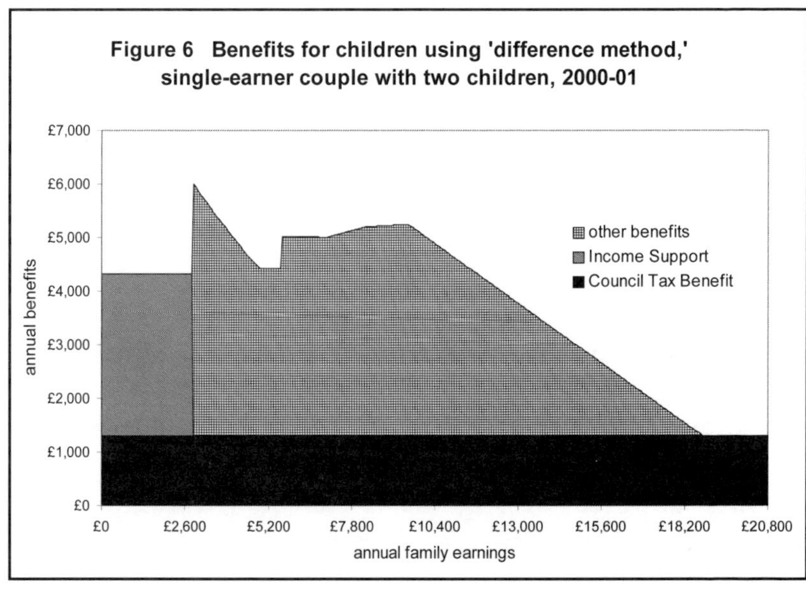
Figure 6 Benefits for children using 'difference method,'
single-earner couple with two children, 2000-01
£7,000
£6,000
£5,000
£4,000
£3,000
£2,000
£1,000
£0
annual benefits
other benefits
Income Support
Council Tax Benefit
£0
£2,600
£5,200
£7,800
£10,400
£13,000
£15,600
£18,200
£20,800
annual family earnings

Figure 5 shows the family benefits for a couple with two children. Out of work, this family type would receive about £10,900 in Child Benefit, Income Support, Housing Benefit and Council Tax Benefit – if the family had no other income. Income Support is reduced pound for pound for any earnings above £520 per year. Once in work of 16 hours or more per week, the Working Families Tax Credit comes into effect, initially at a flat level but including an increase at 30 hours work per week, before starting to taper away. It runs out at wages of about £18,800 for this family type. These figures assume one earner. If there were two earners, with the same total gross earnings, benefits would be lower and the couple also cannot combine two times 15 hours work to reach the 30 hour threshold.[4]

Figure 6 shows the difference between the couple with two children and what a childless couple would receive. Out of work, the couple with children receives just over £4,000 more in benefits than a childless couple. The working family with children starts off by being about £6,000 better off than the working childless couple. But, as with the lone-parent family, there is some fluctuation in the difference measure at these lower wage levels because of the way the income tests interact. Couples with two children and earning below average male earnings are typically about £5,000 better off than childless couples in the same earnings range.

Comparing Figure 3 with Figure 5 shows that couples with two children do not receive twice the level of support of lone parents with one child, despite being twice as large a family unit. For example, at gross earnings of £10,000, the couple with two children would receive about £5,000 in family benefits and the lone parent about £3,300. This difference is due mainly to the fact that first children receive higher levels of support than second and subsequent children. As well, the amount of Working Families Tax Credit does not vary with the number of adults in the household, so two-parent families and lone-parent families receive the same amount if they have the same earnings and same number of children.

Integrated Child Credit

As noted above, a new system is due to be introduced from 2003 which will replace most existing child payments, though Child Benefit will remain. There is much that is still to be decided about the specifics of the way this new system will operate (e.g., how the income tests will work), but for illustrative purposes we can assume that the Integrated Child Credit will be equivalent to the current child credit in Working Families Tax Credit plus the Children's Tax Credit (as the Treasury does in its discussion of this in HM Treasury 2000b) and so we can illustrate the structure of the new system.[5] Figures 7 and 8 show how Child Benefit and Integrated Child Credit together might look for our two model family types.

The proposed new system produces a relatively simple profile. For a lone parent with one child, families with gross earnings of between £0 and about £13,200 would receive about £2,500 in total, and the second plateau would be found at wages between about £16,500 and £32,000. For a couple with two children, families on gross earnings of between £0 and about £12,500 would get about £4,400. The benefit is then reduced as earnings rise until another plateau is reached and families with gross earnings between about £20,000 and £32,000 receive about £1,740. The Integrated Child Credit would run out completely at gross earnings of about £40,000, but the universal Child Benefit would continue in payment. For both family types, therefore, Integrated Child Credit payments go fairly high up the income distribution and the second plateau will include many middle-income families.

This picture shows the Integrated Child Credit and Child Benefit in isolation and does not include adult benefits or housing-related benefits (and so is not directly comparable to Figures 3 and 4 above). In practice, of course, much will depend on the relationship between the Integrated Child Credit and these other income-tested benefits, which is as yet unclear. This matter is discussed further below.

POLICY ISSUES

As noted at the start, these policy changes represent a new departure for the UK. Although there is little direct talk of redistribution, there is a strong focus on tackling poverty and promoting opportunity at both individual and community levels. Here we consider four policy issues which are at the centre of current debate: the goal of eliminating child poverty in twenty years, the impact on children of the strong work focus to current policy, the future of child support policy and the issues raised by the proposed Integrated Child Credit.

Eliminating child poverty

A central goal of current policy is the elimination of child poverty in twenty years, with a reduction by half in ten years. As we have seen, policies to achieve this target include higher levels

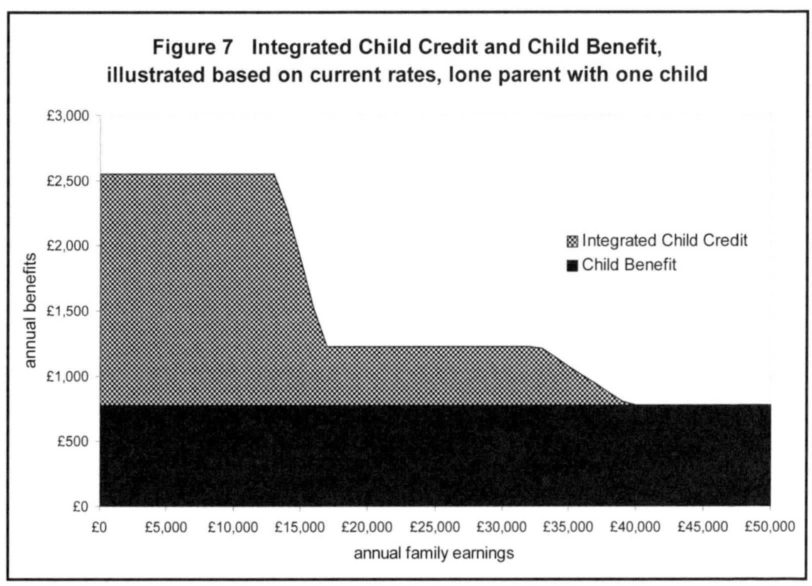

Figure 7 Integrated Child Credit and Child Benefit, illustrated based on current rates, lone parent with one child
£3,000
£2,500
£2,000
£1,500
£1,000
£500
£0
annual benefits
Integrated Child Credit
Child Benefit
£0
£5,000
£10,000
£15,000
£20,000
£25,000
£30,000
£35,000
£40,000
£45,000
£50,000
annual family earnings

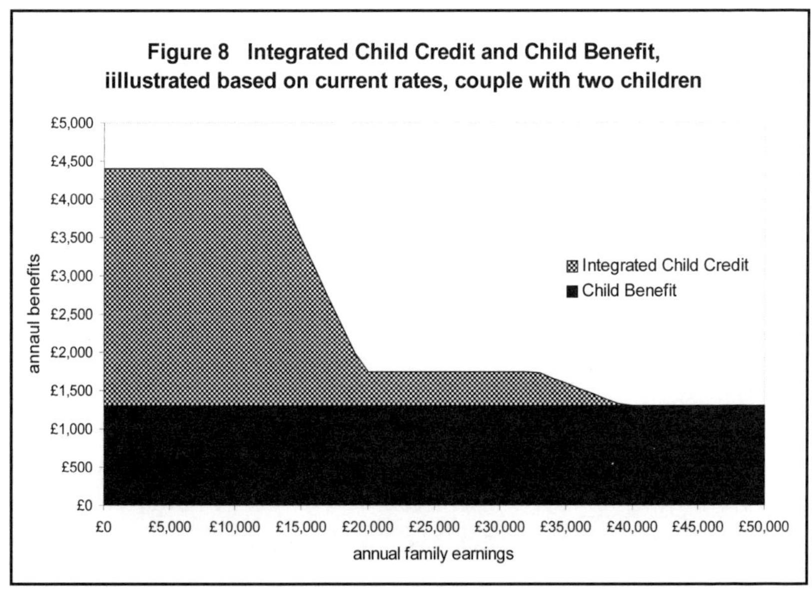

Figure 8 Integrated Child Credit and Child Benefit, iillustrated based on current rates, couple with two children
£5,000
£4,500
£4,000
£3,500
£3,000
£2,500
£2,000
£1,500
£1,000
£500
£0
annaul benefits
Integrated Child Credit
Child Benefit
£0
£5,000
£10,000
£15,000
£20,000
£25,000
£30,000
£35,000
£40,000
£45,000
£50,000
annual family earnings

of financial support, changes in the structure of financial support and a range of new family policy initiatives.

There is no doubt that the tax and benefit changes introduced since 1997 have been redistributive towards families with children. The average household with children will gain by £850 per year, with the highest gains (about £1,500 to £1,560) at the lowest two deciles [HM Treasury 2000a]. Hills [2000] compares the impact of the budget measures introduced since 1997 with what would have happened if benefits and taxes had simply been uprated (i.e., indexed) for inflation and finds that low-income couples with children have gained between £1,300 and £3,000 per year. These tax and benefit changes are likely to have a positive impact on child poverty. The Treasury [2000a] estimate that about 800,000 children will be lifted out of poverty by the measures introduced in the 1998 and 1999 budgets. Piachaud and Sutherland [2000] make a similar estimate and also calculate that the measures reduce the size of the poverty gap (the aggregate deficit below the poverty line) by about a quarter. Following the changes announced in the 2000 budget, the Treasury estimate that between 1.2 and 1.9 million children will be lifted out of poverty by 2001 (1.2 million using a poverty line of 60 percent of median household income, and 1.9 million using a poverty line of below 50 percent of the median).

However, as Hills points out, the estimates of the impact on child poverty are based on estimating "a reduction in the numbers *compared to those if no changes had been made*" [Hills 2000: 27]. The initiatives may not actually translate into such a fall in the numbers in poverty, which will also depend on what happens to market income and employment levels (discussed below) as well as on the achievement of high levels of take-up for these new tax credits. And even if these measures succeed in the goal of reducing child poverty levels by half, that would still leave over two million children in poverty. These children are likely to be the hardest to reach: Many are children in lone-parent families and many are young children. The very poorest and most disadvantaged children – some ethnic minorities, groups such as travellers and asylum seekers, and children leaving local authority care – also need extra help.

The adequacy of Income Support/Jobseekers Allowance to meet needs also remains an important political issue [Lister et al. 1999; Land 1999; Holman 2000]. Much of the research evidence from the 1980s and 1990s showed that Income Support levels were far from adequate, especially for families with children [Bradshaw 1987; Cohen et al. 1992; Kempson 1996; Middleton et al. 1997; Parker 1998]. In the past few years there have been some substantial increases in the children's rates of benefit, as described above. Benefit rates for families with children are now much closer to Parker's (1998) 'low cost but acceptable' budget, taking inflation into account.[6] Nevertheless, couples with two children are still over £1,000 per annum below the 'low cost' budget and lone parents with two children almost £700 below.

It also could be argued that adequacy should mean a higher standard than the low-cost budget and that children in families on benefit require higher levels of support if they are to be kept out of both poverty and social exclusion. Linking benefit increases to wages rather than to prices would ensure that such families were able to keep pace with rising living standards. In addition, the Social Fund – which provides loans to Income Support/Jobseekers Allowance families that have to be repaid from current benefit – adds to the hardship experienced by families on benefit. Families repaying Social Fund loans are living on incomes below the safety net level, and the system is both unpopular and poorly targeted [Huby and Dix 1992]. There is much still to reform in this part of the social security system.

Work-based welfare

Taking children out of poverty, and keeping them out, also will require high and sustained levels of employment for their parents. As noted above, living in a workless household is one of the most common factors associated with childhood poverty. Piachaud and Sutherland [2000] estimate that if 1.5 million more parents move into employment, then another million children could be lifted out of poverty.

Employment is being supported by two main sets of policies. First there are measures to 'make work pay' – to boost income from work, especially for low-paid workers. These include a National Minimum Wage (for the first time in the UK), lower starting rates of tax and National Insurance contributions, the Working Families Tax Credit and other in-work benefits, and various measures intended to help people make the transition from unemployment to work (e.g., benefit 'run ons' whereby benefits remain in payment for the first few weeks in work). Secondly, there are initiatives to 'make work possible' by new measures intended to help parents reconcile work and family life (e.g., parental leave, extended maternity rights) and, most importantly, the 'New Deal' programs [CM 4445 1999; Millar 2000a]. These measures are targeted upon young people, long-term unemployed people, older workers, disabled people, lone parents and the partners of unemployed claimants. For some groups, notably young people and the long-term unemployed, participation is compulsory and they must take part in employment, training or voluntary/environmental work options. For other groups, including lone parents and partners (the latter refers mainly to women married to unemployed men), participation is voluntary and the main support offered is access to a 'personal adviser' who gives information and advice on job seeking and training opportunities. However, from 2001 it will be compulsory for all new benefit claimants to attend a 'work-focused' interview (although not necessarily to go on to seek work, depending on circumstances).

The issue of compulsion to seek work is controversial, especially in respect of groups such as lone parents. But more generally, there also is concern that high levels of parental employment may not best meet the needs of children. It would mean children spending longer periods away from home, travelling to child care, in after-school care, with childminders and so on [Ridge 2000]. The 'working week' for children – school plus care – will increase, including for young children (the aim is to get most three year-olds and all four year-olds in nursery education). The quality of care offered to children thus will be very important, and not just the costs of that care. Some commentators argue that society should be doing more to value socially useful caring work – which might include financially supporting full-time parental care for both married and lone mothers [Land 1999; Hirsch 1999]. Expecting, or requiring, all parents to work is not necessarily seen as the best way forward.

Child support

Child support has been a topic of great controversy in the UK since the Conservative government introduced the *Child Sup-*

port Act in the late 1980s [Millar, 1996; Bradshaw and Skinner, 2000]. This legislation replaced the court-based system of determining the financial obligations of separated parents with a system based on a standard formula and operated by a new agency (the Child Support Agency) set up within the Department of Social Security. This change proved to be very controversial from the start – complex to operate and perceived as inequitable by many of those involved, especially the separated fathers who often felt they were being asked to pay too much and without due regard of their circumstances. The system rapidly became almost unworkable and was subject to various reforms in the first few years. The current government has produced reform plans that include a simpler formula, with generally lower payments and more streamlined administration [CM 3992 1999]. These changes are due to come into effect the end of 2001.

Only about a quarter of lone-parent families receive child support payments, and the child support system has not led to any increase in this percentage [Social Security Select Committee 1999]. Child support is of greatest value to working families, as it is not taken into account when in-work benefits such as Working Families Tax Credit are calculated (it is partly taken into account for families in Income Support). Child support can help boost the 'income package' of such families, but it is increasingly clear that it can play only a small role in the incomes of lone-parent families since many separated parents cannot afford to pay very much [Bradshaw et al. 1999] and compliance remains a problem for others. The reforms will get rid of some of the worst aspects of the current system, but child support is likely to remain a controversial policy area.

The proposed Integrated Child Credit

The Integrated Child Credit proposal represents a radical new departure, but one which has some clear attractions in the context of current policy goals [HM Treasury 2000b]. It would abolish the division between working and non-working families and so should improve work incentives (by making the transition into work much simpler) as well as being more socially integrative (by making most families part of the same system). It will be paid to the main carer, just like Child Benefit, and so get directly into the family budget. It could be an important element in meeting the promise to eliminate child poverty. But, despite the apparent simplicity, the Integrated Child Credit presents some major operational challenges in respect of both design and delivery [Institute for Fiscal Studies 2000; Kelly 2000; Millar 2000b; Hirsch 2000].

On the design side, the Integrated Child Credit is intended to fulfil two main roles. For some families – those with no income from work – it will be their only source of income for children. It therefore must be set at a level sufficient to meet subsistence needs. But for other families – those with income from work – it will be making a contribution to children's needs, though not necessarily meeting the full amount. It would be costly, and some would argue wasteful, to take a subsistence level benefit very far up the income distribution. At the same time, however, having a flat structure across a wide range of earnings would help to keep the income testing to a minimum.

Keeping the income testing simple also requires a system that is not necessarily fine tuned to current circumstances, either in respect of the time period over which entitlement is assessed or the time period over which the award is made. The contrast between the way in which Income Support and Working Families Tax Credit are currently assessed and paid illustrates this point. Income Support is intended to meet current needs, so entitlement is based on current weekly income, and any changes in income or circumstances bring an immediate change in benefit levels: The system is highly responsive to change. Working Families Tax Credit is a top-up for low wages, so entitlement is based on wages over a period of several weeks (to get a measure of typical wages) and, once awarded, the amount remains the same for six months, regardless of changes in income or circumstances: The system is fairly unresponsive to change.

Which model is more appropriate for the Integrated Child Credit? If it is very responsive to change, this will mean lots of families undergoing repeated income tests, and the advantages of simplicity and non-intrusiveness would be lost. If it is not very responsive to change, there is a danger that families experiencing significant falls in income will not receive the financial help they need when they need it. Other families whose incomes rise nevertheless would continue to receive high levels of financial support for their children. Decisions are still to be made about the time period over which income will be measured, the time period over which the credit will be paid, and the types of changes in income and circumstances to be notified.

Collecting the information necessary for the assessment also poses challenges. The Integrated Child Credit is to be administered by the Inland Revenue, but that does not mean entitlement can be assessed on the basis of existing tax information. There are two main problems. The first is that the UK tax system is based on the individual and not the family, so it would be necessary to combine records in some way to measure family income. Secondly, most people in the UK pay their income tax through the 'Pay-As-You-Earn' (PAYE) system and do not complete tax returns. Even among those who do so, the amount of information on family circumstances (e.g., number of children and whether single, married or cohabiting) contained in tax records is limited. The UK cannot easily follow other countries in using its current tax records to assess entitlement without extending the information collected through the tax system (either through PAYE or tax returns) and requiring more people to supply this information. The alternative is to introduce a special claim form, as has been done for the new Children's Tax Credit.

The Integrated Child Credit will be a cash payment to the main carer. This feature generally has been welcomed because it gets the money more directly into the family budget and maintains the privacy of individuals vis-à-vis their employers. But it does raise the question of why the Inland Revenue is to be responsible for the program's administration rather than the Department of Social Security. The Integrated Child Credit, it could be argued, is a tax credit in name only and is actually more like any other social security cash benefit. The government argues that tax credits are perceived as less stigmatizing than benefits and that the Integrated Child Credit will include many families that have not previously had any need for contact with the Department of Social Security (other than claiming Child Benefit) but always have been in the tax system. However, if we make a distinction between assessment and delivery, it could be argued that both departments should be involved, as in other countries (for example, the benefit could be assessed by the Inland Revenue and delivered by the Department of Social Security).

Finally, there are important decisions to be made about how the Integrated Child Credit will interact with existing benefits, in particular Housing Benefit, the child care element of the Working Families Tax Credit and child support payments.

In addition, the tax credit proposals also include a new Employment Tax Credit for adults. This benefit would be available to all low-paid adults as a top-up to wages, not just to those with children, probably on the basis of family (not individual) income. Thus families with children potentially will be eligible for three separate in-work credits (the Integrated Child Credit, the Employment Tax Credit and the Child Care Tax Credit) as well perhaps as Housing Benefit. It is not clear that this situation represents a simplification from the point of view of families claiming these various credits, especially if there are separate and different income tests. Other complications include what to do about in-kind benefits (such as free school meals and free welfare foods for children, free prescriptions and hospital fares for adults) that currently are available to Income Support/Jobseekers Allowance recipients but not to those receiving Working Families Tax Credit. The impact on total income, on effective marginal tax rates and on the financial incentives to work (for both one- and two-earner families) cannot be assessed until we know more about these interactions. Clearly there remain many issues of delivery and design to be resolved over the next year or two.

EVALUATION

Looking at the system of support for children as whole in the UK, how well is it operating? We consider this question in respect of coverage, adequacy, simplicity, incentives to work and care, and social integration.

The financial support given through benefits and taxes is very important to families in the UK, and this is true of both the universal and the income-tested benefits. Child Benefit plays an important role in the family budget; "it tides families over when the money runs out, provides a reliable source of income in times of hiatus or crisis, gives women a source of income independent of a spouse, lends some recognition to the costs and importance of child-rearing, and allows mother money to spend on children" [Bradshaw and Stimson 1997: 51-52]. All families receive Child Benefit and about a third of children are in families receiving income-tested benefits that generally are well targeted on the lowest income deciles [Hills 1997]. The proposed Integrated Child Credit will include families across a wide range of earnings, so its coverage will be high. The government had reaffirmed a commitment to maintaining the universal Child Benefit for children, a policy which also is supported by the main anti-poverty advocacy groups.

The issue of adequacy is harder to evaluate. Child Benefit is intended as a contribution to the costs of children and, as such, the level clearly represents a political decision about what society is able/willing to transfer in this way. There is no statutory requirement to uprate Child Benefit and in the 1980s the value was allowed to decline in real terms. The current Labour government has been uprating Child Benefit, but when the Integrated Child Credit is introduced this may lead to 'competition' between the two benefits for future resources. Benefits for children in poor working families have seen the largest increase in recent years, in line with the commitment to work-based welfare, but so too have benefits for children of non-working parents. These benefits are now getting closer to a 'low cost but acceptable' standard, but there is still a gap to be closed if benefits are to meet subsistence costs. In comparison with our EU partners, UK financial support for children is relatively low [Bradshaw et al. 1993; Bradshaw 1999].

Simplicity is an important goal, but one that has to be judged within the context of the different and varying aims and objectives of the tax and benefit systems. Child Benefit clearly scores high on this criterion, but otherwise there is quite a confusing array of benefits/tax credits, each with its own income tests and claiming procedures. Lack of knowledge of what is available and how to get it remains a problem in respect of claiming benefits, probably more so than issues of stigma. For families moving from out-of-work to in-work benefits, the transition can still cause problems, though the 'New Deal' personal advisers are playing an important role in providing information about the different types of support available and in helping families to claim their entitlements. The Integrated Child Credit should help in this respect, being both simpler and available to both working and non-working families. However, it will be very important to monitor take-up of the Integrated Child Credit, as experience suggests that new benefits take some time to achieve high take-up levels and we do not know if the same will be true of tax credits. As discussed above, there are many decisions to be made about the details of the Integrated Child Credit but, if it is to work, it must involve a simpler form of income testing – one that requires less information, less often.

Since increasing work incentives is an important policy goal, benefits for children must be assessed against this objective as well. The current tax/benefit system has two sorts of potential barriers to entry into work – those caused by the level of support and those caused by the structure of the support – and for working families there also may be financial disincentives to work extra hours or for high wages. The incentive structures may be different for one-earner and two-earner families. In general, families are better off in work than out of work, and the recent policy has strengthened this through increases to in-work benefits and other measures such as the National Minimum Wage, the lower starting rates of income tax and reductions in National Insurance contributions. Measures to ease the transition to work also have been introduced, and again the Integrated Child Credit should help in this respect.

In two-parent families, these measures have boosted the incentives for at least one adult in the family to enter work, but they may be reducing work incentives for the other. In-work benefits for families can be conceptualized as providing a wage replacement for a second earner, rather than simply as a wage supplement for a single earner [Millar et al. 1997]. But keeping 'second earners' out of the workforce may not be a desirable goal in the longer term, either for the economy as a whole or for the individuals concerned. Many of these second earners are women and absence from the labour market can incur a significant cost to them, including if they become lone parents and need to be able to support themselves through paid employment.

There is also an issue of the 'incentive to care,' as it might be called in parallel to the incentive to (paid) work. Provisions such as parenting or carers payments can be used explicitly to support care work and/or to compensate parents for the indirect costs of children (i.e., the loss of earnings associated with full-time child care). Or they can be used to keep second earners out of the labour market. These sorts of issues and debates are becoming more prominent in policy discussions, not least because of the increasing attention given to the problems that people – both women and men – face in reconciling work and family life. They raise some important but difficult issues that cannot be considered without explicit discussion of the gendered impacts of policy.

Finally, social integration is an important policy goal in the UK and is one of the driving forces behind the current and future reforms. Child Benefit brings all children together into one system, and it is intended that the Integrated Child Credit should do the same for its eligible children. On the other hand, the extension of income testing that will be created by the Integrated Child Credit may be seen as socially divisive rather than socially integrative, and it could be argued that raising the universal Child Benefit would have been a more integrative move than the introduction of the new income-tested tax credit.

CONCLUSION

This is a period of very rapid policy change for the UK. Many of the measures described above, both financial and service based, represent a new direction for the UK. Family policy has never before been so explicit. No government before has made such a clear commitment in respect of child poverty. Children have become much more visible in the past few years and their needs increasingly recognized. But the voices of children themselves remain relatively silent in all of this and finding ways to develop more child-centred policies may be the next important step.

ENDNOTES

1. These amounts for first children in Income Support/Jobseekers include the 'family premium' paid to all those with children, per family and not per child. It is logical to include this benefit as part of the support for a first child although it does not appear in the children's 'scale rates' (see Table 3).

2. With thanks to Matt Barnes for his work on producing these figures.

3. To examine the complete impact of the tax and benefits system, it would be necessary to include both the benefits/tax credits received by the families (as positive amounts) and the payments made in income tax, National Insurance contributions and indirect taxes (as negative amounts). These graphs show the net amount of benefit received at various levels of gross income – the shape and size of benefits for children (not the total impact of taxes and benefits).

4. Each earner is taxed individually and each has his/her own tax allowances. A two-earner couple pays less in income and payroll taxes than a one-earner couple with the same total gross wage. This, in turn, reduces entitlement to income-tested benefits (which are based on net income) and so overall the impact on disposable income is similar. For example, at total gross wages of £10,400 per year, the one-earner couple pays about £1,770 in taxes and National Insurance contributions and receives about £5,200 in benefits. At the same gross earnings, but divided 60/40 between two earners, income taxes and National Insurance amount to just under £470 and benefits to about £4,056. This means that both types of family (i.e., one-earner and two-earner) have a disposable income of around £13,800, made up in slightly different ways. In practice, many two-earner couples have combined net earnings that take them above eligibility for in-work benefits. Median gross annual earnings in April 1999 were about £19,400 for men in full-time jobs, £14,700 for women in full-time jobs and £5,500 for women in part-time jobs [Office of National Statistics 1999].

5. This slightly overestimates the Integrated Child Credit, as it is based on adding the Children's Tax Credit to the child element of the Working Families Tax Credit. In practice, the Children's Tax Credit comes into effect first and leads to a small increase in net income. The Working Families Tax Credit therefore is slightly lower, because it is based on that slightly higher net income.

6. Parker [1999] calculates budgets for two family types – a couple and a lone parent, each with two children aged 4 and 10 – by estimating the cost of a budget derived from a range of sources, including nutritional advice. Her 1998 'low cost' total, excluding rent, was about £170 per week for the couple and about £133 for the lone parent. At that time, Income Support (minus rent) was about £131 for a couple and about £105 for a lone parent. Couples were thus about £39 short of the low cost budget and lone parents about £27 short. If we uprate the low cost budgets to April 2000 by the standard retail price index less housing, the budgets for a couple with two children becomes about £178 compared with £155 that would be received in Income Support/Jobseekers Allowance – a shortfall of about £23. For a lone parent, the budget becomes about £139 compared with Income Support of £124 – a shortfall of about £14. Thus the gap has closed significantly, but families with children – particularly two-parent families – remain below this (not very generous) budget standard.

REFERENCES

Bradshaw, J. (1999). "Comparing Child Poverty." *Poverty.* 104:15-19.

Bradshaw, J. (1987). *Budgeting on Benefit.* London: Family Policy Studies Centre.

Bradshaw, J., J. Ditch, H. Holmes and P. Whiteford. (1993). *Support for Children: a Comparison of Arrangements in 15 Countries.* London: HMSO.

Bradshaw, J. and C. Stimson. (1997). *Using Child Benefit in the Family Budget.* London: HMSO.

Bradshaw, J., C. Stimson, C. Skinner and J. Williams. (1999). *Absent Fathers.* London: Routledge.

Bradshaw, J. and C. Skinner. (2000). "Child support: the British fiasco." *Focus,* 21(1): 80-85.

Brown, J. (1988). *Child Benefit: Investing in the Future.* London: Child Poverty Action Group.

Child Poverty Action Group. (1999). *Welfare Benefits Handbook.* London.

CM 4445. (1999). *Opportunity for All: Tackling Poverty and Social Exclusion.* London: The Stationery Office.

CM 3992. (1999). *Children First: a New Approach to Child Support.* London: The Stationery Office.

Cohen, R., J. Coxall, G. Craig and A. Sadiq-Sangster. (1992). *Hardship Britain: Being Poor in the 1990s.* London: Child Poverty Action Group.

Department of Social Security. (2000a). *Households Below Average Income, 1994/5 to 1998/9.* London.

Department of Social Security. (2000b). *Opportunity for All - One Year On: making a difference*. London.

Department of Social Security. (2000c). *The Changing Welfare State: Social Security Spending.* London.

Department of Social Security. (1999). *Social Security Statistics 1999.* London.

Dilnot, A. and J. McRae. (1999). *Family Credit and the Working Families Tax Credit.* London: Institute for Fiscal Studies.

Ditch, P, S. Pickles and P. Whiteford. (1992). *The New Structure of Child Benefit: a Review.* London: Coalition for Child Benefit.

Ford, R. and J. Millar. (1998). *Private Lives and Public Responses: Lone Parenthood and Future Policy in the UK.* London: Policy Studies Institute.

Gordon, D., L. Adelman, K. Ashworth, J. Bradshaw, R. Levitas, S. Middleton, C.Pantazis, D. Patsios, S. Payne, P. Townsend and J. Williams. (2000). *Poverty and Social Exclusion in Britain.* York: York Publishing Services for the Joseph Rowntree Foundation.

Gregg, P., S. Harkness and S. Machin. (1999). *Child Development and Family Income.* York: York Publishing Services for the Joseph Rowntree Foundation.

HM Treasury. (2000a). *Budget March 2000.* London.

HM Treasury. (2000b). *Tackling Poverty and Making Work Pay - Tax Credits for the 21st Century. The Modernisation of Britain's Tax and Benefit System.* Number 6. London.

HM Treasury. (2000c). *Spending Review 2000: New Public Expenditure Plans 2001-2004.* London.

HM Treasury. (1999). *Supporting Families Through the Tax and Benefit System.* London.

Hills, J. (2000). *Taxation for the Enabling State.* London: London School of Economics, Centre for the Analysis of Social Exclusion, CASE paper number 41.

Hills, J. (1997). *The Future of Welfare: A Guide to the Debate.* York: York Publishing Services for the Joseph Rowntree Foundation.

Hirsch, D. (2000). *A credit to children: The UK's radical reform of children's benefits in an international perspective.* York: York Publishing Services for the Joseph Rowntree Foundation

Hirsch, D. (1999). *Welfare Beyond Work.* York: York Publishing Services for the Joseph Rowntree Foundation.

Hole, D. (1998). *Options for the UK Tax Return System.* York: York Publishing Services for the Joseph Rowntree Foundation.

Holman, B. (2000). "At the hard end, poverty lives." *New Statesman,* May 15: 23-24.

Howarth, C., P. Kenway, G. Palmer and R. Miorelli. (1999). *Monitoring Poverty and Social Exclusion.* York: York Publishing Services for the Joseph Rowntree Foundation.

Huby, M. and G. Dix. (1992). *Evaluating the Social Fund.* London: HMSO.

Institute for Fiscal Studies. (2000). *Green Budget.* London.

Kelly, R. (2000). *Reforming the Working Families Tax Credit.* London: The Fawcett Society.

Kempson, E. (1996). *Life on a Low Income.* York: Joseph Rowntree Foundation.

Land, H. (1999). "New Labour, New Families?" In D. Hartley and R. Woods eds. *Social Policy Review 11.* University of Luton: Social Policy Association.

Lister, R., J. Goodee and C. Callender. (1999). "Income Distribution Within Families and the Reform of Social Security." *Journal of Social Welfare & Family Law.* 21 (3): 203-220.

Micklewright, J. and K. Stewart. (2000). "Child Well-being and Social Cohesion". *New Economy:* 18-23.

Middleton, S., K. Ashworthy and I. Braithwaite. (1997). *Small Fortunes: Spending on Children, Childhood Poverty and Parental Sacrifice.* York: York Publishing Services for the Joseph Rowntree Foundation.

Millar, J. (2000a). *Keeping Track of Welfare Reform: The New Deal Programmes.* York: The Joseph Rowntree Foundation.

Millar, J. (2000b). "The Integrated Child Credit: Issues of Policy and Delivery." *Poverty,* summer.

Millar, J. (1996). "Poor Mothers and Absent Fathers." In H. Jones and J. Millar eds. *The Politics of the Family.* Aldershot: Avebury.

Millar, J., S. Webb and M. Kemp. (1997). *Combining Work and Welfare.* York: The Joseph Rowntree Foundation.

Office for National Statistics (ONS). (1999). *Family Spending 1998/99.* London.

Office for National Statistics (ONS). (1999). *New Earnings Survey 1999.* London.

Parker, H. (1998). *Low Cost but Acceptable, a Minimum Income Standard for the UK: Families with Young Children.* Bristol: Policy Press.

Piachaud, D. and H. Sutherland. (2000). *How Effective is the British Government's Attempt to Reduce Child Poverty?* London: London School of Economics, CASE paper 38.

Rahman, M. Palmer, G., Kenway, P. and Howarth, C. (2000). *Monitoring poverty and social exclusion 2000.* York: York Publishing Services for the Joseph Rowntree Foundation.

Ridge, T. (2000). *Childhood Poverty and Social Exclusion.* University of Bath: unpublished PhD thesis.

Social Security Select Committee. (1999). *The 1999 Child Support White Paper, 10th Report.* London: The Stationery Office.

UNICEF. (2000). *A League Table of Child Poverty in Rich Countries.* Innocenti Report Card Issue number 1. Florence.

ANNEX 1: PERSONAL INCOME TAX SYSTEM, UK

Unit of taxation

Individual with individual personal allowances (see below).

Pay-as-you-earn versus annual reconciliation

Pay-As-You-Earn (PAYE), deducted weekly or monthly. At the end of the year, there is a reconciliation between gross earnings and level of PAYE paid and either the PAYE code is adjusted to recoup or repay any difference or the amount is deducted/added to the next wage packet. There is no reconciliation with capital taxes, etc., unless a tax return form is completed (see below).

Who is responsible for submitting tax returns

Those required to complete tax returns are: the self-employed, higher rate taxpayers (who may have to pay higher rate taxes on investment income), people with complex tax affairs, non-taxpayers and lower rate taxpayers who have paid excess tax under PAYE [Hole 1998].

Coverage

In 1996/97, there were about 9 million tax return forms issued, out of about 27 million individual taxpayers, so only about one-third of taxpayers complete tax returns (these figures refer to all taxfilers, not just families).

Federal/state/local

Local property taxes are collected by Local Authorities and (as noted in text) can be reduced for poor people. There are no local sales taxes.

Progressivity

Income Tax Personal Allowances 2000-01	
Aged under 65	£4,385
Aged 65-74	£5,790
Aged 75 and above	£6,050
Married couples [1]	
Age 65 before 6.4.200 £5,185	
Age 75 and above	£5,255
Minimum amount	£2,000
Income limit for age related allowances	£17,000
Widow bereavement allowance (deaths before 5.4.2000)	£2000
Blind persons allowance	£1,400

[1] Tax relief for these allowances is restricted to 10 percent.

Tax Rates [1] for 2000-01 from April	
Starting rate 10%	£1-£1,520
Basic rate 22%	£1,521-£28,400
Higher rate 40%	Over £28,400

[1]Bands of taxable income after taking the tax allowances above into account.

Note also National Insurance contributions, paid at rate of 10 percent of gross on weekly earnings between £76 and £535.

Administrative body

Inland Revenue.

ANNEX 2: BASIC NATIONAL STATISTICS, UK

GDP and population

GDP: £843,725 million in 1998
Population: 59 million

Labour force

26.9 million in employment, 1.8 million unemployed (according to International Labour Office definition), 17.3 million inactive (1998)

Children as percentage of population

20.5 percent under 16

Families with children as percentage of all households

49 percent (couples with children 40 percent, lone parents with children 9 percent) in 1996

Average number of children

1.7 children per family

Among families with children under 18

a. Single parents as percent of total, male and female:
22 percent of all families with children are lone-parent families, 1.8 percent lone fathers and 20.2 percent lone mothers

b. Families with different levels of adult employment:

Number of Children in Families (Millions), 1997-98				
	Couple	Lone parent	All	% of total
2 working adults	4.6	-	4.6	36%
1 working adult	2.7	1.0	3.7	29%
No working adult	1.0	1.8	2.8	22%
Self-employed	1.6	neg.	1.6	13%
All	9.9	2.8	12.8	100%

c. Mother-only families employed as percentage of mother-only families

About 46 percent (compared to about 65 percent of married mothers)

Child poverty rate

Households Below Average Income figures: equivalent income of less than half of mean income after housing costs 1997-98 - 4.4 million children, 34 percent of all children.

UNICEF figures: equivalent income of less than half of median before housing costs 1995 - 21.3 percent of children

Median income by family type

Mean gross income in 1998-99 (from Family Expenditure Survey):

a. With children: 2 parent – £31,408 annual (£604 weekly); 1 parent: £10,192 annual (£196 weekly)

b. Without kids: 2 adult, non-retired – £31,668 annual (£609 weekly); single, non-retired – £15,756 annual (£303 weekly)

Mean, equivalized net income, all households, 1998-99 (from Households Below Average Income): £16,796 annual (£323 weekly)

Median, equivalized net income, all households, 1998-99 (from Households Below Average Income): £13,832 annual (£266 weekly)

TABLE 1
UNIVERSAL BENEFITS

	Child Benefit
Eligibility rules 1. Who is entitled to benefits	1. Child lives with claimant, or claimant contributes to the maintenance of the child at a rate of at least the amount of child benefit for that child. 'Child' means under 16 years, or under 19 years and in full-time recognized education.
2. Reciprocal responsibilities	2. None.
3. Budget caps	3. Open-ended.
Benefits description 1. Amounts per child	1. Rates from April 2000: Eldest eligible child £780; Other children (each) £520; Lone parent rate £912 (Note: The lone parent rate of child benefit was abolished for new claimants from 6 July 1998.)
2. Income-related structure	2. and 3. not applicable.
3. Definition of income	
4. Indexing	4. Secretary of State has 'power' to uprate but no duty to do so.
Delivery features 1. Administrative arrangements	1. Benefits Agency (dss.gov.uk/ba/GBI/5a8eea2.htm) introduced 5 April 1977.
2. How people get enrolled	2. By post on claim form, health workers usually provide forms to mothers of new born children.

	Child Benefit
3. Responsiveness	3. Normally awarded until the child no longer qualifies on age or education criteria. Any changes in circumstance that might affect entitlement must be reported.
4. Payment procedures	4. Generally paid every four weeks, for three weeks in arrears and one week in advance. Paid to either parent, but usually the mother, by 'order book' (i.e., book of cheques that can be cashed at post offices) or by ACT (automatic credit transfer).
5. Verification procedures	5. Benefits Agency checks records.
6. Aboriginal peoples	6. Not applicable.
7. How program is delivered	7. Benefits Agency, through a single administrative centre.
8. How program is financed	8. General taxation.
9. National/state integration	9. Not applicable.

Sources: Tables 1-3, DSS (1999) and CPAG (1999).

TABLE 2
NON INCOME-RELATED BENEFITS

	Child Dependency Increases to National Insurance Benefits	Guardians Allowance Child's Special Allowance	Disability Living Allowance
Eligibility rules 1. Who is entitled to benefits	1. May be payable with the following National Insurance benefits: retirement pension, widows benefit, short-term incapacity benefit at the higher rate and long term incapacity benefit, invalid care allowance, severe disablement allowance, higher rate industrial death benefit, unemployability supplement and short-term incapacity benefit if beneficiary over pension age. Claim for any child for whom child benefit is received.	1. *Guardians Allowance* is paid to someone looking after a child as part of their family because both the child's parents are dead; or one of the parents is dead and the other is missing or, is serving a prison sentence of 5 years or more; or they were divorced or never married. *Child's Special Allowance* to a divorced woman whose former husband died before April 1987, on the basis of his National Insurance contributions.	1. Has two elements. The 'mobility' component is paid at two rates. The higher rate is for people unable to walk, or with severe mental or physical disabilities. The lower rate is for those who need help or guidance and for a child beyond what is normally needed. For people aged 5 to 65. The 'care' component is paid at three rates for people with differing needs for care, for people aged 0-65.
2. Reciprocal responsibilities	2. None.	2. None.	2. None.
3. Budget caps	3. Open-ended.	3. Open-ended.	3. Open-ended.

	Child Dependency Increases to National Insurance Benefits	Guardians Allowance Child's Special Allowance	Disability Living Allowance
Benefits description 1. Amounts per child	1. First child £517, others £590.	1. As Child Dependency Increases.	1. Mobility higher rate £1,944, Lower rate £738. Care higher £2,784, middle £1,861; lower £738.
2. Income-related structure	2. Not income-related but no increase is payable for the first child if a cohabiting partner earns at least £145 per week. Entitlement for each child is lost for each complete £19 per week above that.	2. and 3. Not applicable.	2. and 3. Not applicable.
3. Definition of income	3. Not applicable.		
4. Indexing	4. Secretary of State has duty to uprate in line with prices, usually done each April, on basis of price rises over previous year.	4. As Child Dependency Increases.	4. As Child Dependency Increases.
Delivery features 1. Administrative arrangements	1. Benefits Agency (dss.gov.uk/ba/GBI/5a57ca1.htm).	1. Benefits Agency (dss.gov.uk/ba/GBI/5a58486.htm).	1. Benefits Agency (dss.gov.uk/ba/GBI/5a583da.htm).

	Child Dependency Increases to National Insurance Benefits	**Guardians Allowance Child's Special Allowance**	**Disability Living Allowance**
	Guardians Allowance introduced 5th July 1948. *Child's Special Allowance* introduced 18th Feb 1957.	Introduced 1st April 1992	
2. How people get enrolled	2. Through main benefit claim but must complete separate claim form.	2. Claim form to Benefits Agency.	2. Claim form to Benefits Agency
3. Responsiveness	3. Continues as long as main benefit.	3. Continues as long as eligible.	3. Continues as long as eligible, any changes in conditions affecting eligibility must be notified.
4. Payment procedures	4. Paid with main benefit.	4. Paid by order book or ACT.	4. Paid by order book or ACT to parent.
5. Verification	5. Contribution record verified.	5. As for Child Benefit.	5. May be checked medically.
6. Aboriginal peoples	6. Not applicable.	6. Not applicable.	6. Not applicable.
7. How program is delivered	7. Benefits and Contributions Agencies.	7. Benefits Agency.	7. Benefits Agency.
8. How program is financed	8. National Insurance contribution fund.	8. General taxation.	8. General taxation.
9. National/state integration	9. Not applicable.	9. Not applicable.	9. Not applicable.

TABLE 3
INCOME-RELATED BENEFITS

	Income Support Income-tested Job Seekers Allowance	**Working Families Tax Credit Disabled Person's Tax Credit**	**Housing Benefit Council Tax Benefit**
Eligibility rules 1. Who is entitled to benefits	1. All aged over 18 and habitually resident, with income from all sources below the scale rates. For *Income Support:* either aged 60 plus, or a lone parent with a child under 16 living with them, or be incapable of work because of sickness, or be caring for a severely disabled person, some other categories. Not eligible if working more than 16 hours per week. For *Job Seekers Allowance*: must be actively seeking work, and not eligible if working 16 or more hours per week (24 for a partner).	1. Couples or lone parents with one or more dependent children, and one parent must be employed for at least 16 hours a week (including self employed). For *Disabled Person's Tax Credit* must have been receiving a disability benefit. Cannot receive both *Working Families Tax Credit* and *Disabled Person's Tax Credit.* Must be resident in the UK and entitled to work here. For the Child Care Tax Credit, claimants must be employed for at least 16 hours per week. This applies to both members of a couple or one must be	1. For Housing Benefit, must be habitually resident; must either be entitled to Income Support/ Jobseekers Allowance or have a low income; and must be liable to pay rent in respect of the dwelling. For Council Tax Benefit, as above except must be liable for Council Tax Benefit in respect of the dwelling.

	Income Support Income-tested Job Seekers Allowance	Working Families Tax Credit Disabled Person's Tax Credit	Housing Benefit Council Tax Benefit
		working and the other receiving incapacity/disability benefits. The childcare must be registered care.	
2. Reciprocal responsibilities	2. See above.	2. Employment conditions as above. Can add hours from more than one job, but cannot add hours of partner.	2. None.
3. Budget caps	3. Open-ended.	3. Open-ended.	3. Open-ended.
Benefits description 1. Amounts per child	1. Scale rates: Child aged 0-16 £1,383 (from 10.00 £1,609); aged 16-18 £1,651; Family premium (one per family): £741; Disabled child premium £1,157; Lone parent premium (if claimant before 4.98) £826; Single adult/lone parent, under 18 £1,635; 18-24: £2,150; 25 plus £2,714; Couple, both under 18 £3,242; one or both over 18 £4,261.	1. Child age 0-16: £1,331; aged 16-18 £1,370; Disabled child £1,157; *Working Families Tax Credit* for lone parent/couple £2,763; *Disabled Person's Tax Credit* for lone parent/couple £4,414; 30 hour credit (working over 30 hours) £585.00; Child care tax credits 70% of up to £5,200 for one child and up to £7,800 for 2 or more children.	1. As for Income Support/Jobseekers Allowance.

	Income Support Income-tested Job Seekers Allowance	Working Families Tax Credit Disabled Person's Tax Credit	Housing Benefit Council Tax Benefit
2. Income-related structure	2. Amount of benefit is calculated by adding up rates as above and deducting all income received from this source.	2. For each family size there is a maximum of total credits as above. If net income is below the threshold of £4,755, receive maximum. If net income is above threshold, 55p of every excess £ is deducted from the maximum.	2. If receiving Income Support/Jobseekers Allowance or income below that level, get full eligible rent. If net income is above Income Support/Jobseekers Allowance rates, the amount is reduced by 65p for every extra £ for Housing Benefit; by 20p for every extra £ for Council Tax Benefit. Amount is reduced if there are non-dependent people in the household.
3. Definition of income	3. Net family income from all sources, including other benefits. Earnings disregards: £260 for single, £520 for couples, £780 for lone parents. Child Support disregard: £520. Any income above disregarded is deducted £ for £ from benefit. The first £3,000 of capital is ignored, and no ben-	3. Net family income from all sources. Various benefits are disregarded including Child Benefit, some disability benefits and Housing Benefit/Council Tax Benefit. Child Support is disregarded. Capital limits as for Income Support/ Job Seekers Allowance.	3. Net income from all sources, some benefits disregarded (but *not* Working Families Tax Credit and Child Benefit). Other disregards as for Income Support/ Jobseekers Allowance, except higher earnings disregard for lone parents (£1,300). Disregard of child care costs for child under 12 in

	Income Support Income-tested Job Seekers Allowance	**Working Families Tax Credit Disabled Person's Tax Credit**	**Housing Benefit Council Tax Benefit**
	efit is payable if capital above £8,000. For every full £250 between £3,000 and £8,000, benefit is reduced by £52. The value of the main residential home is not counted as capital If child has £3,000 capital, then no Income Support received for that child.		registered child care, if adult working 16 hours, plus up to £3,120 for one child, £5200 for two or more children. Capital limits as for Income Support/ Jobseekers Allowance, except maximum is £16,000.
4. Indexing	4. Secretary of State has power to uprate but no duty to do so. Usually an annual uprating in April, index-linked to prices.	4. As for Income Support/Jobseekers Allowance.	4. As for Income Support/Jobseekers Allowance.
Delivery Features 1. Administrative arrangements	1. Benefits Agency (dss.gov.uk/ba/GBI/ 5a5868a.htm) (dss.gov.uk/ba/GBI/ 5a591f6.htm). Introduced Income Support 1st April 1998 and Job Seekers Allowance 7th October 1996.	1. Inland Revenue (inlandrevenue. gov.uk/wftc/ dss.gov.uk/ba/ GBI/5a58405.htm) (dss.gov.uk/ba/ GBI/5a58405.htm). Introduced 5th October 1999.	1. Local Authorities, although Department of Social Security responsible for setting benefits rates, etc. (dss.gov.uk/ba/ GBI/5a5868 a.htm) (dss.gov.uk/ba/GBI/ 5a58609.htm).

	Income Support Income-tested Job Seekers Allowance	Working Families Tax Credit Disabled Person's Tax Credit	Housing Benefit Council Tax Benefit
			Introduced 1st April 1983.
2. How people get enrolled	2. Claim in person at local Benefits Agency office, no discretion except for extra Social Fund payments.	2. Applications are made to the Inland Revenue using a special claim form. No discretion.	2. If receiving Income Support/Jobseekers Allowance or income below that level, get full eligible rent. If net income is above Income Support/ Jobseekers Allowance rates, the amount is reduced by 65p for every extra £ for Housing Benefit; by 20p for every extra £ for Council Tax Benefit. Amount is reduced if there are non-dependent people in the household.
3. Responsiveness	3. Assessment is based on current income. Once awarded the bene-fits remain in payment as long as eligible but claimants must report any changes in income or circumstances. Annual reviews.	3. Assessment is based on income averaged over 6 weeks if weekly paid (or over 3 months). Once awarded, the benefits remain in payment for 6 months, regardless of any	3. Net income from all sources, some benefits disregarded (but *not* Working Families Tax Credit and Child Benefit). Other disregards as for Income Support/Jobseekers

	Income Support Income-tested Job Seekers Allowance	**Working Families Tax Credit Disabled Person's Tax Credit**	**Housing Benefit Council Tax Benefit**
		changes in income or circumstances.	Allowance, except higher earnings disregard for lone parents (£1,300). Disregard of child care costs for child under 12 in registered child care, if adult working 16 hours, plus up to £3,120 for one child, £5,200 for two or more children. Capital limits as for Income Support/Jobseekers Allowance, except maximum is £16,000.
4. Payment procedures	4. Payments are made by order book or ACT, usually fortnightly. Paid to claimant but couples on Income Support can opt as to who is primary claimant.	4. Payments are made by employers through the wage packet (weekly or monthly) or by order book or ACT (weekly or fortnightly). The first is the method unless family opts to have non-working partner designated as claimant.	4. As for Income Support/Jobseekers Allowance.
5. Verification procedures	5. Benefits Agency checks information at time of claim and	5. Either send pay slips as proof of earnings with claim	5. As for Income Support/Jobseekers Allowance.

	Income Support Income-tested Job Seekers Allowance	Working Families Tax Credit Disabled Person's Tax Credit	Housing Benefit Council Tax Benefi
	may recheck if suspect fraud.	form, or employer can verify directly. For self-employed need statement of accounts. Fraudulent claims can be prosecuted.	
6. Aboriginal peoples	6. Not applica ble.	6. Not applicable.	6. Not applicable.
7. How program is delivered	7. Benefits Agency.	7. Inland Revenue.	7. Local Authorities.
8. How program is financed	8. General taxation.	8. General Taxation.	8. General taxation.
9. National/state integration	9. Not applicable.	9. Not applicable.	9. National scheme delivered by Local Authorities.

TABLE 4
RECENT FAMILY POLICY MEASURES: SUMMARY

New strategies and institutions	Including Ministerial Group on the Family (to develop family policies and co-ordinate family policies across departments), the National Family and Parenting Institute (to act as independent centre of expertise, provide guidance and develop better parenting support, with funding of £2 million over 3 years), Parent Line Plus (a national parenting telephone help line), Annual Poverty Audit (to monitor progress on goal of eliminating child poverty), Teenage Pregnancy Strategy (to reduce rates of teenage pregnancy), the Children's Funds (a network of local and regional funds to support work by the voluntary sector in meeting the needs of children, with funding of £450 million over three years).
Sure Start	In 250 areas, managed by voluntary and statutory agencies in partnership, with a budget of £450 million per annum rising to £500 million in 2003-04. Aims to promote the physical, intellectual and social developments of pre-school children, to equip them for starting school. Currently reaches about 18 percent of poor pre-school children and aims to reach one-third by 2003-04. Services provided include outreach and home visiting, support for families and parents, play, child care, primary health care, community health care, advice about child health and child development, support for special needs, and access to special needs services.
National Child Care Strategy	Investing £470 million to ensure good quality and affordable child care for all 0-14 years, by 2003. Guarantees free nursery places to all 4 year-olds and for up to 60 percent of 3 year-olds. 'Early Excellence Centres' established to develop a range of models of good practice and integrated early education and child care, involving carers, parents and other family services.

Educational Maintenance Allowances	For children aged 16 plus who attend full-time courses at school or college, £30-£40 per week, depending on parental income, paid during term time. Started in September 1999 in 15 pilot areas, will be extended to cover 30 percent of the country and may eventually replace Child Benefit for this age group.
On Track	Aimed at reducing the risk factors that link young people with future criminal behaviour. An initial £27 million will fund 20-30 pilot projects, which will include pre-school education, parent support and training, family therapy, home visits and home/school partnerships.
Family Friendly Employment initiatives	Including improved maternity leave and entitlement to Maternity Allowances extended to women earning below the National Insurance threshold. Sure Start Maternity Grant of £300 for 200,000 mothers in low-income families. Introduction of unpaid parental leave of up to 13 weeks, and some rights to leave for other dependent care.
Community-based initiatives	Including the New Deal for Communities, Health Action Zones, Education Action Zones, Employment Zones.

TABLE 5
BENEFIT RECEIPT BY FAMILIES WITH CHILDREN, DECEMBER 1998

	Families in receipt (000s)	% of all families	Children in receipt (000s)	% of all children	Lone parents % of families in receipt	Take-up (caseload/exp.)[1]	Total expenditure (£m) 1998/99[1]
Child Benefit	6,976	100	12,621	100	NA[2]	100	7,278
One-Parent Benefit	1,037	15	1,648	13	100	NA	5
Family Credit	788	11	1,578	13	51	72/84	2,477
WFTC	1,400	20	NA	NA	44	NA	NA
IS/JSA	1,347	19	2,508	20	77	85/91	14,885
Housing Benefit	1,411	20	2,737	22	66	95/96	11,219
Council Tax Benefit	1,504	22	2,947	23	63	86/87	2,484
Disability Living Allowance	NA	NA	203	1.6	NA	NA	NA
Guardians Allowance	2.9	0.04	3.0	0.02	-	NA	2
Widowed mothers	44.8	0.7	73.2	0.6	100	NA	NA

1. All claimants, not just families with children, figures shown are average for caseload and expenditure.
2. About 24 percent of all families with children are lone-parent families.

Source: Department of Social Security, 1999b.

TABLE 6
CLAIMANTS OF KEY BENEFITS[1], AUGUST 1999

	Families with dependent children (000s)	Number of children under 16 (000s)	% of all children under 16	Family type children under 16 (000s)[2]		Number of children under five (000s)
				in couple families	in lone-parent families	
All[3]	2,215	4,015	34	1,532	2,421	1202
Working Family	757	1,403	12	807	596	396
Unemployed	152	292	2	282	9	105
Sick & Disabled	352	600	5	376	162	116
Lone Parent	920	1,651	14	-	1,651	563
Other	34	70	1	67	3	21

1. Includes Income Support, Jobseekers Allowance, Family Credit, Incapacity Benefit, Severe Disablement Allowance, Disability Living Allowance, Disability Working Allowance.
2. Plus 62,000 where family status not known.
3. This includes all families with children for whom an additional benefits is paid, including 93,000 families with 308,000 young people aged 16 to 18 (22 percent of that age group).

Source: Department of Social Security. *Cross Benefit Analysis, August 1999.*

TABLE 7
EXPENDITURE ON BENEFITS/TAX CREDITS FOR FAMILIES AND CHILDREN, 1988/89 TO 2001/02

	Expenditure £m cash			Expenditure £m in 1998/99 prices		
Year	Children[1]	Families[2]	Total children and families	Children[1]	Families[2]	Total children and families
88/89	4,695	3,742	8,437	6,937	5,528	12,465
89/90	4,738	4,137	8,875	6,533	5,704	12,237
90/91	4,821	4,528	9,349	6,164	5,789	11,853
91/92	5,439	5,578	11,017	6,548	6,716	13,264
92/93	5,955	7,081	13,036	6,940	8,252	15,192
93/94	6,332	7,900	14,232	7,189	8,969	16,158
94/95	6,405	8,599	15,004	7,169	9,624	16,793
95/96	6,644	9,420	16,064	7,228	10,247	17,475
96/97	6,943	9,847	16,790	7,317	10,377	17,694
97/98	7,090	10,049	17,139	7,270	10,304	17,574
98/99	7,297	10,139	17,436	7,297	10,139	17,436
99/00[3]	8,288	10,946	19,234	8,106	10,705	18,811
00/01	8,570	12,844	21,414	8,177	12,255	20,432
01/02	8,853	13,195	22,048	8,241	12,283	20,524

1. Child Benefit, One-Parent Benefit, Guardians Allowance.
2. Maternity Allowance, Statutory Maternity Pay, Maternity Grant, Family Credit, WFTC, IS and HB paid to lone-parent families.
3. From 99/00 estimates for total of both benefits and tax credits.

Source: Department of Social Security (2000c), Tables B3 and B4.

TABLE 8
FINANCIAL SUPPORT FOR FIRST CHILDREN, 1997 AND 2001

Family receiving	1997	2001
Income Support	£1,456	£2,392
Family Credit/Working Families Tax Credit (maximum)	£1,248	£2,600
No benefits, paying standard rate of tax	£ 572	£1,248
No benefits, paying higher rate of tax	£ 572	£ 806

Source: HM Treasury (2000) Chart 5.1.

BENEFITS FOR CHILDREN: THE UNITED STATES

Daniel R. Meyer

INTRODUCTION

The US has often been called a 'reluctant' welfare state [Jansson 1997]. Self-reliance is trumpeted and individual responsibility emphasized, with less stress on communal obligations or corporate responsibility. Substantial research has explored *why* the US seems to differ from other countries, with explanations including a history of emphasis on opportunity, the frontier making it seem as if everyone who put forth effort could succeed, the political power of conservatives and the absence of a countervailing radical force, the limited powers of the central government, and the need for a limited welfare state so that the workforce would continue to expand [Jansson 1997].

In the US context, children are typically seen as primarily their parents' responsibility, not necessarily the responsibility of society. The main role of the state is to provide opportunities through the educational system and to make sure that the labour market 'works' (by setting and enforcing a minimum wage, regulating labour market practices, etc.). Parents are expected to take advantage of the market, and it is usually assumed that individuals can reach moderate levels of economic well-being for themselves and their children if they try.

But this is not the only role of the state. The state has provided *indirect* benefits to families with children through the tax system for nearly a century. Families with children have paid lower income taxes than families without children with the same level of income. However, until the 1998 Child Tax Credit, the main mechanism for this support was an exemption for every individual in a family, with the same amount for adults and children. Thus the chief support for families with children was a favourable tax treatment that was not typically seen as an explicit provision of benefits for children, but seen more as a response to these families' lesser ability to pay taxes.

If parents have great difficulty in the market, state assistance does come into play, but it is clearly a *residual* role, coming into force only when the 'normal' systems have failed. Thus the US has historically provided some cash benefits to families with children, with benefits available to families unable to rely on earnings because of parental disability, unemployment, death or separation. As in many countries, the US has had a two-tiered system, with a more generous tier providing benefits to those with substantial prior connection to the labour force, who receive social insurance benefits, and a less generous tier providing benefits to those with less labour force connection, who must meet income and assets tests to receive welfare.

The lower tier, welfare, has been much more controversial than social insurance, with the program that provides cash to single-parent families, Aid to Families with Dependent Children (AFDC), in turn being much more controversial than the program that provides cash to families that have a child with a disability, Supplemental Security Income (SSI), or the programs that provide in-kind assistance. In fact, programs that provide in-kind assistance to low-income families (medical coverage, food coupons, housing assistance) have grown dramatically and are larger in terms of total expenditures than are the programs that provide cash [Scholz and Levine 2000].

Substantial changes in Aid to Families with Dependent Children occurred in the 1980s, as individual states were encouraged to experiment with various reforms, and in 1988, with the

Family Support Act which required states to develop a variety of programs that could move women from welfare to work. The pace of reform efforts quickened in the 1990s, culminating in the passage of the *Personal Responsibility and Work Opportunities Reconciliation Act* (PRWORA). The *Personal Responsibility and Work Opportunities Reconciliation Act* eliminated Aid to Families with Dependent Children, replacing it with Temporary Assistance to Needy Families (TANF), in which each state designs its own cash program for low-income families. The *Personal Responsibility and Work Opportunities Reconciliation Act* also established lifetime time limits for receiving benefits, and required most individuals to work in exchange for their benefits after a 24-month recipiency period (or shorter, at state option). Because each state was required to develop its own Temporary Assistance to Needy Families program, many states began reviewing the way the income support system for families with children was working, and policy in this area is generally now in a time of review and change.

In the last decade, there also have been two large expansions in the Earned Income Tax Credit (EITC), a program that provides earnings supplements primarily to low-income families with children. Recent reforms also include the new federal child tax credit, described in more detail below, which is intended to assist a wide range of families with the financial burdens of raising children.

Because substantial changes in the government's provision of benefits to families with children have occurred in the last decade, this is a critical time to step back and review US government policies. This paper describes current policy in the US, first with a detailed overview of cash benefits, then a more limited overview of goods and services subsidies. The paper then reviews inputs and outcomes of the 'system' of benefits for children. The report closes with a discussion of current policy issues.

Several preliminary comments precede the description of current policy. First, the US has a federal system, with some benefits provided by the federal government and others provided by states. It is beyond the scope of this paper to provide information on each state, so in this review I focus on Wisconsin, well known as a leader (or outlier) in policies affecting families [Wiseman 1996]. Second, the focus is on child-related benefits, and thus programs in which eligibility does not require having a child and in which the benefit does not vary by family size, like Unemployment Insurance in Wisconsin, are not covered. I consider any features of the tax and transfer system that lead to differences in post-tax, post-transfer income between those with and without children to comprise the 'child-related benefit system.' Thus I take a relatively expansive view of 'benefits,' considering tax expenditures as well as direct benefits. This focus on all features of the tax and benefit system that result in families with children having higher net income than families without children reveals several indirect and hidden features of benefits for children in the US.[1]

INCOME BENEFITS FOR CHILDREN

Universal benefits

The US has no universal cash benefit for all children. While most children receive at least one of the income-related benefits described below, there is no single program that provides income support for all children.

Income-related benefits

Table 1 summarizes three programs for children in which the amount received depends on parental income (but not the amount of assets; benefits available only to those who meet an assets test are discussed in the next section). All three programs are delivered through the income tax code. (Annex 1 provides more detail on the income tax code in the US.) First, there is an exemption in the US tax code for each individual in a taxpaying unit, totaling $2,750 per individual (and thus per child) in 1999, and this exemption is available to all taxpaying units except those with very high incomes. The exemption is an offset to income and is not refundable for those with no tax liability. Because the tax brackets range from 15 percent to 39.6 percent, the value of the exemption ranges from nothing (for those not in a taxpaying range) to $412.50 per child per year (for those in the lowest tax bracket) to a maximum of nearly $1,000 per child.[2]

Additional amounts of support for children are hidden within the tax code but not shown on the table. For example, single individuals receive a standard deduction of $4,300 (in addition to the exemption), while single parents receive $6,350 (there is no difference in the standard deduction for childless married couples and those with children).[3] Another hidden benefit results from different tax bracket cut points: For example, single individuals begin paying 28 percent of their net taxable income when it reaches $25,750; for single individuals with a child, the 28 percent tax bracket does not begin until their net taxable income totals $34,550. Thus, net taxes due for single individuals and individuals with children differ because of the exemption, because of the standard deduction and because of tax bracket differences; all these can be seen as 'benefits for children.'

The second main benefit for children in the federal tax code is a new *non-refundable* credit for children that became available in 1998. Similar to the exemption, the child tax credit is available to most families (although the income limits are lower than for the exemption). The credit is $500 for each child, with no limit on the number of children. The credit is a direct offset to taxes due, but is generally not refundable. (For some families with more than two children, a portion of the credit can be refundable.) Both the credit and the exemption may be taken. Combining these two benefits, families in the lowest income categories receive nothing (because they are not in taxpaying range and both provisions are non-refundable), those in a low-income range would receive a tax off-set of nearly $1,000 per child per year, and those with family incomes of, say, $100,000, receive about $1,500 tax savings per child per year.

Some states also have provisions for families with children. For example, Wisconsin has had a non-refundable credit for children, but it is quite small ($50 per child per year).[4]

These benefits are administered in the US through the income tax system. For the most part, the public generally does not think of them as being part of the income support system for children.

The third main program is the Earned Income Tax Credit (EITC), also described in Table 1. The Earned Income Tax Credit is a *refundable* tax credit, so it is available even to families with incomes below taxpaying range. It is available only to families with earnings, providing nothing to those which do not have earnings. The amount of the benefit has three ranges, initially increasing with earnings, then a flat portion during which families receive the maximum benefit, then decreasing with earnings. Those without children receive a small benefit, up to $347 per year; families with one child can receive benefits up to $2,312 per year, and those with two or more, up to $3,816. Thus the child-related portion of the benefit is about $2,000 for the first child and about $1,500 for the second.

The Earned Income Tax Credit is administered through the income tax system, with the assessment of eligibility and the calculation of the amount done by the Internal Revenue Service. Most families receive a cheque annually from the Internal Revenue Service as part of their annual reconciliation of income taxes. Individuals do have the option of receiving the benefit in their regular paycheques, but recent estimates are that only about 1 percent of Earned Income Tax Credit recipients do so [Hotz and Scholz 2000]. Some of the reasons for the recipients' preference for annual administration include: some individuals are hesitant to inform their employer of eligibility for a low-income program; others are reluctant to ask the employer to do extra processing of their pay; others are concerned that if they received benefits over the course of the year they may have to pay back a portion when the annual reconciliation is done; and others prefer receiving a sizeable cheque from the Earned Income Tax Credit once a year as a way to save for durable goods or other large expenditures.

In 1999, 11 states also had Earned Income credits, patterned after the federal credit [Johnson 1999]. For example, Wisconsin's credit is a refundable portion of the federal credit, but it is available only for families with children. The amount for one and two children is fairly low: 4 percent of the federal credit for one child and 14 percent of the federal credit for two children, but it is generous for three or more children, providing 43 percent of the federal credit.

Income- and asset-tested benefits

As mentioned above, in 1996 welfare reform legislation in the US made a monumental change to the income support system for families with children.[5] The *Personal Responsibility and Work Opportunities Reconciliation Act* eliminated the last-resort cash program for families, Aid to Families with Dependent Children (AFDC), and replaced it with Temporary Assistance to Needy Families (TANF). Each state designs its own Temporary Assistance to Needy Families program, with very few federal constraints other than time limits (a lifetime maximum of five years receiving federal benefits, though states can exempt up to 20 percent of the caseload from this lifetime limit) and work requirements (most individuals must be working in exchange for their grant at least within 24 months of beginning receipt). States have great flexibility in using federal Temporary Assistance to Needy Families funds to design their own programs, as long as they demonstrate that they are spending a certain portion of previous expenditures on programs for low-income families with children.

Because states have so much flexibility, Temporary Assistance to Needy Families is more of a funding stream to states than a uniform program. As stated above, I focus here on Wisconsin's program, Wisconsin Works (W-2), described in more detail in Table 2 (as is Temporary Assistance to Needy Families).

Even before the passage of Temporary Assistance to Needy Families, Wisconsin had begun a radical redesign of its cash assistance to low-income families. It had begun experimenting with a large number of welfare reforms, and there was widespread dissatisfaction with the Aid to Families with Dependent Children program. Thus when states were given wide flexibility to design programs, Wisconsin was ready to institute a major change, and Wisconsin Works (W-2) began in September 1997. To some extent, W-2 has gone further in reform than every other state and thus defines one end of the continuum of state programs. It is unusual in several ways:

- No cash is provided except for those engaged in work or work-like activities. Most other states provide at least some grace period in which one can receive benefits without work.

- Benefits do not vary by family size. The general philosophy is that the income support system needs to mimic the low-skill labour market: Because individuals in the private sector do not get raises when they have more children, neither should individuals receiving benefits.

- The program is primarily administered by private agencies (while it is administered by local governments in most of the counties, it is administered privately in Milwaukee County, where the vast majority of recipients live).

- Recipients get to keep all child support paid on their behalf (in other states, child support paid on behalf of Temporary Assistance to Needy Families recipients is retained by the state, or only a portion is passed through to the family). This practice is consistent with the philosophy that those participating in W-2 should be treated as much like other non-participating citizens as possible.

The Wisconsin Works (W-2) program is built around a 'self-sufficiency ladder.' Individuals in every tier receive case management and assistance in finding and retaining employment. They also can receive other non-cash supports (e.g., child care, health care, assistance with transportation, a short-term loan) from the W-2 agency. The assumption is that nearly everyone can start at or near the top of the ladder. Those most ready for work are placed in the highest tier and receive only the basic services (case management and other non-cash supports, etc.) from the W-2 agency; they receive a market wage from their employer, which can be supplemented with the Earned Income Tax Credit. The second tier, Trial Jobs, provides a temporary job with a private sector employer, with the employer receiving financial support from the state for participating in the program, and the recipient receiving a market wage from the employer and the Earned Income Tax Credit. (The individuals in these two 'upper tiers' can receive basic services from the W-2 agency as well).

If individuals are not deemed ready for either of these tiers, they can be placed in a Community Service Job (CSJ), working for the public sector or a private not-for-profit or even for-profit organization, but here they receive benefits based on the hours they work and a sub-minimum wage and they are not eligible for other federal employment-related supports (e.g., the Earned Income Tax Credit, social insurance). The lowest tier is W-2 Transitions; here the work assignment is determined by a Financial and Employment Planner (caseworker) and may include working in a agency that provides employment to those with developmental or cognitive disabilities, participating in treatment for alcohol or other drug dependencies, caring for one's child if the child has a disability, or some other approved activity. Like those in a Community Service Job, individuals in this tier receive benefits based on the hours they participate and a sub-minimum wage. Finally, those with children less than 13 weeks old are eligible for cash without meeting a work requirement.

Another income- and asset-tested program that provides cash to families with children is the Supplemental Security Income (SSI) program, also described in Table 2. This federal program provides benefits to families with children with a severe disability that meet strict income and asset tests. The number of recipients (and thus the cost) grew rapidly in the early 1990s as a result of a court decision that required a less stringent definition of disability to be eligible. The *Personal Responsibility and Work Opportunities Reconciliation Act* changed the definition of disability to be more stringent. Some states (including Wisconsin) choose to supplement the federal benefit for children with disabilities. Supplemental Security Income also provides benefits to adults with severe disabilities. The federal Supplemental Security Income benefit schedule varies only with the number of individuals with a disability, and thus provides nothing extra when an adult recipient has children. However, states can provide state-funded benefits to these families, and Wisconsin now provides an additional $250 per month for the first child of these low-income parents with disabilities (and $150 per month for each child thereafter).

Social insurance entitlements

Benefits for children paid through the social insurance system are outlined in Table 3. A child whose parent has worked a significant amount, then becomes disabled or dies, is eligible for benefits. In contrast to income- and asset-tested programs, these benefits are generally not controversial even though they provide higher benefits to participants. In Wisconsin and about three-fourths of the states in the US, the Unemployment Compensation program does not provide differential benefits for families compared to individuals, nor does family size enter into either the eligibility criteria or the benefit calculation [Hobbie, Wittenbeurg, and Fishman 1999], and thus it is not reviewed in Table 3.

Total benefits

To gain a sense of the generosity of benefits, I calculate the total amount of child benefits from various sources for prototypical families with various levels of earnings. I begin with a single parent with one child (Figure 1). For the single-parent family, the benefits shown are the incremental benefit received over what a single adult would receive. (Note that in the US, in contrast to many other countries, single individuals with no dependents and no income are generally not eligible for governmental income support unless they have a permanent disability or are temporarily unemployed after a period of working.) Simplifying assumptions include the following: that the family has no other income than earnings and benefits, files taxes by taking standard deductions and pays nothing for child care.

I consider six types of child benefits. First is Wisconsin Works (W-2). Children are a requirement for W-2 receipt, so the total amount of W-2 is a 'child benefit.' Because W-2 requires full-time work (or a 'work-like' activity), I assume W-2 is only relevant for those not earning in the private market. I assume they would work full time in a Community Service Job, which would pay them about $8,000 a year. (Note that while parents cannot generally combine private-sector earnings and W-2 simultaneously, they can participate sequentially; this possibility is ignored here.)

Second, I consider food stamps, an important part of the safety net for low-income families described in more detail in the next section. (I include it here even though it is not a cash benefit because it is an important component of families' budgets and its cash value is easy to calculate.) Gross child-related food stamp benefits at zero income (i.e., the difference between the benefit for a single individual and a two-person family) total $1,440.[6] At other low-income levels, food stamps add a child benefit of about $1,200. The single-parent family loses food stamp benefits at income of about $12,000.

Third, I consider the federal Earned Income Tax Credit, examining the incremental amount for children. There is no benefit for those without earnings, and the child benefit increases with each dollar earned, up to a plateau of about $2,300 at an income of about $5,000; the benefit begins declining at an income of about $14,000.

Fourth, I consider the exemption for children and other features of the tax code. As noted above, the exemption for children is not refundable, so is of no value until the family has enough income that it would owe taxes. Single individuals begin owing taxes at about $8,000 of earnings. The difference in income tax bills for the family with and without children rises to $412 per year for earnings of $10,000 through $32,000, and then gradually increases to $1,914 per year for those earning $46,000 through $66,000. The figure shows that these tax preferences are by far the most generous benefit for those with incomes over $36,000.

Fifth, the non-refundable federal child tax credit is added. As with the exemption, the credit is of no value to those with low earnings, not providing benefits until the family has $10,000 in earnings. At $14,000 of earnings and above, the credit is worth $500; the value declines after $75,000 of earnings and disappears at earnings of $84,000. Finally, I add benefits for children within the Wisconsin tax system. These amounts are quite small, reaching a maximum of $220 at $10,000 of earnings.

The second family type is a married-couple family with two children. I calculate incremental child benefits by comparing amounts of income for this family to a husband-wife family without children. I again use a simplified family in that the family has no other income than earnings and benefits, files taxes by taking standard deductions, only one parent works[7] and the family pays nothing for child care. The amounts of the six benefits are shown in Figure 2.

The W-2 child benefit is the same as the single-parent family, because there are no adjustments for family size within W-2. Food stamps provide a maximum of about $2,200 (about twice as much as the single-parent family, and benefits are available at higher earning levels). The child portion of the federal Earned Income Tax Credit is substantial for this family, providing up to $3,800 in income compared to $2,300 for the single-parent family, and is available at higher earning levels. (The increased benefit is due to the difference between two children and one child, rather than the difference between single-parent families and two-parent families.)

The federal tax preference is not as large for this family as the single-parent family (maximizing at $1,500 instead of $2,500). This counter-intuitive result comes from the different tax treat-

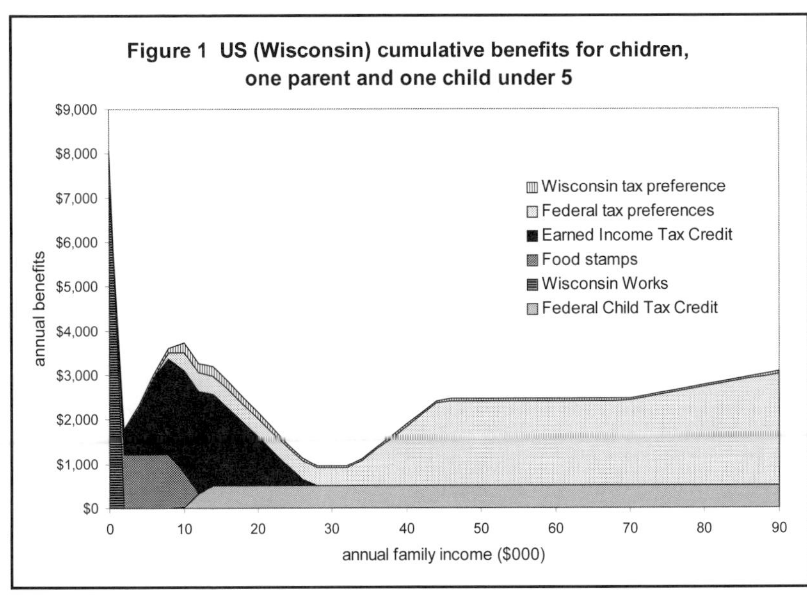
Figure 1 US (Wisconsin) cumulative benefits for chidren, one parent and one child under 5
$9,000
$8,000
$7,000
$6,000
$5,000
$4,000
$3,000
$2,000
$1,000
$0
annual benefits
Wisconsin tax preference
Federal tax preferences
Earned Income Tax Credit
Food stamps
Wisconsin Works
Federal Child Tax Credit
0
10
20
30
40
50
60
70
80
90
annual family income ($000)

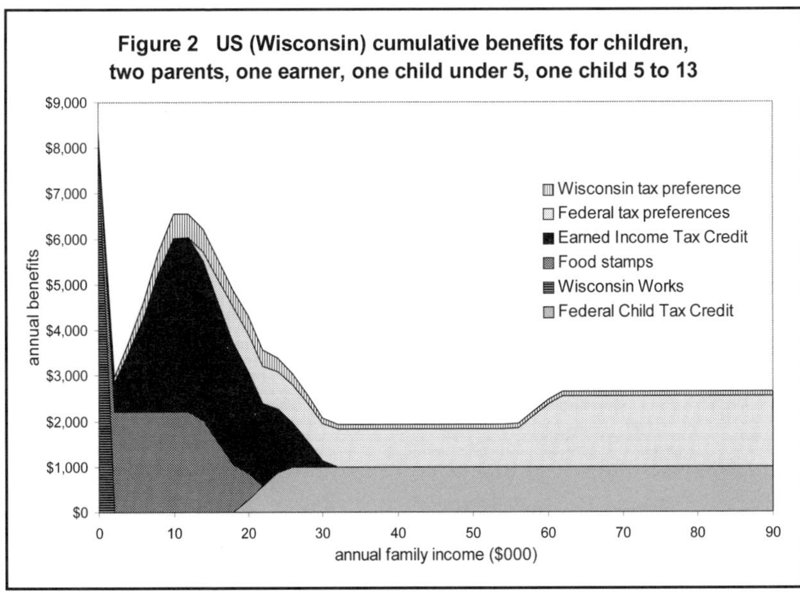
Figure 2 US (Wisconsin) cumulative benefits for children, two parents, one earner, one child under 5, one child 5 to 13
$9,000
$8,000
$7,000
$6,000
$5,000
$4,000
$3,000
$2,000
$1,000
$0
annual benefits
Wisconsin tax preference
Federal tax preferences
Earned Income Tax Credit
Food stamps
Wisconsin Works
Federal Child Tax Credit
0
10
20
30
40
50
60
70
80
90
annual family income ($000)

ment of single individuals and married couples. For families with earnings of $40,000, the tax due before the child tax exemption is about $5,900 for the one-adult family, $4,500 for the one-adult, one-child family, $4,100 for the two-adult family and $3,300 for the two-adult, two-child family. Thus at this level of income, the incremental benefit for children is actually higher for the single-parent one-child family (though the total tax liability is lower for the married-couple two-child family). The child tax credit, in contrast, is explicitly based on the number of children, so totals $1,000 for two-child families with earnings above $24,000. Finally, the Wisconsin tax system provides more for this family than the single-parent family, but the amounts are still quite small, reaching a maximum of about $500.

Both figures demonstrate several inconsistencies across income levels. First, in both family types, there is a very large drop in the amount of total benefits for children going from zero earnings to $2,000. The figures are a little misleading in that the W-2 benefit that comprises most of the child benefit at zero earnings is time limited; one can only receive benefits from a Community Service Job for two years. (Moreover, if one were in the labour market for a portion of the year, and received W-2 benefits for a portion, one *could* receive W-2 benefits at $2,000 of earnings). Ignoring this complication, in the short term, the family would receive more benefits from W-2 than from sporadic, low-wage work. In fact, for both families shown here, total net income is higher at zero earnings than at $2,000 or $4,000.

Second, it is clear that the overall child benefit system in the US/Wisconsin is more about supporting earnings than about meeting needs: The single-parent family gets higher child benefits at $4,000 of earnings than at $2,000, even more at $6,000 and still more at $8,000. Similarly, for the married-couple family, after the initial drop in child benefits from zero earnings to $2,000, child benefits then increase with earnings until the latter reach $12,000. Third, the child benefit system is least generous to families in a middle-income range: Minimum child benefits occur for the single-parent family at $28,000-$32,000 and for the married-couple family at $32,000-$54,000. These families have incomes too high to receive benefits targeted at lower-income families, but do not yet have incomes high enough to receive large amounts of assistance from the income tax exemptions and other tax provisions that are worth more to those in higher tax brackets. Finally, at moderate earnings levels ($42,000-$60,000), child benefits for this single-parent one-child family are higher than those for this married-couple two-child family. This is true only because we are comparing a single-parent family to a two-parent family; within family types, the child benefit for an additional child is always higher. This is a function of a policy regime that primarily delivers child-related benefits through a tax exemption combined with a tax system that has higher rates for single individuals.

IN-KIND BENEFITS FOR CHILDREN

While not the central focus of this paper, non-cash benefits are a critical component of support for families with children in the US. This section provides a sketch of the major programs and policies.

Child care benefits and subsidies

The US provides assistance in paying for child care through a non-refundable tax credit (the Dependent Care Tax Credit or DCTC) in the income tax system. The credit offsets a portion of child care expenditures (covering a higher percentage for low-income families), but because it is not refundable, the Dependent Care Tax Credit actually provides very little support to low-income families. The federal government also provides several other programs to assist with child care, including a variety of other tax expenditures, but in general there is less public financial support for child care in the US than in many industrialized countries.

States also provide assistance with child care as part of their Temporary Assistance to Needy Families program. A new child care subsidy program was put in place in Wisconsin simultaneously with Wisconsin Works. Families with children under age 13 that meet an income test are eligible to have a portion of their child care expenditures covered as long as they use a certified care provider. The new subsidy is available to *all* families with children that meet an income test, and thus is a significant expansion over the previous policy, which was primarily limited to welfare recipients.

Shelter subsidies

Shelter benefits for children are provided indirectly. Local housing authorities administer a variety of assistance programs, including housing vouchers that enable families to rent housing in the private market, and housing units that are either governmentally owned or subsidized. Housing benefits are not fully funded, so in many areas there are very long waiting lists; for example, the waiting list in Milwaukee in June 2000 was estimated to be 3 to 3.5 years [LaRosa 2000]. The benefit is generally a rent subsidy, so the family pays a designated portion of the rent and the government pays the rest (up to a maximum). Because all low-income individuals are eligible, the benefit for *children* is the incremental benefit available that allows a family to receive a larger apartment and a higher public subsidy (because the market rent for a larger apartment is higher but the share of a family's income it must pay in rent is fixed). Families with children may also move up in the queue faster than individuals, so the benefit for children may also be linked to accessing the subsidy.

As in many countries, the income tax system allows homeowners to deduct the interest paid on a mortgage in the calculation of taxable income. The amount of the deduction does not depend on family size, so while the amount of this tax expenditure is substantially larger than the shelter subsidies for low-income families, it is not considered here as a benefit for children.

Food subsidies

The US has three main programs that provide assistance with food for low-income families. The Food Stamp program is federal and provides benefits to low-income families (and individuals) that meet income and asset tests. Traditionally, benefits have come in the form of coupons that can be used to purchase food in participating stores, but more states are now using electronic debit cards.

The Women, Infants and Children (WIC) program provides vouchers for specific, limited types of food for low-income pregnant women, infants and children who are at risk of nutritional deficiencies. The program is administered differently from most income support programs in that individuals enroll through public health centers.

Finally, school lunches and breakfasts, and meals while children are in child care, are partially or fully subsidized for low-income children. The school lunch program is in virtually every school, and lunches are provided free to children from very low-income families and at partial subsidy to children with families with lower incomes. Similar in structure to school lunches, school breakfasts are offered in about half the schools [Rossi 1998]. Other subsidies for food are available to child care centers and to families providing child care in their own homes.

Health care subsidies

The US does not have universal health coverage. In the past, publicly provided health benefits through the Medicaid program were available primarily to families receiving cash welfare. Because the jobs available to welfare recipients did not typically include health insurance, this made staying on welfare rational, since leaving it would open a family to significant health risks. Thus since the late 1980s, Medicaid eligibility began to be 'de-linked' from welfare and made available to different categories of low-income children outside the welfare system. In 1997, the Children's Health Insurance Program (CHIP) was started, which gives states funds to design their own program to provide coverage for low-income children, either by expanding Medicaid or by instituting a new program.

INPUTS AND OUTCOMES

Table 4 provides a summary of the governmental inputs into the cash child benefit system and limited information on recipients. (Note that the table focuses only on cash benefits, though in-kind benefits are larger governmental expenditures.) The Earned Income Tax Credit is clearly the largest benefit program in terms of expenditures, at about $30 billion, followed by the exemption for children and the child tax credit, at about $20 billion, then Temporary Assistance to Needy Families and child benefits within Social Security (each about $12 billion). However, because exemptions for children are not income tested, they help twice as many families as the Earned Income Tax Credit. Even in its most expensive days, Aid to Families with Dependent Children (the precursor to Temporary Assistance to Needy Families) was not a large program, with benefits totaling $23 billion in 1994 (current dollars); caseload declines and fixed funding have meant that current benefits are about $12 billion. Note that overall expenditures for families with children are a very low proportion of GDP, reinforcing the reputation of the US as having a reluctant welfare state.

The final row shows that the largest programs in terms of overall expenditures provide the smallest amounts to individual recipient children. Thus average benefits per child recipient range from $498 per month for children of deceased workers to less than $50 per month for the exemption for children and the child tax credit.

POLICY ISSUES

Brief evaluation

How is the current policy working? In this section I begin with my own evaluation of child benefit policy, considering several criteria, including harmonization, administrative issues, adequacy, work incentives, stigma, equity and accountability.

In terms of *harmonization*, current US policy has some gaps. In particular, families with very low earnings could receive little because their earnings are too low for substantial support from the Earned Income Tax Credit, yet the last-resort program, Temporary Assistance to Needy Families, may provide them with little assistance. Second, the Earned Income Tax Credit's high taper rate leads to substantial effective marginal tax rates in some ranges because it is not offset by any other features of the tax-transfer system. Third, families in the middle-income range receive the least in total child benefits because of the reliance on regressive tax exemptions.

Politicians have often complained about *fraud* in the child benefit system, particularly in Aid to Families with Dependent Children/Temporary Assistance to Needy Families and food stamps, but, more recently, in the Earned Income Tax Credit as well. (Because the other programs are more hidden, there is little current discussion of fraud.) Within Temporary Assistance to Needy Families, there has often been concern about individuals receiving benefits simultaneously with working in the underground economy. This particular type of fraud should lessen, as it is now nearly impossible to meet the obligations required by Temporary Assistance to Needy Families for work or work-like activity while working a substantial amount on the side. Part of the problem with fraud in the Earned Income Tax Credit is that children's living arrangements are part of the eligibility conditions, but the tax system is unable to monitor where a child is living. In my view, the political rhetoric about fraud is not based on empirical demonstrations of widespread problematic fraudulent behavior.

Current US child benefit policy relies very heavily on the market generating substantial employment opportunities. In areas of the country in which this is accurate, the system as a whole *may* do a reasonable job at providing *adequate* supplementary benefits. But, in regions in which this is not true, or if and when a recession occurs, or for individuals unable to make it in the market for whatever reason, benefits clearly are very inadequate. The current benefit regime generally provides only supplements to earnings; if earnings themselves are inadequate (or nonexistent), there are few benefits and the main benefit remaining is time-limited.

One way to assess whether benefits are adequate is to examine measures of child poverty. While the US official measure of poverty is limited in important ways [Citro and Michael, 1995], it provides one measure of economic well-being. According to this measure, poverty among children was 16.9 percent in 1999 [US Census Bureau 2000b]. While this has improved from the 22.7 percent of 1993, the level is still quite high, especially for a time of sustained economic expansion, and I believe the continued high poverty rates suggest that benefits for children are inadequate.

On the other hand, the current system has substantial *work incentives*; in fact, as discussed above, cash benefits are generally available only for a short time unless individuals are working. Expansions to the Earned Income Tax Credit have been found to be associated with substantial increases in the labour force participation of lone mothers (e.g., Meyer and Rosenbaum 1999), but it may have a small negative effect on hours worked among those already working (see Hotz and Scholz 2000, for a review). Similarly, while the focus of policy reforms within Temporary Assistance to Needy Families has generally been to increase the incentive to begin working, the poorly integrated system of multiple means-tested programs results in substantial disincentives to increase the hours of work in some ranges [Wolfe 2000].

Stigma historically has been seen as a major problem in the US transfer system. The stigma associated with receiving benefits may have been lessened by Temporary Assistance to Needy Families; anecdotally, recipients report less stigma, consistent with the idea that the new Temporary Assistance to Needy Families program is more reflective of prevailing norms. Because so much of the child benefit system in the US is now accomplished through the income tax system, this too has lessened stigma. Finally, shifts within the food stamp program away from coupon books and toward electronic debit cards should lessen the public display of recipiency, which is probably linked to stigma. On the other hand, the welfare debate includes many statements *very* critical of welfare recipients, so those who receive last-resort benefits probably still face substantial stigma.

Many observers have serious questions about *equity* in the US system. Poverty rates among children of colour remain much higher than those of Caucasian children; I believe the striking and ongoing disadvantage associated with race and ethnicity in the US reveals substantial inequity. A feature of the most recent welfare reform is that each individual state designs its own last-resort benefit system. This development could lead to substantial cross-state inequities, with similar families being treated differently. Another type of inequity is that families with more needs (particularly large families) receive no more than families with fewer needs under Wisconsin's Temporary Assistance to Needy Families program. Similarly, looking at the child benefit system as a whole, there are several income ranges in which families with lower incomes receive less than families with higher incomes.

Finally, some problems with *accountability* remain in the US child benefit system. Prior to welfare reform, states could experiment with their last-resort benefits, Aid to Families with Dependent Children, but in order to receive a waiver from general program rules, they had to conduct evaluations of the effects of reforms. Usually these evaluations had rigorous experimental designs. Under Temporary Assistance to Needy Families, states are not required to evaluate their program. The federal government has been making additional funds available to states for some evaluation efforts, in particular studies of the economic well-being of those who leave welfare. Some information on these outcomes will be available, but understanding the *impacts* of welfare reform requires a comparison of outcomes after welfare to some other group affected by a different policy regime, and current evaluation efforts in this area are lacking. The aspects of the child benefit system other than Temporary Assistance to Needy Families have been subject to even less evaluation, and, as we have seen, the last-resort program, while generating a substantial amount of interest and policy debate, is actually only a fairly small part of child benefit expenditures. Finally, traditional policy evaluations do not always take into account the perspective (and voice) of recipients, so complete accountability is not necessarily guaranteed by having formal policy or program evaluations.

Current governmental directions

Even though the US has the highest child poverty rate among developed countries [Burtless and Smeeding 2000], the elimination of child poverty is not frequently discussed by policy makers, and explicit proposals to increase spending dramatically on benefits for children are generally not part of the current public debate.

The *Personal Responsibility and Work Opportunities Reconciliation Act* significantly changed child benefits for the lowest-income families in the US. One of the most important features has been the change from open-ended funding for Aid to Families with Dependent Children (with the federal government paying a portion of whatever states spent) to a block grant, in which the federal government provides a set amount of funding and states must provide at least a portion of the funds they were providing under Aid to Families with Dependent Children. Federal funding levels were set based on historical Aid to Families with Dependent Children caseload levels. Because caseloads have radically declined both because of a booming economy and because of welfare changes (see, for example, Schoeni and Blank 2000), nearly all states have had substantial resources available for programs for low-income families. Moreover, the 'maintenance of effort' requirement imposed on them has meant they have an obligation to spend at least a portion of this money on new programs. Thus many states are considering changes to their Temporary Assistance to Needy Families program, or new programs, to assist low-income families.

Some options for new spending are targeted at increasing in-kind benefits (increasing child care options, medical coverage, housing subsidies); some are focused on improving the human capital of recipients; and others are aimed at assisting those with temporary disabilities. On the other hand, in Wisconsin and other states, massive changes already have been made and the policy focus is more on waiting to see how the policies work, perhaps making small incremental changes as problems arise.

On the federal level, most of the social policy action currently involves the level and distribution of tax cuts. In the debate about tax cuts, one focus is on lowering taxes for married couples, but not necessarily only those with children. Another focus is policies affecting seniors; proposals to change Medicare and Social Security (Old Age Insurance) are receiving substantial debate.

Regarding families with children, some legislative attention is being given to lowering the fixed federal funding given to each state for Temporary Assistance to Needy Families programs in the next budgetary cycle. President Clinton proposed an expanded Earned Income Tax Credit for three-child families, but this does not appear likely to pass. From the left, new proposals include community job creation, alternative and broadened unemployment compensation, and increased child care [Sweeney et al. 2000]. From the right, Robert Rector [1999] recently proposed that the next policy reforms should go further in promoting marriage, either by providing additional tax cuts for two-parent families with children or by providing more funding to states that lower the extramarital birth rate. He also proposes strengthening work requirements and capping all welfare spending.

Key issues

One of the key conceptual issues for child benefit policy in the US is how to design policy so that employment is encouraged while adequate benefits are provided for children in families that are not working. Analysts have long recognized a tradeoff between these competing goals. Recent changes in Wisconsin, at least, come down firmly on the side of encouraging employment: Children in families that are not working are given cash only in exchange for their parents working, and even this is limited to two (to five) years. The only exception is that parents with disabilities so serious that they are eligible for Supplemental Security Income can receive supplements of $150-$250 per child per month. How to work within this system for families that have significant difficulties with employment, and yet cannot pass the stringent disability test, remains a large policy challenge. Moreover, how this system will work in times of economic downturn is a critical policy question.

More broadly, there is so much emphasis in the US on working in the paid labour market, particularly for women, that the work that women traditionally have done is being consistently devalued. I believe a key issue for policy is whether (and, in my view, not whether, but how) it will support women in the role of caring, whether caring for children or caring for other family members.

Another key issue is how to increase the responsiveness of the system to income fluctuations. The main income supports to families with children are delivered through the tax system, and thus are generally delivered annually rather than in a timeframe that meets immediate need. (While families could receive the Earned Income Tax Credit in their regular paycheque, few families accept this option.) Even families that apply for W-2 assistance and are placed in a grant-receiving tier (CSJ or W2-T) do not receive their first cheque until after a significant period has passed, because this is the way the working world operates. (They may, however, be given one-time assistance to make it to the first cheque.)

A related issue is how to provide assistance for families that are temporarily unemployed. The Unemployment Insurance system in the US requires substantial recent employment in the regular employment sector before being eligible for benefits. The system is covering fewer and fewer of the unemployed, in part because as work has become more sporadic, they may not have worked the requisite number of hours, and in part because work opportunities for many low-skill individuals occur outside the regular employment sector: Those providing child care and those in limited-term employment or other temporary jobs are generally not covered by Unemployment Insurance. Adapting the social insurance system to fit the new economy and integrating the social insurance system with other benefits to children remain large challenges.

Finally, a particular issue in the US is searching for ways to provide ancillary benefits often provided by employers in the primary employment sector but seldom by employers in low-wage sectors. For example, large companies provide health coverage to families, pensions and sick leave and may offer 'family-friendly' policies like on-site child care and flexible hours. A difficult policy challenge is whether to require employers to provide these types of benefits, whether to deliver them through public programs or whether to allow the inequality that would result from inaction.

CONCLUSION

Many policies providing benefits for children the US are hidden within the tax system. While others are more explicit, the interactions among them create a problematic system. Figures 1 and 2 reveal patterns in the additional amounts that parents receive over those received by non-parents that are very hard to justify. Why should upper-income and lower-income lone parents receive so much more than middle-income lone parents? The differentials are not as great for married couples, but the pattern is similarly problematic. At the same time, poverty rates among children in the US, though at their lowest level in decades, are strikingly high in an international context.

Surely there is room to adjust policies that would increase equity and adequacy simultaneously. I believe there are lessons for the US in the recent reforms in Canada, the United Kingdom and Australia. In an economic period in which the federal government has unprecedented surpluses and states have unprecedented powers to set policy for low-income families, this is an opportune time to consider changes – perhaps momentous changes – in the policies providing benefits to children.

ENDNOTES

1. I do not cover other policies that regulate parental behavior, including policies that govern divorce and child support, though these are obviously also important to the economic well-being of economically vulnerable families with children (for a recent review of child support policy in the US, see Meyer 2000). In addition, several smaller programs are not included, including payments to children in foster care, subsidies for families that adopt children and benefits to children of veterans with a disability.

2. Those in the highest tax bracket cannot receive the full benefit because they are already in the benefit reduction range, and thus the highest value is to those in the second highest tax bracket, 36 percent.

3. About 70 percent of returns use the standard deduction; the remainder itemize deductions [Internal Revenue Service 1998].

4. The Wisconsin child credit, available for tax year 1999, has been replaced in 2000 by a wide variety of state tax reforms.

5. For a recent thorough description of the changes brought about by PRWORA and the changes to state programs made as a result, see Pavetti [2000].

6. In this example, *net* child-related food stamp benefits are actually negative at zero *earnings*: in this simplified example, a single individual with no earnings would have no cash income, and, if he/she could exist, would receive $1,464 in food stamps. Because single parents at zero earnings could receive W-2 and would probably be put in a community service job, they would have higher cash income, so they would receive less in food stamps, $748. The net child 'benefit' in food stamps for this case is thus a negative $716.

7. At a given level of total earnings, the amounts of W-2, food stamps, Earned Income Tax Credit, federal income taxes and the federal child credit for a one-earner couple are identical to those for a two-earner couple. There is a small (maximum $350) credit in Wisconsin available to two-earner couples. Of course, the assumption of no child care expenditures is less tenable in two-earner couples with young children.

REFERENCES

Burtless, G. and T. M. Smeeding. (2000). "The Level, Trend, and Composition of American Poverty: National and International Perspective." Prepared for *Understanding Poverty in America: Progress and Problems* conference, Madison, WI, May 2000.

Citro, C. F. and R. T. Michael, eds. (1995). *Measuring Poverty: A New Approach*. Washington, D.C.: National Academy Press.

Hobbie, R. A., D. C. Wittenbeurg and M.E. Fishman. (1999). "Temporary Assistance for Low-Wage Workers: Evolving Relationships among Work, Welfare, and Unemployment Insurance." In E. Ganzglass and K. Glass eds. *Rethinking Income Support for the Working Poor*. Washington, DC: National Governors' Association.

Hotz, V. J. and J. K. Scholz. (2000). "The Earned Income Tax Credit." Prepared for the NBER Conference on Means-Tested Transfers, May 2000.

Jansson, B. (1997). *The Reluctant Welfare State: American Social Policies: Past, Present, and Future.* 3rd edition. Pacific Grove, CA: Brooks/Cole.

Johnson, N. (1999). "A Hand Up: How State Earned Income Tax Credits Help Working Families Escape Poverty." Washington, DC: Center on Budget and Policy Priorities.

LaRosa, D., Program Management Specialist, Rent Assistance, Housing Authority of the City of Milwaukee. Personal Communication, June 5, 2000.

Meyer, B. D. and D. T. Rosenbaum. (1999). "Welfare, the Earned Income Tax Credit, and the Labor Supply of Single Mothers." Manuscript, Northwestern University.

Meyer, D. R. (2000). "Fathers and the Child Support System." In M. Melli and J. T. Oldham eds. *Child Support: The Next Frontier*. Ann Arbor: University of Michigan Press.

Pavetti, L. A. (2000). "Welfare Policy in Transition: Redefining the Social Contract for Poor Citizen Families with Children and Immigrants." Prepared for *Understanding Poverty in America: Progress and Problems* conference, Madison, WI, May 2000.

Rector, R. (1999). "Welfare: Broadening the Reform." In S. M. Butler and K.R. Holmes eds. *Issues 2000: The Candidate's Briefing Book.* Heritage Foundation. http://www.heritage.org/issues/chap8.html

Rossi, P. H. (1998). *Feeding the Poor: Assessing Federal Food Aid.* Washington, DC: American Enterprise Institute.

Schoeni, R. F. and R. M. Blank. (2000). "What Has Welfare Reform Accomplished?," Working Paper 7627. Cambridge, MA: National Bureau of Economic Research.

Scholz, J. K. and K. Levine. (2000). "The Evolution of Income Support Policy." Prepared for *Understanding Poverty in America: Progress and Problems* conference, Madison, WI, May 2000.

Statistical Abstract of the United States. (1999). Washington, DC: US Government Printing Office.

Sweeney, E., L. Schott, E. Lazere, S. Fremstad, H. Goldberg, J. Guyer, D. Super and C. Johnson. (2000). "Windows of Opportunity: Strategies to Support Families Receiving Welfare and Other Families in the Next Stage of Welfare Reform." Washington, DC: Center on Budget and Policy Priorities.

US Census Bureau. (2000). *Poverty in the United States: 1999.* Current Population Reports, Series P60-210. Washington, DC: US Government Printing Office.

US Census Bureau. (1999). *Money Income in the United States: 1998.* Current Population Reports, P60-206. Washington, DC: US Government Printing Office.

US Congressional Budget Office. (1998). "Projecting Federal Tax Revenues and the Effect of Changes in Tax Law."

US Internal Revenue Service. (1998). *Individual Income Tax Returns: 1996.* Washington, DC: US Government Printing Office.

Wiseman, M. (1996). "State Strategies for Welfare Reform: The Wisconsin Story." *Journal of Policy Analysis and Management*, 15: 515-546.

Wolfe, B. L. (2000). "Incentives, Challenges, and Dilemmas of TANF." Institute for Research on Poverty Discussion Paper 1209-00. Madison, WI.

ANNEX 1: PERSONAL INCOME TAX SYSTEM, US

Unit of taxation

The basic unit of income taxation for federal purposes is a family. There are five filing statuses: single, married filing jointly, married filing separately, head of household (generally unmarried individuals who provide a home for others, typically single-parent families), and qualifying widow(er) with a dependent child. Married couples typically choose to file jointly rather than separately because this filing status is generally treated more generously.

Pay-as-you-earn versus annual reconciliation

Employers are generally required to withhold estimated income taxes from the earnings of employees and to transfer these to the federal and state government regularly. Individuals who are self-employed or have significant sources of unearned taxable income are required to pay estimated taxes quarterly. An annual reconciliation is completed for calendar years, with the return due April 15.

Who is responsible for submitting tax returns

Each individual is responsible for submitting a return if they are required to pay taxes, or if they would like a refund or a refundable credit. Married couples are not required to file unless their gross annual income in 1999 was at least $12,700 (slightly higher if one or both is age 65 or older); single individuals are not required to file unless their income was at least $7,050.

Coverage

In 1996, 120,000,000 tax returns were filed (Internal Revenue Service 1998). The percentage of families filing is probably increasing, given increases in employment and the generosity of the Earned Income Tax Credit.

Federal/state/local

In addition to federal income taxes, most states have income taxes (though some do not). In addition, a few large cities in the US have their own local income taxes. States with income taxes typically link their tax system to the federal system; individuals file a copy of their federal forms with the state form, which is due the same time, and state tax calculations often begin with federal definitions of income, expenses, etc. (though these are generally modified slightly).

Progressivity

In federal income taxes, there are 5 rates (15 percent, 28 percent, 31 percent, 36 percent, and 39.6 percent); the cut-points between rates vary depending on filing status. In 1999, married couples filing jointly receive a standard deduction of $7,200 and an exemption of $2,750 per person, so a married couple with one child, does not have 'taxable income' until its income is at least $15,400 (higher depending on deductions). They the family owes 15 percent of the first $43,050 of taxable income, 28 percent of amounts over $43,050 but less than $104,050, 31 percent of amounts over $104,050 but less than $158,550, 36 percent of amounts over $158,550 but less than $283,150, and 39.6 percent of amounts over

$283,150. Comparable brackets for single parents (head of household) are: less than $34,550 (15 percent); $34,551-$89,150 (28 percent); $89,151-$144,400 (31 percent); $144,401-$283,150 (36 percent), over $283,150 (39.6 percent).

Percentage of refunds versus taxes owed

In 1996, 72 percent overpaid, and 97 percent of these received a refund [US Internal Revenue Service 1998].

Administrative body

The Internal Revenue Service (IRS) is the federal administrative body. States have their own administrative bodies (the Department of Revenue in Wisconsin, for example).

ANNEX 2: BASIC NATIONAL STATISTICS, US

GDP and population

GDP: $8,511,000,000,000 in 1998 (SA 99, #721*)

Population: 270,561,000 in 1998 (SA 99, #2)

Unemployment and labour force participation rate

The total civilian non-institutionalized population age 16 and over in 1998 was 205,220,000. Of these, 131,463,000 were employed and 6,210,000 were unemployed (SA 99, #649)

Percentage of population under 18

25.8 percent in 1998 (SA 99 #14)

Number of families with children under 18 as percent of all households

34 percent in 1998 (SA 99 #73)

Average number of children

Among families with children, mean is 2.01 children.

Among families with children, 41.3 percent have one child, 37.8 percent have two children, 15.4 percent have three children, and 5.5 percent have four or more children. (SA 99 derived from #78 and #14)

Among families with children under 18

a. Single parents as percent of total, male and female:

32 percent of all families with children are headed by single parents, 26 percent by mothers, 6 percent by fathers (SA 99, #76)

b. Families with different levels of adult employment:

60 percent of all children in husband-wife families have both parents employed

65 percent of children in mother only families have an employed mother

84 percent of children in father only families have an employed father (SA 99, #84)

Child poverty rate (½ median LIS)

22.3 percent in 1997 [Burtless and Smeeding, 2000]

Median income by family type (before tax)

a. with children

i. All husband-wife: $57,022 median family income 1998 [Table 6, US Census Bureau 1999]

ii. One parent, female: $20,692 median household income 1998 (Table 12, US Census Bureau 1999). No figure directly comparable for one parent, male, a proxy is $35,681 for male householders, no wife present 1998 (may or may not have children, but do have an individual related by blood in the home) [Table 4, US Census Bureau 1999]

b. without children

i. Husband-wife: $51,323 median family income 1998 [Table 6, US Census Bureau 1999]

ii. Single individuals living alone aged 15 and over, $25,081 1998 [Table 7, US Census Bureau 1999]

*NOTE: Most statistics are from *Statistical Abstract of the United States: 1999.* (Abbreviated as SA)

TABLE 1
INCOME -RELATED BENEFITS

	Exemption for Children	Child Tax Credit	Earned Income Tax Credit
Eligibility rules 1. Who is entitled to benefits	1. All families filing tax returns with children up to age 18 (or 24 if student) for whom the parent provided over half their support. No time limits, no limits by employment status. Limited amounts for married couples with gross taxable incomes over $189,950 or single parents with incomes over $158,300 (1999).	1. All families filing tax returns with children for whom the parent provided over half their support. No time limits, no limits by employment status. Limited amounts for married couples with gross taxable incomes over $110,000 and single parents with incomes over $75,000 (1999).	1. Those with children under age 18 (24 if full-time student) who live with family at least half time. Benefits only for those with earnings. No requirement for particular hours of work, only earnings. No time limits.
2. Reciprocal responsibilities	2.Recipients must file tax form claiming dependent.	2. Recipients must file tax form claiming credit.	2. Recipients must file tax form. Earnings are required.
3. Budget caps	3. Open-ended.	3. Open-ended.	3. Open-ended.
Benefits description 1. Amounts per child	1. Nonrefundable income offset within federal income tax system of $2,750/ child (1999). Value varies by tax bracket.	1. Nonrefundable tax credit within federal income tax system of $500/child.	1. 1999 maximum amount for those with no children, $347/year; for 1 child, $2,312; for 2 or more children $3,816. Age,

	Exemption for Children	Child Tax Credit	Earned Income Tax Credit
			family structure irrelevant.
2. Income-related structure	2. For married-couple families with gross taxable income after deductions of up to $43,050, value is 15% of $2,750 or $412.50/child/year. Married-couple families with higher incomes receive higher values, up to $990/child. Married-couple families with taxable incomes over $312,500 are not eligible.	2. Amount limited for higher-income parents.	2. 1999 Structure: no guarantee for those not working, no minimum benefit. For no children, families receive a subsidy of 7.65 cents for dollar, up to $4,530 in earnings; after $5,670 in earnings, benefits taper off at a rate of 7.65 cents per dollar, disappearing at $10,200. For one child, families get 34 cents for every dollar of earnings, up to $6,800; after $12,460 benefits taper off at 15.98 cents for every dollar, to disappearing point of $26,928. For two or more children, families receive 40 cents per dollar of earnings, up to $9,540; after $12,460 benefits taper off at 21.06 cents per dollar, and the disappearing point is $30,585.
3. Definition of income	3. Taxable income includes earnings, interest, dividends, a por-	3. Taxable income includes earnings, inter-	3. Earnings are only factor, although having other income

	Exemption for Children	Child Tax Credit	Earned Income Tax Credit
	tion of capital gains, etc. (but not child support).	est, dividends, a portion of capital gains, etc. (but not child support).	higher than relatively low levels will make one ineligible.
4. Indexing	4. The exemption amount is indexed, as are the tax brackets.	4. Credit amount not indexed.	4. Subsidy rates are not indexed, but income turning points are indexed.
Delivery features			
1. Administrative arrangements	1. Internal Revenue Service (IRS).	1.Internal Revenue Service. Tax form required. No discretion on part of IRS.	1. Internal Revenue Service.
2. How people get enrolled	2. Tax form required. No discretion on part of IRS.	2. Income on annual basis, credit on annual basis.	2. Anyone who files a tax form can receive benefits; if desired, individuals can receive benefits every pay period, but the vast majority (over 99 percent) receive it annually.
3. Responsiveness	3. Income on annual basis, exemption on annual basis.	3. Filing status determines name on cheque.	3. The benefits are calculated on an annual basis, so even if paid with each paycheque an annual reconciliation is required, with overpayments requiring repayment.

	Exemption for Children	**Child Tax Credit**	**Earned Income Tax Credit**
4. Payment procedures	4. No cheques issued.	4. Generally non-refundable	4. Cheque received by whoever's name is on the tax form.
5. Verification procedures	5. Routine audits.	5. Routine audits.	5. Regular audits. Those found to be ineligible with the error due to "reckless or intentional disregard of the EIC rules" are not eligible for the credit for the next two years; those found to have committed fraud cannot take the credit for ten years.
6. Aboriginal peoples.	6. No special provisions.	6. No special benefits	6. No special provisions.
7. How program is delivered	7. Cheque or direct deposit where there is a refund. National program.	7. Cheque or direct deposit are both options.	7. Annual program administered by IRS. Paycheque program is paid by employer.
8. How program is financed	8. Program cost hidden (tax expenditure).	8. Program cost hidden (standard tax expenditure).	8. Financed through general revenue.
9. National/ state integration	9. State income tax codes also have exemptions or credits.	9. State income tax codes also have exemptions or credits.	9. Some states have state EICs.

Note: Wisconsin's income taxes have a small nonrefundable credit of $50/ dependent.

TABLE 2
INCOME- AND ASSET-TESTED BENEFITS

	W-2 in Wisconsin	**TANF**	**Supplemental Security Income (SSI)**
Eligibility rules 1. Who is entitled to benefits	1. Families with children under age 18. Assistance is contingent on participating in a work placement unless one has a child less than 13 weeks old. Employment must be 40 hours/ week (except for Community Service Jobs, which require 30 hours/week in work training and 10 hours in education/ training; and W-2 Transition, which requires 28 hours in work training and 12 hours in education/ training. Time limits: 24 months in a single tier; lifetime limit of 60 months.	1. Families with children meeting income and asset tests. Time limits: states can set but no longer than 60 months.	1.Children under age 18 (or under 22 if full-time student) with a "medically determinable physical or mental impairment that results in marked and severe functional limitations." No time limits. Law between 1990 and 1996 allowed for eligibility based on individualized functional assessment; since 1996 stricter standard.
2. Reciprocal responsibilities	2. Participants must attend job placement and cooperate with child support agency.	2. Participants must cooperate with child support agency and fulfill requirements set by state. Many states have work requirements.	2. No reciprocal responsibilities.

	W-2 in Wisconsin	TANF	Supplemental Security Income (SSI)
3. Budget caps	3. Not an entitlement, but budget ceiling has not been reached.	3. Federal funding capped.	3. No budget caps.
Benefits description 1. Amounts per child	1. Unsubsidized employment and trial jobs pay market wages. Those in CSJs receive $673/month; those in W2-T receive $628/month. The amount for CSJs and W2-Ts is not adjusted for family size.	1. States can determine.	1. The federal maximum benefit for an individual child was $512/month (2000). States may supplement this amount. (The supplement in Wisconsin in 2000 is $84/month). The amounts vary only by income, and not by age, order, number of children, family structure, or level of disability.
2. Income-related structure	2. Benefit structure simple: flat rate if meet hours requirement. Benefits available to those with incomes less than 115% of the federal poverty line and assets less than $2,500 (excluding vehicle equity up to $10,000 and home equity).	2. Benefit structure: set by states; generally largest amount for non-workers.	2. The SSI program is primarily for seniors and adults with disabilities. For children, a portion of the parents' income is deemed to be available for the child. There are income disregards for earnings.

	W-2 in Wisconsin	TANF	Supplemental Security Income (SSI)
3. Definition of income	3. To calculate eligibility, gross income is used. Child support is ignored in the calculation of benefits for most families (this provision is subject to an experimental evaluation, so a control group of families receives only a portion of that paid on their behalf).	3. Gross income, generally.	3. Income includes earnings, unearned income and nearly every potential source of income.
4. Indexing	4. Benefits are not indexed.	4. Benefits not automatically indexed (states determine).	4. Benefits are indexed to inflation.
Delivery Issues 1. Administrative arrangements	1. Wisconsin Department of Workforce Development sets requirements for program, actual delivery is done by county government or by private agencies, three of them for-profit.	1. Federal agency is the Administration for Children and Families within the Department of Health and Human Services. States make own arrangements.	1. The program is administered by the Social Security Administration.
2. How people get enrolled	2. Individuals enter a job center and see a planner, who	2. State discretion. Individual applications	2. Individuals must apply, have their income verified, and have their

	W-2 in Wisconsin	TANF	Supplemental Security Income (SSI)
	assists the parent in designing an employment plan and helps them connect to other services they may be eligible for. Individuals reapply regularly.	required, with regular reapplications.	disability status approved. Generally reapplications are required annually. There is little discretion in the amounts of benefits, but significant professional discretion is required in determining disability.
3. Responsiveness	3. Payments are made monthly; the accounting period is weekly or even hourly (a family not in their work assignment for an hour can be docked an hourly rate). Changes in family income are irrelevant unless they would make a family ineligible; changes in household composition are also irrelevant unless all children leave.	3. Payments generally monthly.	3. Changes in income need to be reported as they occur; payments made monthly
4. Payment procedures	4. Cheque comes to self-designated "head."	4. Generally cheque to "head."	4. Cheque is in a parent's name.
5. Verification procedures	5. Substantial verification process. Sanctions used frequently, for a variety	5. State discretion.	5. Individuals are certified for particular periods of time, typically one year.

	W-2 in Wisconsin	TANF	Supplemental Security Income (SSI)
	of offenses against program rules.		
6. Aboriginal peoples	6. Three tribal agencies administer the W-2 program for their members.	6. Tribes can negotiate directly with federal government or participate in state program.	6. No special procedures.
7. How program is delivered	7. County governments can deliver program if they have met performance criteria; otherwise any organization can bid to administer the program.	7. State discretion.	7. The federal program is administered by Social Security offices. State supplements can be administered either by the state welfare office or nationally.
8. How program is financed	8. The federal government provides a block grant; the remaining necessary funds come from general revenue.	8. Federal government provides block grant.	8. Financing is from general revenues.
9. National/state integration	9. Federal government requires plan, states have substantial freedom in determining plans.	9. Federal government requires plan, states have substantial freedom in determining plans.	9. Federal program that allows state supplements.

NOTES: Wisconsin's Earned Income Credit is a specified percentage of the federal credit, but only for those with children. For one child, the credit is 4 percent of the federal Earned Income Tax Credit, for two children it is 14 percent of the federal Earned Income Tax Credit, and for three or more children it is 43 percent of the federal Earned Income Tax Credit.

TABLE 3
CONTRIBUTORY SOCIAL INSURANCE ENTITLEMENTS

	Child Benefit within Social Security
Eligibility rules	
1. Who is entitled to benefits	1. Children under age 18 (or 19 if in secondary school) whose parent is retired, has a disability, or is deceased who was fully insured at the time of retirement, disability or death. No current employment is required of the parent, and there are no time limits on receipt. To receive disability benefits, the adult must be unable to engage in "substantial gainful activity" due to a condition that will last at least 12 months (or result in death).
2. Reciprocal responsibilities	2. Beneficiaries have no ongoing obligations.
3. Budget caps	3. The program is an entitlement, financed through a combination of a trust fund and a pay-as-you-go payroll tax.
Benefits description	
1. Amounts per child	1. Benefits are based on "average indexed monthly earnings." Amounts are not related to a child's age. The number of children affects the benefit, but family structure does not.
2. Income-related structure	2. The actual benefit is a percentage of previous earnings, with higher percentages for those with lower earnings.
3. Definition of income	3. Benefits are not means-tested (though they are taxed for moderate-income families).
4. Indexing	4. Benefits are indexed.

	Child Benefit within Social Security
Delivery features	
1. Administrative arrangements	1. The program is administered by the Social Security Administration (federal).
2. How people get enrolled	2. Individuals apply for benefits; survivor's benefits do not require reapplication, nor do retired worker benefits. Benefits based on disability require reapplication every 3 years.
3. Responsiveness	3. Cheques come monthly. Other income is irrelevant, so is not reported.
4. Payment procedures	4. Cheque comes to insured person or designee.
5. Verification procedures	5. Limited verification; earnings records are kept centrally, benefit calculation is straightforward.
6. Aboriginal peoples	6. No special provisions.
7. How program is delivered	7. Employers collect the employer and employee share of the payroll tax; otherwise have no role.
8. How program is financed	8. Financed partly by payroll tax on employers and employees.
9. National/state integration	9. Nationally uniform benefits.

TABLE 4
INPUTS, OUTPUTS AND RECIPIENT CHARACTERISTICS: INCOME BENEFITS FOR CHILDREN

	Exemption for Children	Child Tax Credit	EITC	TANF W-2	SSI	Child Benefit within Social Security
Total (in millions)	$20,000 estimated (1996)	$19,000 projected (2000)	$31,900 (1999)	$12,400 TANF (1999) $115 W2 (1998)	$5,000 for children annualized 6/98 $93 in WI annualized 6/98	$12,370 for children (1998) ($3,300 children of disabled workers; $8,140 survivors of workers; $930 children of retired workers)
Percent of GDP	0.2	0.2	0.4	0.1	0.1	0.1
Percent of government spending	0.5*	0.5*	1.0*	0.4	0.2	0.4
Recipient Characteristics						
Number of families (thousands)	38,780	NA	19,500 (1999)	2,536 TANF (6/99) 27 in WI (6/99)	887 (6/98) 17 in WI (6/98)	NA
Number of children (thousands)	68,138 (1997)	38,000	23,484 (1997)	4,300 TANF (6/99) 19 in WI (6/99)	887 (6/98) 17 in WI (6/98)	2,967 (1998) 1,364 children of disabled parents; 1,364 survivors of workers; 240 children of retired workers
Average monthly benefit	$24/child recipient	$42/child recipient	$113/ child recipient	TANF:$358/ family 1998 W2: $650/ family receiving cash assistance (1999)	$433/child recipient (6/98)	$202/child of disabled parents; $498/child of deceased workers; $324/child of retired workers

NOTES: The SSI program has a separate component for adults with a disability. Eligibility requirements, benefit levels and administrative arrangements are all similar to that described above. Single parents who receive SSI as a result of a disability can receive benefits from the state for children. In Wisconsin, they receive an extra supplement of $150-$250/child/month, called a SSI Caretaker Supplement. This program is administered completely separately from the W-2 program, by the Department of Health and Family Services.

ABOUT THE AUTHORS

Ken Battle is President of the Caledon Institute of Social Policy, Ottawa, Canada.

Michael Mendelson is Senior Scholar at the Caledon Institute of Social Policy, Ottawa, Canada.

Daniel R. Meyer is a Professor of Social Work and an Affiliate of the Institute for Research on Poverty at the University of Wisconsin – Madison in the United States.

Jane Millar is Professor of Social Policy and Director of the Centre for the Analysis of Social Policy at the University of Bath, UK.

Peter Whiteford is Principal Administrator (Social Policies), Non-Member Economies and International Migration Division, OECD, Paris and formerly with the Department of Family and Community Services, Canberra, Australia.